ETHICS IN CRIME AND JUSTICE
⊰ Dilemmas and Decisions ⊱

SECOND EDITION

CONTEMPORARY ISSUES IN CRIME AND JUSTICE SERIES

Roy Roberg, Consulting Editor

ETHICS IN CRIME AND JUSTICE
Dilemmas and Decisions

SECOND EDITION

Joycelyn M. Pollock
SOUTHWEST TEXAS STATE UNIVERSITY

WADSWORTH PUBLISHING COMPANY
BELMONT, CALIFORNIA
A DIVISION OF WADSWORTH, INC.

Criminal Justice Editor: *Brian Gore*
Editorial Assistant: *Jennifer Dunning*
Production: *Scratchgravel Publishing Services*
Production Service Coordinator: *Debby Kramer*
Print Buyer: *Karen Hunt*
Permissions Editor: *Jeanne Bosschart*
Interior Design: *Anne Draus, Scratchgravel Publishing Services*
Copy Editor: *Lorraine Anderson*
Cover: *Stephen Rapley*
Compositor: *Scratchgravel Publishing Services*
Printer: *Malloy Lithographing, Inc.*

This book is printed on acid-free recycled paper.

International Thomson Publishing
The trademark ITP is used under license.

Library of Congress Cataloging-in-Publication Data

Pollock, Joycelyn M.,
    Ethics in crime and justice : dilemmas and decisions / Joycelyn M. Pollock. — 2nd ed.
      p. cm. — (Contemporary issues in crime and justice)
    Includes bibliographical references and index.
    ISBN 0-534-21456-8
    1. Criminal justice, Administration of—Moral and ethical aspects.
  2. Criminal justice, Administration of—United States.   I. Title.
  II. Series.
HV7419.P65   1993
364.973—dc20   93-28076

Foreword

The Contemporary Issues in Criminal Justice Series introduces important topics that until now have been neglected or inadequately covered to students and professionals in criminal justice, criminology, sociology, and related fields. The volumes cover philosophical and theoretical issues and analyze the most recent research findings and their implications for practice. Consequently, each volume will stimulate further thinking and debate on its subject matter, in addition to providing direction for policy formulation and implementation.

The foreword to the first edition opened, in part, with the following statement: "The topic of ethics has always been of critical importance to the field of criminal justice and criminology. Judging from recent reports of frequent ethical violations throughout the criminal justice system, this primer on morality, ethics, and human behavior could not be more timely. The sensitivity and critical nature of the subject matter make it seem surprising that greater attention has not been devoted to this topic." These comments ring as true today, if not more so, as they did when the first edition was published. Consequently, this updated second edition can be considered as timely and important as the ground-breaking original work.

In this edition, Pollock wisely adheres to the original format, which was well grounded in the philosophical and practical dilemmas surrounding the modern criminal justice system, including the police, court, and correctional subsystems. Greatly expanded discussions on determining moral and ethical behavior, crime victims, policy-making, and crime prevention have been added. Furthermore, a new final chapter on "Professionalism, Pride, and Ethics for Real People," a glossary of terms, and "real life" examples have been added; the popular Ethical Dilemmas sections at the end of each chapter have also been updated.

Consistent with the first edition, this work allows us to come away with a better understanding of the complicated moral and ethical dilemmas confronting the criminal justice practitioner, and how these dilemmas may be confronted and dealt with. In fact, the expanded discussions and topics included in this second edition accomplish this end result in an even more comprehensive and meaningful manner. As such, this work continues to be one of the most important contributions to the ethics literature in the field, and should be read and debated by both students and practitioners, with the purpose of better understanding and improving the ethical decisions made by those who work throughout the criminal justice system.

Roy Roberg

Preface

I began work on this book about nine years ago when I was asked to teach a new course entitled Criminal Justice Ethics. Since the first publication of *Ethics in Crime and Justice: Dilemmas and Decisions*, in 1989, several other books in the area have been published and others are in various stages of publication. Panels on ethics now appear at the American Society of Criminology and the Academy of Criminal Justice Sciences conferences where none existed before. Academies and law enforcement institutes now have training units in ethics. In criminal justice, one is encouraged by the interest in establishing ethics centers and the newfound attention to ethics in training.

This increasing interest is understandable and welcome when one considers the events that have occurred since this book first appeared. The videotaped beating of Rodney King and the acquittal of the four charged police officers sparked the Los Angeles riots and brought police brutality into every living room and dinner conversation. Scandals in federal, state, and local governments continue with depressing regularity, even though new ethics commissions are being created at every government level. The overcrowding of prisons has brought public scrutiny to release policies and sentencing issues. Private corrections has become more popular, and many states now must come to terms with the attendant ethical problems of such an innovation. The legal profession was criticized by Vice President Dan Quayle at its own annual bar meeting in 1991. Issues such as mandatory pro bono service and disciplinary procedures are debated in bar journals and national conferences. While all this attention to and discussion of ethics are encouraging, one hopes it is not simply because ethics is a "hot" topic that will be replaced by other issues when the media find a new social problem and/or the public loses interest.

One challenge in teaching ethics is the necessity of presenting enough background in moral analysis while still allowing sufficient time to explore issues specific to criminal justice. Therefore, this volume provides the basic tools needed to analyze moral issues. Although there are many complex issues that could be raised within the description of each ethical system, I have chosen to spend more time on issues specific to criminal justice professionals. It is probably advisable for a criminal justice ethics course to be team taught by a criminal justice professor and a philosophy professor. At least, frequent speakers from the other discipline should be invited to provide more competent analyses of the issues unique to their field of expertise. This will ensure that the course is more than a "bull session" but is also relevant to criminal justice issues. The greatest difficulty in teaching ethics is presenting the concepts and issues in a way that the typical student or practitioner can find meaningful—this book is intended to do just that.

The most astute philosophical propositions have little impact on people if only other philosophers can understand them. This book is aimed at undergraduate students and practitioners who ordinarily do not have the time or inclination to debate minute and esoteric issues in the philosophy of justice or morality. However, that does not mean that they are less capable or less interested in resolving fundamental issues of right and wrong or determining what is necessary to be a moral person. There are no experts in the field of morals and ethics. Every person who has a capacity to reason and to care has exactly the same right as the most esteemed philosopher to make pronouncements regarding the nature of humankind and definitions of morality.

Teaching an ethics course is a rewarding experience. It is always stimulating and students usually enjoy the challenge of dealing with issues that are rarely covered in other courses. If one is lucky enough to get a good cross section of students, including police officers or corrections officers, then the discussions become even more valuable. I must thank all the students in the courses I have taught over the years at the University of Houston–Downtown. They have helped in the revision of this book by providing me with additional ethics issues and by letting me know when something wasn't quite clear. I must also thank the police officers who have participated in the in-service ethics courses I have taught at the Houston Police Academy and those who attended workshops at national conferences. The dilemmas and viewpoints that they bring to these classes are obviously realistic and sincere.

I would also like to thank the reviewers provided by Wadsworth, including Bradley S. Chilton, Washington State University; Walt Copley, Metropolitan State College of Denver; Jane Foraker-Thompson, Boise State University; John Kleinig, John Jay College; and Emilio Viano, American University. Their comments were insightful and thorough. Kathleen Haney and Ray Wright, two philosophy professors at the University of Houston–Downtown, helped me understand some issues important to the discussion in Chapter 2. A number of others over the years have written or talked to me at national conferences about their experiences using the book in college classrooms. Their comments and suggestions have been much appreciated, and I hope that they will find this new edition continues to meet their needs. I would also like to thank Chief Mark Moulton, who, I believe, exemplifies ethical law enforcement administration and is also a good friend.

Over the years, I have been exposed to each of the subsystems of criminal justice. I started as a probation and parole officer in Washington State. I've spent hundreds of hours in prisons for men and for women in several states. I have also talked to, taught, and ridden with many police officers in several cities and volunteered for a couple of years on a police crisis team. Finally, I have clerked in a district attorney's office to complete a law degree. I have become more convinced over the years that despite its problems, the criminal justice system works at all because of the caring and committed people whom one can find in every segment of the system. Almost all have chosen the field because of a fundamental desire to help or work with people. It's also true that there are problems endemic to the system. There are organizational pressures toward lethargy and cynicism that challenge the strongest individual. There is often a lack of strong ethical leadership that would serve to motivate and enthuse workers. Unfortunately, these problems result in some agencies that foster and perpetuate the worst stereotypes of brutal cops, corrupt courts, and sadistic guards. One can only hope that the good people in the system will continue to find rewards in doing their jobs in the best way they can and never give in to the temptation of easy rationalizations for unethical and unprofessional behaviors. This book is dedicated to them.

Contents

⊰ 3 ⊱
Developing Moral Behavior   33

⊰ 4 ⊱
The Principles of Justice   49

⊰ 5 ⊱
Ethics and the Law   70

⚞ **6** ⚟

Ethics and Law Enforcement   91

⫷ 7 ⫸

Ethics and the Courts   136

⫷ 8 ⫸

The Ethics of Punishment and Correction   163

⊰ **9** ⊱

Professionalism, Pride, and Ethics for Real People   200

ETHICS IN CRIME AND JUSTICE
⊰ Dilemmas and Decisions ⊱

SECOND EDITION

᪥ 1 ᪥

Morality, Ethics, and Human Behavior

The words *morals* and *ethics* are often used in daily conversations. For instance, when public officials use their offices for personal profit, or when politicians accept bribes from special interest groups, they are described as *unethical*. When an individual does a good deed, engages in charitable activities or personal sacrifice, or takes a stand against wrongdoing, we might describe that individual as a *moral* person. Very often *morals* and *ethics* are used interchangeably. This first chapter will discuss how these terms are commonly used and some additional concepts related to them.

DEFINING MORAL BEHAVIOR

To begin with, we need to define what is included in the moral arena—that is, what sort of actions one judges as moral or immoral. We see that while some actions are always defined in moral terms, others are not. First of all, most writers agree that morals and ethics refer to *behavior*. We are concerned, for instance, with the act of stealing or the act of contributing to charity, rather than an idle thought that stealing a lot of money would enable us to buy a sailboat or a vague intention to be more generous. We are not necessarily concerned with how people feel or what they think about a particular action unless it has some bearing on what they do. The intention or motive behind a particular behavior is an important component of that behavior; for instance, in ethical formalism one must know the intent of an action in order to be able to judge it as moral, immoral, or neither. However, one must have some action to examine before making a moral judgment. One cannot commit immoral acts and still be thought of as a moral person. One must behave in a moral and ethical manner to be considered so.

Second, judgments of moral or ethical behavior are directed specifically to *human behavior*. A dog that bites is not considered immoral or evil, although we may judge careless pet owners who allow their dogs the opportunity to bite. Neither do we consider drought, famine, floods, or other natural disasters immoral, even though the death, destruction, and misery caused by these events are probably greater than that caused by all combined acts that humans have perpetrated on their victims. Behaviors of animals or events of nature cannot be judged in the same way as actions performed by human beings. The reasons we view them differently may become apparent in the next paragraph. Morality (or immorality) has only been applied to humans because of their capacity to reason. Because only humans have the capacity to be "good," which involves a voluntary, rational decision and subsequent action, only humans, of all members of the animal kingdom, have the capacity to be "bad."

In addition to limiting discussions of morality to human behavior, we also usually further restrict our discussion to behavior that stems from *free will* and *free action*. Guilt is not assigned to persons who are not sufficiently aware of the world around them to be able to decide rationally what is good or bad. The two groups commonly exempt from responsibility in this sense are the insane and the young. We do not judge the morality of their behavior. Although we may punish a two-year-old for hitting a baby, we do so to educate or socialize, not to punish as we would an older child or adult. We incapacitate the mentally ill to protect ourselves against their violence and strange behavior, but we consider them sick, not evil. This is true even if their actual behavior is indistinguishable from that of other individuals we do punish. For example, a murder may result in a death sentence or a hospital commitment, depending on whether the person is judged to be sane or insane, responsible or irresponsible.

Admittedly, at times we have difficulty in deciding whether behavior originates with free will. Historically, the insane and even those with physical illnesses such as epilepsy and leprosy were punished in the belief that they suffered these afflictions because of their own sinfulness. Even today, our views on such problems as alcoholism and drug addiction tend to be mixed. Some believe these are serious illnesses and therefore the person performing the negative behavior associated with the illness is not morally culpable; others believe that drinking or addiction and the consequent behavior is caused by moral weakness. Some people even view AIDS as a moral judgment because they believe that it is an affliction only those with certain lifestyles and sexual preferences can contract.

Attitudes toward *the age of reason* and when a child is said to have reached it also seem to be changing. Many states are now revising their laws regarding the trial and punishment of juveniles because of changing beliefs regarding the age of *rationality* and responsibility. Several states have reduced the age at which a child is considered an adult or have developed procedures allowing youngsters who have committed serious crimes, such as murder, to be remanded to adult courts for trial and sentencing. Part of the impetus for this change has been the apparent increase in crimes by juveniles and in the seriousness of such crimes. Whether this increase is a reality or not is irrelevant; the public believes it to be so and the law responds to public perception. This greater degree of ascribed responsibility is also reflected in new laws regarding the insane. Several states have passed laws that create a "guilty but insane" conviction rather than the previous acquittal "by reason of insanity." This unwillingness to excuse persons determined to be insane for their actions is probably also a result of public fear and a perception of widespread abuse of that legal defense.

Because of a lack of intent, someone who hurts another while doing something negligently or carelessly, such as driving while intoxicated or playing with a loaded weapon, may be less morally culpable than those who intentionally harm others. Because the element of deliberation is missing in negligent and careless actions, someone acting negligently or carelessly cannot be said to choose immoral action. One assumes that an individual who has weighed the consequences and knows the outcome and all the ramifications of the action and then proceeds has greater moral culpability than someone who has proceeded without such deliberation.

The moral culpability of an actor is not necessarily equivalent to legal culpability, although we have used the legal terms *negligence* and *recklessness. Mens rea,* or guilty mind, refers to the mental element in a crime. The four levels of legal culpability, relating to the degree of mental blameworthiness, are negligent, reckless, knowing, and intentional. These concepts are useful for us in moral judgment, yet we should not be misled that moral judgments and legal judgments are always the same. One might not be guilty of a crime and still be considered morally culpable. One might be guilty of a crime and be considered morally blameless. The differences between the law and morality will be discussed in a later section.

Intent and free will presuppose voluntary control over behavior. However, there is an argument that some actions are caused by life circumstances and therefore are not completely voluntary. For instance, an extreme of the liberal perspective on crime defends the idea that people who come from impoverished backgrounds and have known nothing but criminal role models cannot help their subsequent delinquency. According to this viewpoint, we may need to examine the relative freedom of choice for all groups. To paraphrase a famous quote: "It is just as illegal for a rich man to steal a loaf of bread as a poor man, but why would he want to?" This exemplifies the idea that we are all bound by limitations of birth and circumstance. If we were to analyze moral culpability on the basis of life choices, it might be that some people who commit serious crimes are less blameworthy than others who come from better backgrounds and commit less serious crimes because of their respective life positions. For instance, the embezzler who already makes a good salary might be more culpable than the mugger who has no job and steals because it is the only thing he or she knows how to do.

Finally, we usually discuss moral or immoral behavior only in those cases where the behavior significantly *affects others.* For instance, throwing a rock off a bridge would be neither good nor bad unless you could possibly hit or were aiming at a person below. If no one were there, your behavior would affect no one; if someone were, however, you might endanger that person's life. All the moral dilemmas we will discuss in this book involve at least two parties, and the decision to be made affects the other individual in every case. In reality, it is difficult to think of any action as completely isolated and without effects on others. Even self-destructive behavior is said to harm the people who love us and who would be hurt by such actions. We sense that this is an important aspect of judging morality when we hear the common rationale of those who, when caught, protest, "But nobody was hurt!" Indeed, even a hermit living alone on a desert island may engage in immoral or unethical actions. Whether he wants to be or not, the hermit is part of human society, and therefore some people would say that even he might engage in actions that could be judged immoral if they degrade or threaten the future of humankind, such as committing suicide or polluting the ocean.

One's actions toward nature might also be defined as immoral, and so relevant actions include not only actions done to people, but also to animals and to nature. To abuse or exploit animals can be defined as immoral—judgments can be made against cockfighting, dog racing, laboratory experimentation on animals, and even hunting. The growth of environmental ethics reflects increasing concern for the future of the planet. The rationale for environmental ethics may be that any actions that harm the environment affect all humans. It may also be justified by the belief that humankind is a part of nature—not superior to it—and should not use the earth for selfish purposes.

Thus far, we know morality and ethics concern the judgment of behavior as right or wrong. Furthermore, they concern only voluntary human behavior that affects other people, the earth, and living things.

Another comment we should make about behavior and morality is that philosophers distinguish between moral duties and *supererogatories*. Duties refer to those actions that an individual must perform in order to be considered moral. For instance, everyone may agree that one has a duty to support one's parents if able to do so, one has a duty to obey the law (unless it is an immoral law), and a police officer has a moral and ethical duty to tell the truth on a police report. These duties exist in one's personal life, and unique ethical duties exist in every profession. Other actions, considered supererogatories, are commendable but not required. A Good Samaritan who jumps into a river to save a drowning person, risking his or her own life to do so, has performed a supererogatory action—there is no moral condemnation of those who stood on the bank, because the action was above and beyond anyone's moral duty. Of course, if one can help save a life with no great risk to oneself, then a moral duty does exist in that situation, and police officers may have an ethical duty to get involved in certain life-threatening situations that others do not. There are also what are called *imperfect duties*. These are general values that one should uphold, but without specific application to when or how. For instance, most ethical systems would support a general duty of generosity, but there is no specific duty demanding a certain type or manner of generosity. Finally, there are many actions one performs during the course of a day, a year, and a lifetime that have no moral implications at all.

Morals and Ethics

One might ask at this point whether there is a difference between morals and ethics. The difference can be described in the following way: *morals* and *morality* refer to what is judged as good conduct (*immorality* is, of course, bad conduct). The term *moral* is also used to describe someone who has the capacity to make value judgments and discern right from wrong (Souryal 1992, 15). *Ethics* refers to the study and analysis of what constitutes good or bad conduct (Barry 1985, 5; Sherman 1981, 8).

There are several branches or schools of ethics. *Metaethics* is "the highly technical discipline investigating the meaning of ethical terms including a critical study of how ethical statements can be verified" (Barry 1985, 11). *Normative ethics* and *applied ethics* are concerned with the study of what constitutes right and wrong behavior in certain situations. Normative ethics determines what people ought to do and defines moral duties. Applied ethics is the application of ethical principles to specific issues. *Professional ethics* is an even more specific type of applied ethics relating to the behavior of certain professions or groups.

To many people, *ethics* has come to mean the definition of particular behaviors as right and wrong within a profession. Very often, in common usage, *morality* is used to speak of the total person, or the sum of a person's actions in every sphere of life, and *ethics* is used for certain behaviors relating to a profession. While discussions of morality and immorality can often get tied up with sin and other religious concepts, professional ethics is usually restricted to an analysis of behavior relevant to a certain profession. For instance, the medical profession follows the Hippocratic Oath, a declaration of rules and principles of conduct for doctors to follow in their daily practices; it dictates appropriate behavior and goals. Most professions, in fact, have their own set of ethical standards or canon of ethics.

Even though professional ethics typically restricts attention to areas of behavior relevant to the profession, these can be fairly inclusive and enter into what we might consider the private life of the individual. For instance, rules regarding relationships with patients, for doctors, or students, for professors, are usually included in codes of ethics for these professions. We are very much aware of how private behavior can affect a person's professional reputation in politics. When politicians are embroiled in controversial love affairs or are exposed as spouse abusers, these revelations have definite effects on their future, even if the behavior has nothing to do with competency in their field. It is clear that in some professions anyway—typically those involving public trust such as politics, education, and the clergy—there is a thin line between what may be judged as moral or immoral and what is judged in the realm of professional ethics.

It does not make a great deal of difference for our purposes whether we use the formal or colloquial definitions of *morals* and *ethics*. This text is an applied ethics text, in that we will be concerned with what should be defined as right and wrong behavior in the professions relevant to the criminal justice system and how people in these professions make decisions in the course of their careers. It is also a professional ethics text, because we are primarily concerned with professional ethics in criminal justice.

Law and Morality

Our laws legislate many aspects of our behavior. Laws, in the form of statutes and ordinances, tell us how to drive, how to operate our business, and what we can and cannot do in public and even in private life. They are the formal, written rules of society. Yet, they are not comprehensive in defining moral behavior. There is a law against hitting one's mother (assault) but no law against financially abandoning her; yet both are considered morally wrong. We have laws against "bad" behavior, such as burglarizing a house or embezzling from our employer, but we have very few laws prescribing "good" behavior, such as helping a victim or contributing to charity. The exception to this would be "Good Samaritan laws," which exist in some states and are quite common in

Europe. These laws make it a crime to pass by an accident scene or witness a crime without rendering assistance.

We have so many laws that not all of them are enforced regularly and people routinely break them and go unpunished. Some actions prohibited by law are thought to be private decisions of the individual and not especially wrong or harmful. Many people object to sodomy laws and other laws regulating sexual behavior because they feel this is private behavior and outside the parameters of social control; others object to the 55-mile-per-hour speed limit law. When laws prohibit behaviors that are not universally condemned, such as laws prohibiting alcohol, drugs, and prostitution, enforcement is more subject to criticism and, not incidentally, more prone to corruption because the ability to rationalize underenforcement or preferential treatment is greater.

We have had laws in the past that were or are now considered immoral—for instance, the internment of Japanese Americans during World War II and pre–Civil War laws that mandated the return of runaway slaves to their owners. An important question in the study of ethics is whether one can be a good person while obeying a bad law. Civil disobedience is the voluntary disobedience of what is considered an unjust or immoral law. Chapter 5 discusses morality and immorality in relation to the legal system in more detail.

Many times what is legal or illegal is confused with what is right or wrong; however, the two are not synonymous. Many use the law as their only source for judging moral behavior. In this view, if something is not illegal, it must be all right. Politicians, for instance, who are exposed for behaviors that violate public trust and/or take advantage of their position for private gain often justify their actions by the excuse that there was no law against such behavior. This rationalization is not satisfactory to us, of course, because the law is the "basement" of appropriate behavior—not the definition of it. One can follow the law to the letter and still violate professional ethics.

Regulations, Standards, and Ethics

In addition to laws, we have a vast number of *regulations* governing the activities of occupations from physician to plumber and organizations from governmental agencies to private clubs. Regulations typically come from a governmental authority and often specify sanctions for noncompliance; *standards* may come from private or public bodies and are often used as a basis for some type of accreditation; *guidelines* may come from a professional group and are usually recommendations rather than directions. Distinctions can be made between these terms, although often they are used interchangeably. These rules for behavior do not carry the formal sanctions of criminal law, but some may carry civil liabilities. Typically, the behavior in question is specific to that particular organization or occupation. Regulations and standards set down parameters of ideal behavior. Most regulations are from the state and federal governments. For instance, the Food and Drug Administration prescribes certain procedures and rules for pharmaceutical companies to follow in developing, testing, and distributing drugs. The Environmental Protection Agency watches over industry to make sure safe methods for disposal of hazardous wastes are implemented.

Noncompliance with standards and regulations is not equated with immoral behavior as readily as is criminal lawbreaking. Although fines may be levied against the construction supervisor who ignored Occupational Safety and Health Agency standards or the auto maker who violated standards of the Consumer Safety Board, ordinarily they are not considered criminals, even when these actions result in injury or death. Jeffrey Reiman (cited in Scheingold 1984, 23) observes the different reporting styles between a mining accident and a murder:

> Why do 26 dead miners amount to a "disaster," and six dead suburbanites a "mass murder"? "Murder" suggests a murderer, while "disaster" suggests the work of impersonal forces. But if over 1000 safety violations had been found in the mine—three the day before the first explosion—was no one responsible for failing to eliminate those hazards? And if someone could have prevented the hazards and did not, does that person not bear responsibility for the deaths of 26 men? Is he less evil because he did not want them to die although he chose to leave them in jeopardy? Is he not a murderer, perhaps even a mass murderer?

In fact, sometimes superficial compliance or outright violation of standards is considered good business practice. Examples of businesses or individuals in business routinely violating standards and/or regulations include insider information trading on Wall Street, toxic waste dumping in industry, and marketing of unsafe products in manufacturing. One example of what was considered good business practice being redefined as illegal is the law prohibiting hiring of illegal aliens. Many businesses had not been willing to follow standards against hiring illegal aliens because the lower labor costs resulted in greater profits. Redefinition from a regulatory infraction to a crime sometimes occurs when the behavior is persistent or the public becomes enraged over a particular incident or accident. When rules or standards are violated, other relevant criminal charges may be imposed as well. For instance, if a company blatantly violates safety regulations by forcing employees to work with toxic chemicals, company officials may be charged with negligent manslaughter if a worker dies. This is extremely rare, however, and there is usually a great deal of difference between the sanctions related to a violation of regulations and criminal lawbreaking.

It is interesting to observe that often regulations and rules for behavior seem to expand in inverse relation to the practiced ethics of a particular profession or organization. Often, when a breakdown in ethical behavior is detected, there is an attempt to bring people back in line with the formulation or expansion of rules. It seems, however, that in any profession, the most effective ethical guides are not those that specify behavior, but rather those that are consistent with and support an organizational ideal. People can find many ways of violating the spirit of an administrative rule while complying with its exact wording. Current examples abound of politicians routinely engaging in behavior or contracts involving conflicts of interest but no actual lawbreaking and lawyers who get around their code of professional responsibility by complying with the letter but not the spirit of the rule. In Chapter 6 we will discuss how impossible it is to specify all the ethical issues police officers may confront in their careers, and the ethical code for police officers does not attempt to do so. Rather, it gives general guidelines for priorities and goals while expecting the individual to make the correct decision in a specific situation.

Decision makers in organizations often, however, feel it is necessary to give employees extensive lists of rules. In an office these may include injunctions not to take supplies, not to make personal telephone calls, and not to spend more than fifteen minutes on breaks. These are very different from the ethical standards of honesty and integrity in the workplace. Where ethical standards are nonexistent, it is doubtful that multitudinous rules of behavior will suffice to eliminate wrongdoing.

Ethics, Morals, and Values

Value is defined as desirability, worth, or importance. Values, as judgments of worth, are often equated with moral judgments of goodness or right. We see that both can be distinguished from factual judgments, which can be empirically verified. Note the difference between the factual judgments "He is lying" and "It is raining" and the value judgments "She is a good woman" or "That was a wonderful day." The latter two judgments are similar to the moral judgments we will be discussing in later chapters. Some writers indicate that value judgments and moral judgments are indistinguishable since neither can be verified (Mackie 1977; Margolis 1971). Just as some believe there are no universal moral standards, some also feel that values are relativistic and individual. For these people, values are not universal and are subjective rather than objective; thus, they are not "truth," but rather something closer to opinion (Mackie 1977, 22–24).

Individual values form value systems. All people prioritize certain things they consider important in life. Behavior is generally consistent with values. For instance, some individuals may believe financial success is more important than family or health. In this case we may assume that their behavior will reflect the importance of that value and that therefore these persons will be workaholics, spending more time at work than with family and endangering their health with long hours, stress, and lack of exercise. Others may place a higher priority on values such as religious faith, wisdom, honesty, or independence than other values such as financial success or status. Discussions concerning values imply a choice or judgment. If, for instance, you were confronted with an opportunity to cheat on an exam, your values of academic success and honesty would be directly at odds. The choice you make in that particular situation may be decided by your value system. Some individuals value success above all other factors and will lie, cheat, and steal to achieve the standard of success to which they aspire. Others may hold honesty so dear that they would not steal even if it were in their best interests to do so—for instance, if they were starving and there were no other way to obtain food. Very often we live our lives without taking a close look at the value system that influences our behavior.

Values and morals are somewhat related, since one's values may dictate one's moral beliefs. Moral standards, for instance, derive from the value one places on such things as honesty, integrity, and trust. Universalists would not hesitate to add, however, that all values are not equal. Valuing money over life, for instance, would be wrong, as would valuing pleasure over charity. An explicit value system is a part of every ethical system, as we will see in the next chapter. Typically, the values involved in most ethical systems are the values of life, respect for the person, and the continued survival of society.

MORALS AND MORAL BEHAVIOR

One of the most difficult things to understand about human behavior is the disjunction between morals and behavior. We all can attest to the fact that believing something is wrong does not always prevent us from doing it. Very often, in fact, we engage in acts that we believe are bad, such as lying, stealing, cheating. In any group of people (such as a college class), a majority will have engaged in some type of wrongful act at least once.

Why do people engage in behavior they believe to be wrong? Criminology has tried in vain to explain why people commit unlawful acts. Psychological experiments show that a large percentage of schoolchildren will cheat when given an opportunity, even though they know it is wrong (Lickona 1976). Those in professions espouse ethical principles and then often are exposed for engaging in extremely unethical practices. Theories that endorse everything from learning to biological predisposition abound, but we still haven't answered fundamental questions of causation. Psychology and psychiatry attempt to explain what happens after the action has taken place; for instance, defense mechanisms such as rationalization and denial help absolve guilt. Personality theory may help us to predict what types of individuals are likely to engage in deviance. Yet with all these scientific and philosophical attempts to explain human action, we are still left with troubling questions when we read or hear about people who kill, steal, or otherwise offend our sense of morality. People's inhumanity to people is one of the great mysteries of life.

Our society ironically seems to endorse one set of beliefs while glorifying just the opposite. Examples of this glorification include that of Al Capone and Jesse James, who are in some ways cultural heroes even though they were known criminals. We have also glorified business executives when their actions could be defined as exploitative. We are dismayed by the amount of violence and crime in our society, yet the television shows that play on these themes are the most popular. We abhor lying, but politicians who tell the truth are rejected by voters. We profess to be a country that cherishes our Constitution and due process rights, but we clap and cheer in movie theaters when Dirty Harry types illegally kill the bad guys. Why do we idolize people who have done things we know and believe to be wrong? Some say we sublimate our wish for excitement and our greed through their exploits. Many of the ideals of success in this society involve aspects of ruthlessness and aggression, traits hard to reconcile with an ideal conception of the good person. At least in Western culture, a "good" person who upholds the ideals of honesty, charity, and selflessness is considered somewhat of a weakling or chump. The fact that our society has mixed values regarding what is considered good and desirable is reflected both in our popular culture and in individual action.

CONCLUSION

How does one determine what is ethical? Can one teach professional ethics and expect ethical behavior to result, and if so, how does one go about it? Does knowing a code of ethics in any given profession necessarily mean an individual will follow it? What are the unethical practices of criminal justice professions? These questions will be addressed in the following chapters, and in the last chapter we will return to the fundamental question: Why be moral?

Human beings tend to have quite complicated ideas about right and wrong, good and bad, and the moral and ethical. In this text, we will restrict our discussion primarily to issues in criminal justice and social control. This chapter closes with some discussion questions to answer in class or in a journal. Ethical dilemmas are also presented to force readers to make difficult decisions regarding their own value systems. Throughout the text, ethical dilemmas will be presented relevant to the topics discussed in each chapter. It is important that readers seriously reflect on the situations and also examine the rationale behind their decisions.

DISCUSSION QUESTIONS

1. Do you agree that a child before the legal age of reason is not morally culpable for his or her actions? Why or why not? What should the age of reason be?
2. What are some situations in which the individual cannot be considered rational or, alternatively, not acting from free will? Is the behavior that results moral or immoral?
3. Can you think of any act that an individual might engage in that does not affect other people? Describe.
4. Describe or collect recent newspaper stories regarding immoral or unethical conduct.
5. Why do people believe a practice (say, stealing) to be wrong and then go ahead and engage in that behavior anyway?
6. Describe a moral person.
7. Have you ever felt guilty after doing something? Why did you do it, then?

⤏ ETHICAL DILEMMAS ⤎

Please read and respond to the following situations. Be prepared to discuss your ideas.

Situation 1

Brenda S. was a rich businessman's daughter. She had had the best of everything all her life. Her future would have been college, a good marriage to a successful young man, and a life of comparative luxury, except that she was kidnapped by a small band of radical extremists who sought to overthrow the government by terror, intimidation, and robbery. After being raped, beaten, and locked in a small, dark closet for many days, continually taunted and threatened, Brenda was told she must participate with the terrorist gang in a bank robbery, or otherwise she and her family would be killed. During the course of the robbery, Brenda shot a bank guard. Was her action moral or immoral? What if she had killed the guard? What if the terrorists had her mother or father, too, and told her if she didn't cooperate, they would kill her parents immediately? What would you have done in her place?

Situation 2

You are a sales representative for a large auto parts manufacturer. It seems to be a fairly common practice for the merchandising agents of distributors to receive large sums of money in return for contracts. You have been asked by one such agent for a $50,000 "fee" for a $1-million contract with his company. Would you pay him? Is it ethical given the fact that everyone else is doing it? What if the contract were essential for the survival of your company (and your job)?

Situation 3[1]

In Europe, a woman is near death from a special kind of cancer. There is one drug that the doctors think might save her. It is a form of radium that a druggist in the same town has recently discovered. The drug is expensive to make, but the druggist is charging ten times what the drug cost him to make. He paid $200 for the radium and is charging $2000 for a small dose of the drug. The sick woman's husband, Heinz, goes to everyone he knows to borrow the money, but he can get together only about $1000, which is half of what it costs. He tells the druggist that his wife is dying and asks him to sell the drug cheaper or let him pay later. The druggist says, "No, I discovered the drug and I'm going to make money from it." Heinz is desperate and considers breaking into the man's store to steal the drug for his wife. Should he steal the drug? Why or why not? If Heinz doesn't love his wife, would this make a difference in your answer? Why or why not?

Situation 4

You are taking an essay exam in a college classroom. The test is closed book and closed notes, yet you look up and see that the person sitting next to you has hidden a piece of paper filled with notes under his blue book, which he is using to answer some questions. What would you do? Would your answer change if (a) the test was graded on a curve? (b) the student was a friend? (c) you knew the student was flunking the course and was going to lose a scholarship he needed on order to stay in school?

---

[1]From Lawrence Kohlberg, *The Psychology of Moral Development* (San Francisco: Harper & Row, 1984), p. 186.

2

Determining Moral
and Ethical Behavior

Each of us has opinions about social issues, such as abortion, adultery, and capital punishment. We also judge the morality of actions—both our own and those of others. We usually do not make decisions about right and wrong haphazardly or arbitrarily. Whether we recognize it or not, we all have moral or ethical systems that help us make decisions regarding specific behaviors. For instance, when someone asks us our views on any of the subjects just mentioned, we respond by judging the action as right or wrong, moral or immoral. Our response is not a factual statement, as if the person had asked us whether the action were legal or illegal. We may use facts to help us decide issues, and very often discussions get caught up in factual rather than moral questions. For instance, in judging the morality of abortion, a relevant fact is when, on average, a fetus can survive outside the womb. While this fact is important, it is not the same thing as the concept of life. The fact of viability can be proven, but the concept of life cannot—for what is life? What is death, for that matter—cessation of brain activity? Can someone be dead and then come back to life through medical technology, and if so, where does that leave traditional definitions of life and death? There is no agreement on when life begins or when it ends, but one's concept of life affects one's moral beliefs about abortion and the use of "life-supporting" technology.

In any moral judgment, it is important to identify and agree upon facts. Concepts may or may not be agreed upon but are also important to identify. For instance, one's concepts of duty, friendship, and loyalty are usually at the heart of professional ethical dilemmas that involve whistle blowing. These concepts as well as honesty and integrity, affect one's moral and ethical decision making. A moral judgment is one that probably was made with the help of basic moral principles. These moral principles are embedded in ethical systems. This chapter presents descriptions of a number of ethical systems.

ETHICAL SYSTEMS

Our principles of right and wrong form a framework for the way we live our lives. But where do they come from? Before you read on, answer the following question: If you believe it is wrong to steal, why do you believe this to be so? You probably said it is because your parents taught you or because your religion forbids it or maybe because society cannot tolerate people harming one another. Your answer is an indication of your *ethical system*. Ethical systems are the source of moral beliefs. They are the underlying premises from which you make judgments. Typically, they are beyond argument. That is, although ethical decisions may become the basis of debate, the decisions are based on fundamental "truths" or propositions that are taken as a given by the individual employing the ethical system.

C. E. Harris (1986, 33) refers to such ethical systems as "moral theories" or "moral philosophies," and defines them as a systematic ordering of moral principles:

> The order of reasoning from moral judgments, through more general moral principles, and finally to a basic moral principle, gives the outline of any moral theory. A moral theory has three levels: The level that you eventually arrive at when you trace your moral convictions back to your most basic moral principles is the moral standard. The intermediate moral principles are moral rules. The moral statement that begins the discussion is a moral judgment.

To put this discussion in our terms, an ethical system is a *moral theory* or basic set of principles of right and wrong. We don't consciously think of ethical systems, but we use them to make judgments all the time. For instance, we may say that a woman who leaves her children alone to go out drinking has committed an immoral act. That would be the *moral judgment* Harris refers to. Moral rules that underlie this judgment might be, "Children should be looked after," "One shouldn't drink to excess," or "Mothers should be good role models for their children." These basic moral rules are derived from an infrastructure of moral principles that is at the heart of all moral decision making. In this chapter we will not discuss all possible ethical systems, nor do we claim that the short descriptions here are enough to give the reader a total picture of each of the systems mentioned. A reader would be well advised to consult texts in philosophy and ethics for more detail. However, we will explore some of the most prevalent views on ethics; specifically, religious ethics, natural law, ethical formalism (Kantism), utilitarianism, the ethics of virtue, the ethics of care, and egoism. These ethical systems generate moral rules; for instance, in the example just given, we might say, "Children should be looked after," because the utility derived from caring for children is a relative good for all of society and outweighs the individual utility (or good) that might be derived from the mother's very transitory pleasure. In this case, our ethical system would be utilitarianism. The moral rules of utilitarianism are consistent with the premise that what is good is that which results in the greatest utility for the greatest number.

Ethical systems have been described as having the following characteristics (Baelz 1977, 19):

1. They are prescriptive; certain behavior is demanded or proscribed. They are not just abstract principles of good and bad, but rather have substantial impact on what we do.
2. They are authoritative; they are not ordinarily subject to debate. Once an ethical framework has been developed, it is usually beyond question.

3. Moral considerations arising from ethical systems are logically impartial or universal. If something is considered wrong it is wrong for everyone. Relativism has no place in an ethical framework.
4. They are not self-serving. They are directed towards others; what is good is good for everyone, not just the individual.

Notice that in the last instance, ethical frameworks are described as "not self-serving." We will discuss one ethical system, egoism, that is indeed self-serving; in fact, it is the very basis of the system that what is good for the individual is good in itself. Although egoism is included in this chapter, it should be noted that it is widely rejected as an ethical system. In fact, some authors prefer to view egoism as the lack of an ethical system and as an example of ethical relativism.

Let us now explore some of the basic ethical systems that might shape our moral and ethical principles. Remember, this is by no means a comprehensive list, nor are the systems fully explained herein. One should turn to philosophical texts for a more complete understanding of these ideas.

Religious Ethics

Probably the most frequent source of individual ethics is religion. Religion might be defined as a body of beliefs that address fundamental issues such as, "What is life?" and "What is good and evil?" A religion also provides moral guidelines and directions on how to live one's life. For instance, Christians are taught the Ten Commandments, which prohibit certain behaviors defined as wrong. The authority of *religious ethics*, in particular Christian ethics, stems from a willful and rational god. For believers, the authority of God's will is beyond question and there is no need for further examination because of this perfection. If God's character is perfection, or perfect good, what is said to be right or good cannot be questioned as long as it comes from the authority of God. The only possible controversy comes from human interpretation of God's commands. Indeed, these differences in interpretation are the source of most religious strife.

Religious ethics is, of course, much broader than simply Christian ethics. Religions such as Buddhism, Confucianism, Judaism and Islam also provide a basis for ethics, since they provide explanations of how to live the "good life" and also address other philosophical issues, such as "What is reality?" Pantheistic religions, those of primitive hunter-gatherer societies, promote the belief that there is a living spirit in all things. A basic principle follows from this belief that life is important and one must have respect for all things, including trees, rivers, and animals. There must be a willful and rational god or god figure, however, before there can be a judgment of right and wrong, and thus before a religion can serve as the basis for an ethical system. Those religions that do have a god figure consider that figure to be the source of principles of ethics and morality.

It is also true that of the religions we might discuss, many have very similar basic moral principles. Many religions have their own version of the Ten Commandments; in this regard, Islam is not too different from Judaism, which is not too different from Christianity. The Golden Rule of "Do unto others as you would have them do unto you" is echoed in Hinduism ("Do naught to others which, if done to thee, would cause thee pain: this is the sum of duty"), in Buddhism ("In five ways should a clansman minister to his friends and familiars . . . by treating them as he treats himself"), in Confucianism ("What you do not want done to yourself, do not do unto others"), and in Judaism ("Whatsoever thou wouldest that men should not do unto thee, do not do that to them") (Reiman 1990, 147). However, while what is right and wrong stems always from the authority of God and the basic rights and wrongs are not too different, particular tenets of behavior may vary from religion to religion because of different interpretations of God's will. Dancing may be immoral to some; drinking, working on Sunday (or Saturday), abortion, and so on are all viewed differently by various religions.

One issue in Western religious ethics is how to determine God's will. Some believe that God is inviolable, and positions on moral questions are unchanging. This is a legalist position. Others feel that God's will varies according to time and place—the situationalist position. According to this position, situational factors are important in determining the rightness of a particular action. Different decisions may be made about behavior as a result of the situation surrounding it (Borchert and Stewart 1986, 157).

According to Barry (1985), human beings can "know" God's will in three ways. The first is through individual conscience. That is, an individual's conscience is the best source for discovering what God wants one to do. If one feels uncomfortable about a certain action, it is probably wrong. The second way we might discover God's will is by referring to religious authorities. They can interpret right and wrong for us and are our best source if we are confused about certain actions. The third way is to go directly to the Bible, Koran, or Torah, as the source of God's law. Some believe that the written word of God holds the answers to all moral dilemmas (Barry 1985, 51–54).

Strong doubts exist as to whether any of these methods are true indicators of divine command. Our consciences may be no more than the products of our psychological development, influenced by our environment. Religious authorities are after all only human, with human failings. Even the Bible, as we know, seems to be used by various groups, all of whom disagree yet can find support within its pages. For instance, some may conclude that capital punishment is prohibited by religious ethics ("Vengeance is mine saith the Lord"); however, others might use other references from the Bible to support capital punishment ("an eye for an eye").

The question of whether people can ever know God's will has been explored through the ages. Thomas Aquinas (1225–1274) believed that human reason was sufficient not only to prove the existence of God but also to discover God's divine commands (Borchert and Stewart 1986, 159). Others feel that reason is not sufficient to know God and that it comes down to unquestioning belief, so that reason and knowledge must always be separate from faith. These people believe that one can only know whether an action is consistent with God's will if it contributes to general happiness, because God intends for us to be happy, or when the action is done through the "holy spirit"—that is, when someone performs the action under the influence of true faith (Borchert and Stewart 1986, 164–171).

These two positions—that one can use reason to understand God and that one must rely on faith—do not help us much when we have a sincere confusion over what to do or what is right. Some who argue on the basis of religious ethics do so from a legalist view: what is considered wrong is always wrong. An example is the Catholics' absolute condemnation of suicide. Others may argue from a situationalist perspective: God's will may depend on situational circumstances. For instance, lying may be wrong unless it is to protect an innocent; or stealing may be wrong unless it is to protest injustice and to help unfortunates. In fact, some would say it is impossible to have an a priori knowledge of God's will because that would put us above God's law since we ourselves would be "all-knowing"; rather, for any situation, if we are prepared to receive them, we can know God's divine commands through faith and conscience.

The example of abortion illustrates how an ethical system based on religion might resolve a moral dilemma. The Catholic church has stated unequivocally that abortion is wrong. This judgment, based on the interpretation of God's will, condemns those who usurp God's power over life and death. If one accepts the pope as the true and only representative of God on earth, there is no choice to be made regarding abortion. This is a legalist view based on religious authority. Other religions and disaffected Catholics base their arguments on God's will also; the difference is in interpretation. If one uses evidence from the Bible to support a pro-choice stand, the basis of the belief is still a religious ethical system. There are others who do not deny that religious doctrine forbids abortion, yet support it anyway based on other ethical systems, such as the ethics of care, utilitarianism, or egoism, with the accompanying belief that God is merciful and would forgive the abortion. Obviously this stand is still influenced by a religious ethical system because of the belief that God would condemn the action while also forgiving it.

Very often issues are not as clear-cut as the abortion question seems to be. For instance, given the moral dilemma of Heinz in Chapter 1, could one make a choice using religious ethics? You will recall that Heinz had to make a moral choice between his wife's life and breaking the law. If one decides that Heinz should steal the drug, can this answer be supported by religious ethics? Some religions, for instance, hold that cure is in the hands of God and humans should not interfere. If one was raised with this religious belief, it would be simple to decide that it was God's will whether Heinz's wife should live or die and that therefore it would be wrong for him to steal. Other religions might hold that life is more important than law or that a person is God's instrument and that God shows intent by a sign. In this case Heinz might decide that God intended for him to get the drug—otherwise the druggist would not have been able to invent it— and therefore he must act out God's will by stealing it.

Many ethical issues are not as difficult. Stealing from your place of employment is obviously wrong; one need look no further than the Ten Commandments to determine that issue. Putting in a day's honest work for a day's pay is also dictated by religious ethics because to do otherwise would be a type of stealing. Basic values of charity and humility are also prescribed by religious ethics.

Thus far we have concentrated mostly on Christianity, although we mentioned that other religions can also serve as the basis of a religious ethical system. In fact, Christianity is not the most prevalent religion in the world, nor is it the oldest. Islam, Buddhism, Confucianism, and Hinduism each present fundamental truths about what is good and the nature of morality. We do not have time to do more than briefly list some of the major tenets of each, and the reader must keep in mind that there are other religions that we have not discussed at all.

Islam   One of the newest yet largest religions is Islam. Like Christianity, this religion recognizes one god, Allah. Jesus and other religious figures are recognized as prophets, as is Muhammed, who is considered the last and greatest prophet. Islam has the Koran, which is taken much more literally as the word of Allah than the Bible is taken by most Christians. There is a great deal of fatalism in Islam; *Im Shallah,* meaning "If God wills it," is a prevalent theme in Moslem societies. On the other hand, there is recognition that if people choose evil, they do so freely. The five pillars of Islam are: (1) repetition of the creed (*Shahada*), (2) daily prayer (*Salah*), (3) almsgiving (*Zakah*), (4) fasting (*Sawm*), and (5) pilgrimage (*Hajj*). One of the other features of Islam is the idea of the holy war. In this concept, the faithful who die defending Islam against infidels will be rewarded in the afterlife (Hopfe 1983).

Buddhism   Siddhartha Gautama (Buddha) attained enlightenment and preached to others how to do the same and achieve *nirvana* —the release from suffering. He taught that good behavior is that which follows the "middle path" between hedonistic pursuit of sensual pleasure and asceticism. Essentials of Buddhist teachings are ethical conduct, mental discipline, and wisdom. Ethical conduct is based on universal love and compassion for all living beings. Compassion and wisdom are needed in equal measures. Ethical conduct can be broken into right speech (refraining from lies, slander, enmity, and rude speech); right action (abstaining from destroying life, stealing, and dishonest dealings, and helping others lead peaceful and honorable lives); and right livelihood (abstaining from occupations that bring harm to others, such as arms dealing and killing animals). To follow the "middle path" one must abide by these guidelines (Kessler 1992).

Confucianism   Confucius taught a humanistic social philosophy that included central concepts such as *Ren,* which is human virtue and humanity at its best as well as the source of moral principles; *Li,* which is traditional order, ritual, or custom; *Xiao,* which is familial love; and *Yi ,* which is rightness, both a virtue and a principle of behavior— that is, one should do what is right because it is right. The doctrine of the mean exemplifies one aspect of Confucianism that emphasizes a cosmic or natural order. Humans are a part of nature and are included in the scheme of life. Practicing moderation in one's life is part of this natural order and reflects a "way to Heaven" (Kessler 1992).

Hinduism   In Hinduism, the central concept of *Karma* can be understood as consequence. Specifically, what one does in one's present life will determine what happens in a future life. The goal is to escape the eternal birth-rebirth cycle by living one's life in a moral manner so that no bad Karma will occur (Kessler 1992). People start out life in the lowest caste but if they live a good life, they will be reborn as members of a higher caste, until they reach the highest *Brahman* caste and only at that point can the cycle end. An early source for Hinduism was the Code of Manu. In this code are found the ethical ideals of Hinduism, which include pleasantness, patience, control of mind, nonstealing, purity, control of the senses, intelligence, knowledge, truthfulness, and nonirritability (Hopfe 1983).

To summarize, the religious ethics system is widely used and accepted. The authority of the god figure is the root of all morality; basic conceptions of good, evil, right, and wrong come from interpretations of the god figure's will. Many people throughout history have wrestled with the problem of determining what is right according to God, and current controversies within and between religious groups illustrate the unresolved difficulties that continue to exist.

Natural Law

In the *natural law* ethical system, there is a universal set of rights and wrongs, similar to many religious beliefs, but there is no reference to a specific supernatural figure. Originating with the Stoics, natural law is an ethical system wherein no difference is recognized between physical laws—such as the law of gravity—and moral laws. Morality is part of the natural order of the universe. Further, this morality is the same across cultures and times. In this view, Christians simply added God as a source of law (as other religions added their own prophets and gods), but there is no intrinsic need to resort to a supernatural figure since these universal laws exist quite apart from any religion (Maestri 1982).

The natural law ethical system presupposes that what is good is what is natural and what is natural is what is good. The essence of morality is what conforms to the natural world; thus, there are basic inclinations that form the core of moral principles. The preservation of one's own being, for instance, is a basic, natural inclination, and thus is a basic principle of morality. Actions consistent with this natural inclination would be those that preserve one's own life, as in self-defense, but also those that preserve or maintain the species, such as a prohibition against murder. Other inclinations are peculiar to one's species—for instance, humans are social animals, and thus sociability is a natural inclination that leads to altruism and generosity. These are natural and thus moral. The pursuit of knowledge or understanding of the universe might also be recognized as a natural inclination of humans, and thus, actions that conform to this natural inclination are moral.

Another thread of this ethical system is that all have inherent rights by virtue of their existence. Souryal (1992) describes natural law as the "steward" of natural rights. This country's founders might be described as natural law theorists. In the Constitution, "natural rights" endowed by the creator are recognized. Natural law theory is either extremely pessimistic about the nature of humankind or optimistic. A pessimistic version of natural humanity is Hobbes's "war of all against all," and "the law of the jungle" is used to describe a natural state where the strong prey upon the weak. On the other hand, there is also the belief that humans are naturally more inclined toward altruism and sociability than aggression. In this view, the natural state of humankind is one of peaceful coexistence, and it is only when civilization thwarts natural impulses that we see negative and immoral behaviors emerge.

Natural law can be applied to the ethical dilemmas we have discussed thus far. In the example of abortion, natural law ethics would probably condemn the decision to abort unless it was to save the life of the mother, since it runs counter to a natural inclination to preserve life. In the Heinz example, one can see that it would be a natural response to help a loved one, consistent with the natural sociability characteristic. Natural law ethics would support stealing the drug.

Natural law theory defines good as that which is natural. The difficulty of this system is identifying what is consistent and congruent with the natural inclinations of humankind.

Ethical Formalism

Immanuel Kant (1724–1804) believed moral worth comes from doing one's duty (Kant, 1949). Just as there is the law of the family (father's rule), the law of the state and country, and the law of international relations, there is also a universal law of right and wrong. Morality, according to Kant, arises from the fact that humans, as rational beings, impose these laws and strictures of behavior upon themselves. People, as flesh and spirit combined, are in constant dynamic conflict over base desires and morality; only by appealing to higher reason can they do what is right. Kant's *categorical imperative* states that "man must act only according to the maxim whereby one can at the same time will that it should become a universal law." At all times one is obliged to behave in a manner one would hope all people would follow. This is an absolute command. According to Kant, *hypothetical imperatives* are commands that designate certain actions to attain certain ends; an example is "*If* I want to be a success, *then* I must do well in college." A categorical imperative, by contrast, commands action that is necessary without any reference to intended purposes or consequences (Kant 1949, 76):

> This imperative is categorical. It concerns not the material of the action and its intended result but the form and the principle from which it results. What is essentially good in it consists in the intention, the result being what it may. This imperative may be called the imperative of morality.

In Kant's view, pure reason demands that one must abide by moral dictates—the categorical imperative—to avoid chaos. Moral laws come from within and their expression places the person in the true order of the universe.

Ethical formalism is a *deontological* approach: the important determinant for judging an act to be moral or not is not its consequence but only the motive or intent of the actor. This is different from *teleological* approaches, which look at the ends of an act—in other words, the act's consequences—to determine moral judgments. Egoism and utilitarianism are teleological in that they posit that acts are good if they contribute to either an individual good, in egoism, or the general welfare, in utilitarianism. Ethical formalism judges the intent of the actor. According to Kant, the only thing that is intrinsically good is a *good will*. If someone does an action from good will, then even if it results in bad consequences, it can be considered a moral action. On the other hand, if someone performs some activity that looks on the surface to be altruistic but does it with an ulterior motive—for instance, to curry favor or gain benefit—then that act is not moral. For instance, Gold, Braswell, and McCarthy (1991) offer the example of a

motorist stranded by the side of the road; another driver who comes along has a decision to help or pass by. If the decision is made to stop and help, this would seem to be a
good act. Not so, according to ethical formalism, unless it is done from a good will. If
the helper stops because he or she expects payment, wants a return favor, or for any
other reason other than a good will, then the act is only neutral—not moral. Only if the
help springs from a good will can we say that it is truly good. A consequentialist would
say the act is good because the end result is good for all. For an action to be moral, then,
the actor must perform it from a good will and the action must not violate the categorical imperative.

A system such as ethical formalism is considered an absolutist system—if something is wrong, it is wrong all the time, such as murder or lying. To assassinate evil ty-
rants like Hitler or Idi Amin might be considered moral under a teleological system because of the action's consequence of ridding the world of dangerous people. However,
in the deontological view, if the act and intent of killing is wrong, it is always wrong;
thus, assassination must also be considered immoral in all cases. Even lying is deemed
to be immoral in this system, despite some good arguments for the case that at times,
lying might be beneficial. For instance, Kant used an example that if someone asked to
be hidden from an attacker in close pursuit, and then the attacker asked where the potential victim was hiding, it would be immoral to lie about it. This seems wrong to
many and serves to dissuade people from seeing the value of ethical formalism. However, according to Kant, lying or not lying is not the determining factor in that scenario
or in any other. All good things and all bad things that happen to any individual are
caused by luck—not any human action. The attacker may not kill the potential victim;
the victim may still be able to get away; the attacker may be justified—the point is that
no one person can control anything in life so the only thing that makes sense is to live
by the categorical imperative.

Another point Kant made, however, was that a lie is only a lie when the recipient is
led to believe he or she is being told the truth. The attacker in the previous scenario or
an attacker who has one "by the throat" demanding one's money has no right to expect
the truth; thus, it would not be immoral to not tell this person the truth. Only if you led
the attacker to believe that you were going to tell the truth and then did not would it
violate the categorical imperative. In other words, Kant distinguishes untruths from
lies. To not tell the truth when the attacker doesn't deserve the truth is not a lie; but if
one intentionally and deliberately sets out to deceive, then that is a lie—even if it is being told to a person who doesn't deserve the truth (Kant 1981).

The following are some of the principles of Kant's ethical formalism (Bowie 1985,
157):

1. Act only on that maxim through which you can at the same time will that it should
   become a universal law. In other words, for any decision of behavior to be made,
   examine whether that behavior would be acceptable if it were a universal law to be
   followed by everyone. For instance, a student might decide to cheat on a test; but
   for this action to be moral, the student would have to agree that everyone should be
   able to cheat on tests. In the situation involving Heinz and the expensive drug, for

one to approve of Heinz's stealing, one would have to agree that it would be morally acceptable for everyone in similar situations to steal.

2. Act in such a way that you always treat humanity, whether in your own person or that of any other, never simply as a means but always at the same time as an end. In other words, one should not use people for one's own purposes. For instance, suicide might be considered immoral if one has the goal of making relatives or other people feel guilty and hurt. This would be contrary to Kant's second principle because the person would be using his or her own body as a means to an end. Another example would be offering a gift to someone in the hope that they will do something in return; this would also be using them as a means for one's own ends. Even otherwise moral actions, such as giving to charity or doing charitable acts for others, would be considered immoral if done for ulterior motives such as self-aggrandizement.

3. Act as if you were, through your maxims, a lawmaking member of a kingdom of ends. This principle directs that the individual's actions should contribute to and be consistent with universal law. Also, because we freely choose to abide by moral law and these laws are self-imposed rather than imposed from the outside, they are a reflection of the higher nature of humans.

Additional elements of Kant's philosophy include the idea that one must freely perform acts consistent with the categorical imperative in order for those actions to be moral. This relates to our earlier discussion of free will, where we questioned whether unintended action or irrational action can ever be moral. Kant proposed that an action can only be moral when there is free will and intent; otherwise the action is only neutral. Finally, Kant repudiated the idea that actions are moral because they make people happy or even that a moral life will make the individual happy. Kant believed that although a moral life may make a person happy, that is not a certainty, nor the reason to be moral (Borchert and Stewart 1986, 212).

This ethical framework is somewhat difficult to understand, but very simply it follows from the beliefs that an individual must follow a self-imposed moral law and that one is capable of using reason to determine right actions since one can evaluate any action using the principles just listed.

Applying Kant's principles, let us see whether ethical formalism can help us solve some ethical dilemmas. We can use the abortion example again. The first principle states that one must act in such a way that the behavior could be universal. If we believe abortions to be morally acceptable, we have to agree to abortion rights as a universal law.

The second principle states that we must not treat others as a means to an end. We might consider that the mother is treating the unborn fetus as a means since the removal of the fetus would result in the end of the inconvenience or problems caused by the pregnancy. On the other hand, most ethical formalists would probably not consider the unborn as persons with inherent rights; thus, we might decide that the mother is being treated as a means to an end if she is denied an abortion since she is treated only as the means for the baby's birth. This interpretation obviously depends on one's definition of life. This illustrates a situation where facts and concepts are important in deciding moral dilemmas. Most anti-abortionists would argue that the unborn fetus is already a living human deserving of respect. Most pro-choice advocates argue that life begins at some later point than conception, often in the second trimester or the fifth month, or at the point of viability. The Catholic church used to hold the view that human life begins at the moment of "quickening," or when the woman first feels the movement of the fetus in her womb. One's concept of life determines when the fetus is deserving of respect when applying the second principle, which is important to the resolution of the dilemma.

The third principle might be interpreted to mean that all of our behavior must be autonomous and of free will to be judged as moral or immoral. We would have to make a decision freely in order for it to be moral. If a person was frightened into having a baby or pressured into aborting it, neither of these actions would be judged in moral terms.

Turning to the situation of Heinz, the categorical imperative would probably judge stealing the drug to be immoral. We would be unlikely to accept a universal law allowing theft of things we can't afford. Furthermore, remember that Kant was not concerned with the consequences of the action; therefore, the drug's use in keeping Heinz's wife alive is irrelevant in deciding the morality of the theft. According to ethical formalism, it is pure luck that she is sick in the first place, and stealing the drug will not ensure her survival since she may be hit by a bus the day after she takes the drug, or the drug may not work, or Heinz may get killed stealing the drug. One cannot justify an otherwise immoral act because of the good consequence that may or may not result.

Criticism is directed at the Kantian view that morality is limited to duty. One might argue that duty is the baseline of morality, not the highest aspiration of it. The Kantian view might even hold that there is no moral duty to another. Another problem with the Kantian view is the priority of motive and intent over result. It may be seriously questioned whether the intention to do good, regardless of result or perhaps with negative result, is always moral. Many would argue that the consequences of an action and the actual result must be evaluated to determine morality (Maestri 1982, 9–10).

Other writers present variations of deontological ethics that do not depend so heavily on Kant. The core elements of any deontological ethical system are the importance placed on intention and judging the act itself rather than the consequences of the act; the universal law application; and the prohibition against treating people as a means.

Utilitarianism

Utilitarianism is a teleological ethical system; what is good is determined by the consequences of the action. Jeremy Bentham (1748–1832), one proponent of utilitarianism, believed that the primary determinant of the morality of an action is whether the action contributes to the good of the majority. Human nature, according to Bentham, is to maximize pleasure and avoid pain, and a moral system must be consistent with this natural fact.

Nature has placed mankind under the governance of two sovereign masters, pain and plea-sure. It is for them alone to point out what we ought to do, as well as to determine what we shall do. On the one hand, the standard of right and wrong, on the other the chain of causes and effects, are fastened to their throne. They govern us in all we do, in all we say, in all we think; every effort we can make to throw off our subjection, will serve but to demonstrate and confirm it. In words, a man may pretend to abjure their empire: but in reality he will remain subject to it all the while. The principle of utility recognizes the sub-jection, and assumes it for the foundation of that system. (Bentham, cited in Borchert and Stewart 1986, 183)

The "utilitarian doctrine asserts that we should always act so as to produce the greatest possible ratio of good to evil for everyone concerned" (Barry 1985, 65). That is, if you can show that an action significantly contributes to the general good, it is good. In situations where one must decide between a good for an individual and a good for society, then society should prevail, despite the wrong being done to an individual. This is because generally the utility or good derived from that action outweighs the small amount of harm done (because the harm is done only to one whereas the good is multi-plied by the many who benefit). For instance, if it could be shown that using someone as an example would be an effective deterrent to crime whether or not the person was actually guilty, then the wrong done to that person by this unjust punishment might be outweighed by the good resulting for society. This is assuming citizens would not find out about the injustice and lose respect for the authority of the legal system, which would be a negative effect for all concerned.

Bentham did not judge the content of utility. He considered pleasure a good whether it derived from vice, such as avarice or greed, or from virtue, such as charity and kindness. Later utilitarians, primarily John Stuart Mill (1806–1873), recognized and placed a value on the type of pleasure and utility. Some kinds of utility are judged better than others. For instance, art offers a different utility for society than alcohol. On the other hand, who is to determine what utility is to be ascribed to these pleasures? A value judgment is certainly being made, but the question is whose criteria should be used (Borchert and Stewart 1986, 190).

In one widely used hypothetical moral dilemma, a woman and her children are hiding in a cabin that is being attacked by Indians. If one of the babies starts crying, should the woman suffocate the baby to save the rest of the children and herself? Ethical formalism would condemn the action because the baby's death would be a means to an end (survival); and the universal law (that everyone should act in the same way under similar circumstances) could not be applied since it is unlikely anyone would agree that babies should always be sacrificed to save others. Remember, if Kant were forced to de-fend the view that the woman should risk the lives of the other children, he would say that she doesn't know for sure that they will be killed if she does not suffocate the baby and she doesn't know whether they may be killed even if she does suffocate the baby—maybe the cabin will be burned down and they will all perish.

Religious ethics would also probably not support such an action; if God wanted the others to survive, the Indians would go away or not hear the baby. Utilitarianism, on the other hand, may very well provide the basis for defining that action as moral since the good derived from the baby's death would be the survival of the rest of the children. Of course, some might interpret the situation differently. For instance, the baby's death might result in a callousness toward human life among those involved and thus in the long term cause more negative results than positive utility.

Utilitarianism has two forms: act utilitarianism and rule utilitarianism. The basic difference between the two can be summarized as follows. In *act utilitarianism*, the basic utility derived from an action is alone examined. We look at the consequences of any action for all involved and weigh the units of utility accordingly. In *rule utilitarianism*, one judges that action in reference to the precedent it sets and the long-term utility of the rule set by that action. We might use the example of Heinz again to illustrate this point. Act utilitarianism would probably support stealing the drug because the utility of his wife's survival would outweigh the loss to the druggist, who could always make up more of the drug. Therefore, the greater utility of the theft would lead to a judgment that the theft was moral. On the other hand, rule utilitarianism would be concerned with the effect that the action would have if made into a rule for behavior. The rule that anytime an individual could not afford a drug, he or she could steal it, would result in a general state of lawlessness and a general disrespect for the law. Such a rule would not result in the greatest utility for the greatest number. With rule utilitarianism, then, we are not only concerned with the immediate utility of the action but also with the long-term utility or harm if the action were to be a rule for all similar circumstances. If we reject Heinz's proposal to steal the drug, it may result in his wife's death, but in the long term, laws against theft, which provide general good for all, will be protected.

These differences are also apparent in a utilitarian argument about the morality of abortion. Act utilitarianism might evaluate the obvious harm to the fetus against the positive utility to the mother. The long-term harm to the fetus if it were born into a hostile and poverty stricken family would also need to be considered. In act utilitarianism, then, we would be concerned with the total utility to the fetus, to the mother, and to society compared with the disutility to all. It may very well be the case that abortion is judged moral for one woman and immoral for another, because of different situational elements and consequences. Rule utilitarianism would evaluate the long-term utility derived if we were to translate the action into a general rule. Would a situation where all women could obtain abortions on demand result in a net gain of happiness and utility for society or a net loss? However one answers that question, it is clear that this is a different decision-making process than that described for act utilitarianism.

Criticism of the utilitarian framework centers around the difficulty of measurement and implementation. How does one measure the pleasure derived from an action? No measuring device exists to help us; therefore, the equation determining what is good is hypothetical at best. Further, as discussed earlier, pleasure is not defined and it is unclear whether pleasure must be the same for all people or can be individually defined. Another argument against utilitarianism focuses on the assumption that happiness is derived from pleasure. As other systems indicate, it may be that happiness derives from something else, such as doing one's duty or altruistic sacrifice (Maestri 1982, 6).

Also, there is little concern for individual rights in utilitarianism. Note this is extremely inconsistent with natural law and ethical formalism. In both natural law and ethical formalism, it is presumed that each individual has inherent rights and must be treated with respect and not be used as a means to an end. Under utilitarianism, the rights of one individual may be sacrificed for the good of many. For instance, Churchill allowed Coventry to be bombed in World War II so the Germans would not know the Allies had cracked the Germans' secret military radio code. Several hundred English people were killed in the bombing raid. It was a calculated risk for greater long-run gains: bringing the war to an end sooner. In a well-known hypothetical dilemma, five people are in a lifeboat with only enough food and water for four. It is certain that they will survive if there are only four; it is also certain that they will all perish if one does not go overboard. What should be done? Under Kantian ethics, it would be unthinkable to sacrifice an innocent even if it means four others may live. Under utilitarian ethics, it is conceivable that the murder might be justified.

In summary, utilitarianism differs from the other two ethical frameworks in that it holds that morality must be determined by the consequences of an action. Society and the survival and benefit of all are more important than any individual. This is a functional theory of right and wrong—something is right when it benefits the continuance and good health of society. Rule utilitarianism may be closer to the principles of Kantism, since it looks at general universal laws; the difference between the two is that the laws themselves are judged right or wrong depending on the motives behind them under ethical formalism, while utilitarianism looks to the long-term consequences of the behavior prescribed by the rules to determine their morality.

The Ethics of Virtue

Each of the foregoing ethical systems seeks to define "What is good action?" The *ethics of virtue* instead asks the question, "What is a good person?" This ethical system rejects the approach that one might use reason to discover what is good. Instead the principle that to be good, one must do good applies. Virtues that a good person possesses include thriftiness, temperance, humility, industriousness, honesty, and so on.

The roots of this system are in Aristotle who defined virtues as "excellences." These qualities are what enable an individual to move toward the achievement of what it takes to be human. Habits of moral virtue are more easily instilled when "right" or just laws also exist. Moral virtue is a state of character where choices are consistent with the *principle of the golden mean*. This principle states that virtue is always the median between two extremes of character. For instance, liberality is the mean between prodigality and meanness; proper pride is the mean between empty vanity and undue humility, and so on (Albert, Denise, and Peterfreund 1984). Hume might also be considered as endorsing the ethics of virtue, although we will also discuss Hume in the next section since he believed that morality is a matter of cultivating character traits that give a person inward peace of mind and consciousness of integrity and that make a person good company to others (Baier 1987). A current philosopher defines virtues as those dispositions that will sustain us in the relevant "quest for the good, by enabling us to overcome the harms, dangers, temptations and distractions which we encounter, and which will furnish us with increasing self-knowledge and increasing knowledge of the good" (MacIntyre 1991, 204).

Moral virtue comes from habit. This is why this system emphasizes character. The idea here is that one does not do good because one reasons out what the good action is using utilitarianism or ethical formalism; rather, one does good because of the patterns of a lifetime. If one has a good character, she or he will do the right thing; but if one has a bad character, she or he will usually choose the immoral path. In *Character and Cops: Ethics in Policing*, Edwin Delattre uses an excerpt from a police chief's biography to illustrate an individual who represents the ethics of virtue:

> One Friday, just before Christmas in 1947, Seedman helped lug into the Safe and Loft office dozens of cartons of toys that had been recovered from a hijacking case. There were dolls, teddy bears, stuffed animals of all kinds.
>
> Ray McGuire, busy overseeing the operation, suddenly looked up and saw that it was close to three o'clock. "I'm never going to get to lunch," he said. "I was going to stop at Macy's to pick up some toys for my girls." One of the detectives mentioned he had to do the same at Macy's. McGuire handed him a twenty-dollar bill. "Pick up a pair of dolls for me, will ya?" (Seedman and Hellman 1974, cited in Delattre 1989: 41)

It never even occurred to McGuire to take any of the dolls and toys surrounding him, because that would be stealing. Delattre writes, "The habit of not even considering greedy behavior, of not speculating about ways to profit from office, prevents such conduct from ever occurring to us" (Delattre 1989, 41). A Kantian ethicist might say that McGuire applied the categorical imperative to the situation and concluded that the action of taking a doll could not be translated into a universal law. A utilitarian formulation would have McGuire weigh the relative utilities of taking the doll or not. However, in the ethics of virtue, as Delattre indicates, if one has developed a habit of integrity, it may be that taking advantage of the situation never even occurs to that person. Under this moral system, those individuals who possess the necessary virtue will act morally and those who don't will act immorally.

It should also be noted that some of us have some virtues and not others. There are many other virtues besides those already mentioned, including compassion, courage, conscientiousness, devotion, and so on. Some of us may be completely honest in all of our dealings but not generous. Some may be courageous but not compassionate. Therefore, we all are moral to the extent that we possess moral virtues; some of us are more moral than others. One difficulty is in judging the primacy of moral virtues. For instance, often in professional ethics there are conflicts that involve honesty and loyalty. If both are virtues, how does one resolve a dilemma where one must be sacrificed?

Let us see how this ethical system can be applied to the examples we have used thus far. One can see that it is more difficult to do so because this system is not a reasoning or formulistic approach. In the abortion dilemma, the ethics of virtue would not help us decide whether that act is moral or not. If a woman holds all moral virtues (or at least relevant moral virtues), then one must conclude that she will do what is right. In Heinz's dilemma, his action will depend on his choice between the virtue of honesty and the virtues of compassion or loyalty to his wife. Which virtue is more important?

One sees that while this ethical system probably explains more of individual behavior than the others since most people do not reason out their actions when they are faced with many choices of behavior, it is difficult to apply to true dilemmas.

The Ethics of Care

The *ethics of care* is another ethical system that does not depend on universal rules or formulas to determine morality. The emphasis is on human relationships and needs. It has been described as a feminine morality since women in all societies are the childbearers and consequently seem to have a greater sensitivity to issues of care. Noddings (1986, 1) points out that the "mother's voice" has been silent in Western, masculine analysis: "One is tempted to say that ethics has so far been guided by Logos, the masculine spirit, whereas the more natural and perhaps stronger approach would be through Eros, the feminine spirit."

The ethics of care is founded in the natural human response to care for a newborn child, the ill, and the hurt. Carol Gilligan's work on moral development in psychology, discussed in more detail in the next chapter, identified a feminine approach to ethical dilemmas that focuses on relationships and needs instead of rights and universal laws. She found that in their responses to ethical dilemmas, some women were resistant to solving the dilemmas given the restraints of the exercise. They wanted to know what would happen after the fact; they wanted to know what the person felt; and they wanted to know other elements that were deemed not relevant if one was applying ethical principles as predetermined by Kohlberg's moral development scale (also discussed in the next chapter). These women were ranked fairly low on the moral development scale, yet Gilligan proposed that theirs is not a less developed morality but rather a different morality. The most interesting feature of this approach is that while a relatively small number of women actually voiced these principles, no men did. She attributed this to the fact that in Western society, we all are socialized to Western ethics, which are primarily concerned with issues of rights, laws, and universalism (Gilligan 1982).

Applying the ethics of care to the examples we've been using leads not to different solutions necessarily, but perhaps different questions. In the abortion example, the discussion has largely been phrased in the terms of the rights of the mother versus the rights of the child. In an ethical system based on care we would be concerned with issues of needs and care. What would happen to the mother if she chose the abortion, what would happen if she did not? Would the child receive the care needed if born? Would it meet the needs of the mother to give birth and then put her child up for adoption? How could her needs be met? With Heinz's dilemma, the solution would probably be to steal the drug since the relationship with his wife is more primary than the relationship with the druggist, but the ethics of care would be concerned with how Heinz and the druggist might come to some understanding about payment, or some other means for both to get their needs met.

Other writers point to some Eastern religions, such as Taoism, as illustrations of the ethics of care (Gold et al. 1991). In these religions, a rigid, formal, rule-based ethics is rejected in favor of gently leading the individual to follow a path of caring for others.

In criminal justice, the ethics of care is represented by the rehabilitative ethic rather than the just-deserts model. The interest in the motives and needs of all concerned rather than retribution is consistent with the ethics of care. In personal relationships, the ethics of care would promote empathy and treating others in a way that does not hurt them. In this view, meeting needs is more important than securing rights.

Egoism

Very simply, *egoism* postulates that what is good for one's survival and personal happiness is moral. The extreme of this position is that all people should operate on the assumption that they can do whatever benefits themselves. Others become the means to ensure happiness and have no meaning or rights as autonomous individuals. *Psychological egoism* is a descriptive principle rather than an ethical prescription. Psychological egoism refers to the idea that humans naturally are egoists and that it would be unnatural for them to be any other way. All species have instincts for survival, and self-preservation and self-interest are merely part of that instinct. Therefore, it is not only moral to be egoistic, it is the only way we can be and any other explanations of behavior are mere rationalizations. *Enlightened egoism* is a slight revision of this basic principle, adding that the objective is long-term welfare. This may mean that we should treat others as we would want them to treat us to ensure cooperative relations. Even seemingly selfless and altruistic acts are consistent with egoism, since these benefit the individual by giving self-satisfaction. Under egoism, it would be not only impossible but also immoral for someone to perform a completely selfless act. Even those who give their lives to save others do so with the expectation of rewards after life. This system completely turns around the priorities of utilitarianism to put the individual first, before anyone else and before society as a whole. To quote from Harris (1986, 47):

> Egoism as a moral philosophy originated in ancient Greece, but the modern emphasis on the individual in competition with other individuals has given it special prominence. The egoistic moral standard states that actions are right if and only if they produce consequences that are at least as good for the self-interest of the egoist as the consequences of any alternative action. Each egoist must personally define self-interest and propose a hierarchy of goods within that definition. Most egoists will be concerned with the fullest realization of their self-interest over a lifetime rather than during only a short period of time.

Let us see how egoism would be used to solve the ethical dilemmas we have been discussing thus far. In the case of abortion, a morality of self-interest would evaluate the benefit to the woman. If it benefited the woman, it would be considered moral. The only case in which the abortion might be considered immoral under egoism is if the mental stress from the abortion would be long-standing and outweigh the benefit of having the abortion in the first place. In our second recurring example, obviously self-interest would dictate that Heinz steal the drug if his wife was dear to him and it was reasonably certain he would not be caught. However, a more difficult decision would exist if Heinz thought he would be punished for the crime. In that case, self-interest would be behind saving his wife as well as avoiding punishment. If Heinz loved his wife so much he could not live without her, then he would be willing to take the punishment; if he did not love his wife, self-interest would lead him to protect himself and let her die.

Obviously, egoism is rejected by many philosophers and laypersons because it violates the basic tenets of an ethical system. Universalism is inconsistent with egoism, because to approve of all people acting in their own self-interest is not a logical or feasible position. It cannot be right for both me and you to maximize our own self-interests, because it would inevitably lead to conflict. Egoism would support exploitive actions by the strong against the weak, which seems wrong under all other ethical systems. Psychological egoism is also a relevant concept in natural law (self-preservation is natural) and utilitarianism (hedonism is a natural inclination). In response to the view that humans are naturally selfish and self-serving, one can point to examples just as plentiful that indicate that humans are also altruistic and self-sacrificing. Which is the true nature of humankind?

ETHICAL RELATIVISM AND UNIVERSALISM

Ethical relativism describes those moral systems in which what is good changes depending on the values and life circumstances of the individual or group, and in which what is bad is relative to the needs and interests of the people engaged in the behavior in question. The generation of the 1960s encapsulated this belief in the phrase "You do your thing and I'll do mine." What is right is determined by culture and/or individual belief; there are no universal laws.

One may look to anthropology and the rise of social science to explain the popularity of this idea. Over the course of studying different societies—past and present, primitive and sophisticated—anthropologists have found that there are very few universals across cultures. Even those behaviors often believed to be universally condemned, such as incest, have been institutionalized and encouraged in some societies (Kottak 1974, 307). Basically, this view defines good as that which contributes to the health and survival of society. So, for instance, societies where women are in ample supply may endorse polygyny and societies that have a shortage of women may accept polyandry; hunting and gathering societies that must contend with harsh environments may hold beliefs allowing for euthanasia of burdensome elderly, while agricultural societies that depend on knowledge passed down through generations may revere their elderly and accord them an honored place in society.

In criminology, cultural differences in perceptions of right and wrong are important to the subcultural deviance theory of crime, wherein some deviant activity is explained by subcultural approval for that behavior. The example typically used to illustrate this is that of the Sicilian father who kills the man who raped his daughter, because to do otherwise would violate values of his subculture emphasizing personal honor and retaliation (Sellin 1970, 187). This individual is seen as enacting what he learned; he is deviant in the wider society but conforms to his own subculture. In effect, he is doing right and wrong at the same time. We might also look at occupational subcultures for examples of relativism. For instance, certain types of police behavior may be considered acceptable by the police subculture even while being contrary to general societal morals. This is especially true of actions such as use of force or willingness to overlook a law. The basic premise of *cultural relativism* is that what is judged as good and bad depends on the society in which one lives, and in some cases the group one belongs to. This view, of course, is impossible to reconcile with universal views of morality.

Cultural relativism usually concerns behaviors that are always right in one society and always wrong in another. What is more common, of course, is behavior that is judged to be wrong most of the time but acceptable in certain instances. For example, killing is wrong except possibly in self-defense and war; lying is wrong except when one lies to protect another. If an action is wrong, why isn't it always wrong? Relativity is difficult to reconcile with ethical systems that propose universal truths.

Even absolutist systems may accept some exceptions. The *principle of forfeiture* associated with deontological ethical systems holds that people who treat others as means to an end or take away or inhibit their freedom and well-being, forfeit the right to protection of their own freedom and well-being (Harris 1986, 136). Therefore, people who aggress first forfeit their own right to be protected from harm. This would permit capital punishment even under the moral proscription against taking life and possibly provide justification for lying to a person who threatens harm.

Of course, this still leaves a lot of questions unanswered. Many feel that it is acceptable for a police officer to accept gratuities, but object to politicians accepting gifts from special interest groups. Some may feel that accepting free coffee and free dinners is fine but nothing more. Some feel that it is wrong for police officers to take such things, but see nothing wrong with police administrators soliciting businesses to provide free catering to management meetings. In other words, in making moral judgments, one often tries to draw a fine line between right and wrong when considering the same type of behavior. This line is subjective and variable according to the seriousness attached to the action. For instance, one might believe that lying for a good cause is moral and that small lies are also acceptable, but somewhere between small and large lies is a line; on one side the action is acceptable, on the other it is wrong. Relativism arguably allows for adaptation to specific circumstances, but the argument for universalism over relativism is that it is impossible to determine what is right and wrong after the removal of moral absolutes, and subjective moral discretion leads to egoistic rationalizations.

OTHER ISSUES

Before we move on, we need to make a few additional points regarding ethical systems. As mentioned previously, ethical systems are not moral decisions as such; rather, they provide the guidelines or principles to make moral decisions. It may often be the case that moral questions are decided in different ways under the same ethical system—for instance, when facts are in dispute. When there is no agreement concerning the accepted facts in a certain case, it is confusing to bring in moral arguments before resolving the factual issues. Capital punishment is supported by some because of a belief that it is a deterrent to people who might commit murder. Others believe that capital punishment is wrong regardless of its efficacy in deterrence. Most arguments about capital punishment get confused during the factual argument about the effectiveness of deterrence. "Is capital punishment wrong or right?" is a different question from "Does capital punishment deter?" The second question might be answered through a study of facts; the former can only be answered by a moral judgment.

Another thing to consider is that none of us is perfect—we all have committed immoral or unethical acts. Even when we know something to be wrong, we sometimes still perform the act. Very few people have such strong moral codes that they never lie or never cause another person harm. Further, very few people are consistent in the use of one ethical system in making moral decisions. Some of us are fundamentally utilitarian, some predominantly religious, but we may make decisions using other ethical frameworks at times. Ethical systems help us to understand or analyze morality but knowing them is no guarantee that we will always act morally and ethically.

CONCLUSION

In this chapter we have explored some of the major ethical systems. Ethical systems are ordered principles that define what is right or good. Each of these ethical systems answers the question "What is good?" in a different way. Under a religious ethical system, what is good is that which conforms to God's will. Under natural law, what is good is that which is natural. What is good under ethical formalism is that which is consistent with the categorical imperative. Under utilitarianism, what is good is that which results in the greatest utility for the greatest number. Under the ethics of care, what is good is that which meets the needs of those involved and doesn't hurt relationships. Under egoism, what is good is that which is best for the individual. The ethics of virtue is the only ethical system that is slightly different in that the question is not so much "What is good?" as "Who is good?" That question is answered by referring to the virtues—a virtuous person is good. Sometimes the same conclusion to an ethical dilemma can be reached using several different ethical systems, but sometimes using different ethical systems may result in contradictory answers to the determination of goodness. Ethical systems are more complex to apply than they are to explain. For instance, utilitarianism is fairly easy to understand, but the measurement of utility for any given act is often quite difficult. We will use these same ethical systems to resolve some of the ethical dilemmas that are presented in subsequent chapters.

DISCUSSION QUESTIONS

1. Use any of the ethical systems to resolve the dilemmas at the end of this chapter. Compare your responses with others.

2. If you had to choose, which ethical system would you say reflects your views most closely? Why?
3. Is there a universal truth relating to right and wrong, moral and immoral? If you answered yes, what are the principles of such a system?

⊶ ETHICAL DILEMMAS ⊷

Please read and respond to the following situations. Be prepared to discuss your ideas.

Situation 1

You are a Christian Scientist, as is your family. One of the teachings of this belief system is that medical science detracts from faith and that sickness can be cured through prayer and reliance on God. Christian Science nurses attend to the ill and practice some home remedies for maladies, and even at times agree to the intervention of medical experts, but most illness is treated with prayer. Your child is severely ill with high fever, vomiting, and convulsions. The representative of the church tells you that the illness is made worse because you do not believe that prayer is helping; thus, in order for the child to get better, you must pray more and not think about taking the child to the hospital. What would you do?

Situation 2

You are on a medical ethics committee that has to decide which transplant candidate is to get a donated liver. Among those on the list are a fourteen-year-old boy who can probably continue on dialysis for the time being with no deterioration of health, a businessman who has promised to give the hospital $3 million for liver disease research as soon as he gets a liver transplant, a much-beloved nun whose health creates a high risk that the operation will not be successful but is first on the list to receive the next organ, and a relative of the organ donor who happens to have liver disease. Who would you vote for and why?

Situation 3

You are in a lifeboat along with four others. You have only enough food and water to keep four alive for the several weeks you expect to be adrift until you float into a shipping lane and can be discovered and rescued. You will definitely all perish if the five of you consume the food and water. There is the suggestion that one of you should die so that the other four can live. Would you volunteer to commit suicide? Would you vote to have one go overboard if you chose by straws? Would you vote to throw overboard the weakest and most sickly of the five? If you were on a jury judging the behavior of four who did murder a fifth in order to stay alive, would you acquit them or convict them of murder?

3

Developing Moral Behavior

In the previous chapter, we explored a variety of philosophical definitions of morality. In this chapter, we will take a different approach and ask the question "How does an individual develop into a moral person?" As we have seen, philosophers have looked to God, natural law, reason, intuition, and emotion to determine morality. There are fundamental questions as to the nature of morality—whether it is subjective and of human construction or whether it is apart from and only discoverable by humans, thus universal and objective. Philosophers are still debating these ancient questions, but the more recent science of psychology helps us understand how individuals develop their own moral systems and definitions of morality.

PSYCHOLOGICAL THEORIES OF MORAL DEVELOPMENT

Psychology seeks to answer such questions as "How does one become moral?" and "Do moral beliefs determine behavior?" The two most important contributions of psychology to this discussion are Kohlberg's moral stage theory and behaviorism or learning theory.

Kohlberg's Moral Stages

The contributions of Piaget and Kohlberg have become essential to any discussion of moral development. Piaget believed that we all go through stages of cognitive, or intellectual, growth. These stages parallel moral stages of development, and together they describe a systematic way of perceiving the world. Piaget studied the rules children develop in their play. These rules reflect the perceptions they hold of themselves and others and move from egocentrism to cooperativeness. Kohlberg carried on with Piaget's work and more fully described the stages each individual passes through in moral and cognitive development (Boyce and Jensen 1978, 87–95).

Two-year-olds do not understand the world in the same way as twenty-year-olds do. This lack of understanding also affects their moral reasoning ability. The infant lacks sensitivity toward others and has a supreme selfishness regarding his or her needs and wants. Infants are not concerned with others because they are only vaguely aware that others exist. An infant's world is confined to what is within reach of his or her hands and mouth. Even a mother is only important as the source of comfort and food. Very slowly the infant becomes aware that others also have feelings and needs. This awareness leads to empathy and a recognition of right and wrong. At later stages, abstract reasoning develops, which leads to the ability to understand more difficult moral concepts.

The following are some characteristics of these cognitive and moral stages (Hersh et al. 1979, 52):

1. They involve qualitative differences in modes of thinking, as opposed to quantitative differences. The child undergoes dramatic changes in perceptions; for instance, in an early stage the realization occurs that what one does has an impact on others. An infant realizes that when she pulls someone's hair, the person reacts; when she cries, someone comes; and when she performs certain behaviors, she is praised.
2. Each stage forms a structured whole; cognitive development and moral growth are integrated. Perceptions of the world and the corresponding moral framework are similar among all individuals at that particular stage. Simplistically, this means that a child cannot be sensitive to others until he is cognitively aware of them or be sensitive to larger issues such as world hunger until he is able to grasp the reality of such conditions.
3. Stages form an invariant sequence; no one bypasses any stage and not all people develop to the higher stages. In fact, according to Kohlberg, very few individuals reach the highest level; the majority reach the middle level and stay there.
4. Stages are hierarchical integrations; that is, each succeeding stage encompasses and is more comprehensive and complicated than the stage that precedes it.

Kohlberg describes three levels of moral reasoning; included in each level are two stages. The levels and stages are described as follows (Barry 1985, 14–16; Kohlberg 1976):

Level l (preconventional level)   At the preconventional level, the person approaches a moral issue from the viewpoint of personal interests. The major concern is the consequences of the action for the person. For instance, young children do not share toys with others because they see no reason to do so. They derive pleasure from them, so to give them to others is not logical. Even if the toys belong to others, there is a predisposition for children to appropriate them. Mothers know the tears and tantrums associated with teaching a child that toys belonging to others must be given back. Young children at play first start sharing, in fact, when they perceive benefit to themselves, such as giving someone their doll in exchange for a game or a ball; or they grudgingly share because they fear a spanking from their mothers if they do not.

Stage 1 has a *punishment and obedience orientation*: what is right is what is praised, what is wrong is what is punished. The child submits to an authority figure's definition and is concerned only with the consequences attached to certain behaviors, not with the behavior itself. Stage 2 has an *instrument and relativity orientation:* the child becomes aware of and is concerned with others' needs. What is right is still determined by self-interest, but the concept of self-interest is broadened to include others. Relationships are important to the child and he or she is attached to parents, siblings, and best friends, who are included in the ring of self-interest.

Level 2 (conventional level)   At the conventional level, people perceive themselves as members of society, and living up to role responsibilities is paramount in believing oneself to be good. Children enter this level when they are capable of playing with other children according to rules. In fact, games and play are training grounds for moral development, since they teach the child that there are defined roles and rules of behavior. For instance, a game of softball becomes a microcosm of real life when a child realizes that he or she is not only acting as self, but also as a first baseman, a role that includes certain specific tasks. Before this stage, the child runs to the ball regardless of where it is hit. Thus, in a softball game with very young children playing, one may see all the players run after the ball and abandon their bases, because they have difficulty grasping the concept of role responsibilities. Furthermore, although it would be more expeditious to trip the runners as they leave the base so they can be tagged out, the child learns that such behavior is not "fair play" and is against the rules of the game. Thus, children learn to submerge individual interest to conform to rules and role expectations.

Stage 3 has an *interpersonal concordance orientation:* the person performs conventionally determined good behavior to be considered a good person. The views of "significant others" are important to the self-concept. Thus, individuals control behavior so as to not hurt others' feelings or be thought of as bad. Stage 4 has a *law-and-order orientation:* the individual is concerned not just with immediate other people, but with the rules set down by society. The law becomes all-important. Even if the laws themselves are wrong, one cannot disregard them, for that would invite social chaos.

Level 3 (postconventional level)   A person at the postconventional level moves beyond the norms and laws of a society to determine universal good—that is, what is good for all societies. Few people reach this level, and their actions are observably different from the majority. Gandhi, for instance, might be described as a person with postconventional morality. He did not subscribe to the idea that laws must be obeyed and carried out peaceful noncompliance against the established law to conform to his belief in a higher order of morality. At this level of moral development, the individual assumes the responsibility of judging laws and conventions.

Stage 5 has a *social contract orientation:* the person recognizes larger interests than current laws. This individual is able to evaluate the morality of laws in a historical context and feels an obligation to the law because of its benefits to societal survival. The orientation of stage 6 is *universal ethical principles:* the person bases moral judgments on higher abstract laws of truth, justice, and morality.

Kohlberg has advanced the possibility of a seventh stage, which has been described as a "soft" stage of ethical awareness with an orientation of cosmic or religious thinking.

It is not a higher level of reasoning, but qualitatively different. According to Kohlberg, in this seventh stage, individuals have come to terms with such questions as "Why be just in a universe that is largely unjust?" It is a different question from the definition of justice that forms the content of the other stages. In this stage one sees oneself as part of a larger whole and humanity as only part of a larger cosmic structure (Kohlberg 1983; Power and Kohlberg 1980).

Critics of Kohlberg

Some believe Kohlberg's theory of moral development has several serious flaws. First, the stages tend to center too much on the concept of justice, ignoring other aspects of morality. Second, the stages, especially stages 5 and 6, may be nothing more than culturally based beliefs regarding moral issues. In fact, a heavy value emphasis is pervasive in the theory regarding right and wrong. Others say Kohlberg overemphasizes reason in moral decisions and ignores emotional factors. Other studies have found significant cultural differences in the age at which children reach the different stages of moral development.

Kohlberg's research also can be described as sexually biased since he primarily interviewed boys. Subsequent studies have found that females tend to cluster in stage 3 because of their greater sensitivity to and emphasis on human relationships. This is a relatively low level of moral development and lower than the law-and-order stage, where men tend to be clustered. Unless one believes that women generally are less moral or less intellectually developed than men, this is a troubling finding and one that calls into question the hierarchical stage theory.

Carol Gilligan (1982, 1987), a student of Kohlberg's, researched this apparent sex difference in morality and developed a theory that postulates that women may possess a *different* morality from men. Most men, it seems, analyze moral decisions with a rules or justice orientation (stage 4), while many women see the same moral dilemma with an orientation toward needs and relationships (stage 3). Gilligan labels this a "care perspective." A morality based on the care perspective would be more inclined to look at how a decision affects relationships and addresses needs whereas the justice perspective is concerned with notions of equality, rights, and universality. This ethics of care has been described as one of the ethical frameworks in Chapter 2.

In one study, while both men and women raised justice and care concerns in responses to moral dilemmas, among those who focused on one or the other, men exclusively focused on justice while half of the women who exhibited a focus did so on justice concerns and the other half focused on care concerns (Gilligan 1987). It was also found that both male and female respondents were able to switch from a justice to a care perspective (or back again) when asked to do so; thus, their orientation was more a matter of perspective than inability to see the other side.

A justice perspective arguably represents the dominant male Western philosophical position, exemplified by Kant's categorical imperative, rule utilitarianism, and even the golden rule. It also seems to be true that the care perspective seems more consistent with some Eastern philosophies that are less judgmental and more accepting of human failings. The fact that the justice moral system is the dominant one is not surprising given that Western philosophy has its roots in Platonic and Aristotelian philosophies, which were completely male-centered and defined the male perspective as representative of the human experience. Nor is it surprising that many women use the justice perspective in analyzing moral dilemmas, since socialization would ensure that they absorb these concepts. What Gilligan points out in her research is that the care perspective completely drops out when one uses only male subjects—which is what Kohlberg did.

Although these criticisms do not necessarily negate the validity of a stage sequence theory, they do call into question the specifics of movement through the stages and possibly the order of the stages (Boyce and Jensen 1978, 124–29). The importance of Kohlberg's work is in the link he makes between moral development and reason. This concept originated with Kant and even earlier philosophers, but Kohlberg gives it a psychological rather than philosophical slant. Also important in Kohlberg's work is the guidance it provides to education. According to the theory of moral stages, one can encourage movement through the stages by exposing the individual to higher stage reasoning. The procedures for encouraging moral growth include presenting moral dilemmas and allowing the individual to support his or her own position. Through exposure to higher reasoning, one sees the weaknesses and inconsistencies of lower level reasoning (Hersh et al. 1979). Kohlberg clearly indicates what is needed for moral growth; despite reservations about his descriptions of the moral stages, these guidelines to encourage moral development seem valid and are supported by other authorities.

Learning Theory and Behaviorism

Learning theorists agree that morality is cognitive but do not believe individuals go through stages of moral development. Rather, children learn what they are taught, including morals and values as well as behavior. In other words, right or wrong is not discovered through reasoning; rather, all humans are shaped by the world around them and form completely subjective opinions about morality and ethics. This learning can take place through *modeling* or by *reinforcement.*

In modeling, values and moral beliefs come from those one admires and aspires to identify with. If that role model happens to be a priest, one will probably develop a religious ethical system; if it happens to be a pimp or a sociopath, an egoistic ethical system may develop. If the identification is broken, moral beliefs may change. It is no surprise that when asked who has been important in their moral development, most people say their parents, since parents are the most significant people in one's life during important formative years. Although we may not hold exactly the same views and have exactly the same values as our parents, there is no doubt that they are influential in our value formation.

Another way learning theorists explain moral development is that whatever is reinforced with rewards becomes permanent, whether it be moral beliefs or behavior. Also, behavior is more easily stabilized and tends to come before permanent attitude change, so for any type of behavior, if it is reinforced and stabilized, consistent beliefs develop to explain it. When there is disagreement between one's attitudes and behavior, the discomfort that results is called *cognitive dissonance.* Often the result is the development of attitudes to support one's behavior. The child who is told constantly to share toys and is disciplined upon refusal is learning the value and moral principle of sharing. As an adult this value may be manifested by lending one's lawn mower to a neighbor or contributing to charities. On the other hand, if a child is never punished for aggressive behavior and instead is rewarded—for instance, by always getting the desired object—then aggressiveness and the accompanying moral principle of "might makes right" develops.

Furthermore, Bandura (cited in Boyce and Jensen 1978, 123–24) states that there is a developmental approach to teaching, keyed to what the child is capable of understanding:

> According to the social learning view, people vary in what they teach, model and reinforce with children of differing ages. At first, control is necessarily external. In attempting to discourage hazardous conduct in children who have not yet learned to talk, parents must resort to physical intervention. As children mature, social sanctions increasingly replace their children's behavior. Successful socialization requires gradual substitution of symbolic and external controls for external sanctions and demands. . . . Evidence that there are some age trends in moral judgment, that children fail to adopt opinions they do not fully comprehend, and that they are reluctant to express views considered immature for their age can be adequately explained without requiring elaborate stage propositions.

According to learning theorists, even the most altruistic behaviors provide rewards for the individual. For instance, acts of charity provide rewards in the form of good will from others and self-satisfaction. Acts of sacrifice are rewarded in similar ways. Honesty, integrity, and fairness exist only because they have been rewarded in the past and are part of the behavioral repertoire of the individual. The moral principles of "honesty is right," "integrity is good," and "fairness is ethical" come after the behavior has been stabilized, not before. This theory is very different from the view that moral principles influence actions.

There is obviously no place in this theory for universalism, absolutism, or the idea that a moral truth exists apart from humans that is not of their construction but that awaits their discovery. It is completely humanistic in that morality is considered a creation of humans that explains and rationalizes learned behavior. Behavior is completely neutral: an infant can be taught any behavior desired and the accompanying moral beliefs consistent with that behavior.

Another important question is whether one can predict behavior from moral beliefs. Psychologists who have studied "immoral" behavior, such as lying and cheating among adults and children, have found it hard to predict whether or when people will perform these behaviors and have found little consistency between behaviors and beliefs. At least one study did find beliefs and actions that matched. "Honesty scores" for people in three organizations were compiled from an attitudinal questionnaire about beliefs. It was found that the organization with the highest average honesty score had the least employee theft, and the organization with the lowest average honesty score had the most employee theft (Adams 1981). However, Kohlberg cites the Hartshone and May study, which found no correlation between different tests of honesty, and another study in which a group of women prisoners were found to have the same rank orderings of vices as female college students. He uses these studies as support for the proposition that one cannot measure a trait in isolation and expect to find consistency between values and action (Kohlberg and Candel 1984, 499–503).

Learning theory might explain, to some degree, why some people have behavior patterns that conflict with their expressed moral beliefs. Let us take the politician who talks about a war on crime and the integrity of his or her platform and then accepts bribes from contractors for county road work. This is fairly easy to explain using learning theory: this individual has been rewarded for corrupt behavior with lucrative financial rewards and lack of exposure; the stand against crime and dishonesty has netted rewards in the form of votes and popularity. Consequently, both actions are reinforced and will continue until the reward structure changes.

In another example of a difference between belief and action, individuals who believe stealing is wrong may be influenced by immediate reward for wrongdoing if they have not internalized a strict sense of morality regarding stealing. In other words, all of us know that stealing is wrong and thus we avoid the action because in the past we have been punished when we have stolen. Thus, stealing becomes associated with negative reinforcement. In the past this might have been pain (a spanking); in the present, it is associated with unpleasant feelings of guilt. Nevertheless, if that association between stealing and pain or guilt tends to be weak, then the immediate reward of money or material possessions will overpower the weak negative reinforcement of guilt. Applying the same line of reasoning to professional ethics, one might assume that if the code of ethics is weak and there are immediate rewards for unethical behavior, then the individual will perform that behavior.

Much research exists to support a learning theory of moral development. For instance, it was found that large gains in moral maturity could be achieved by direct manipulation of rewards for such beliefs. Contrary to Kohlberg's view that an individual comes to a realization of moral principles through cognitive development, this theory proposes that one can encourage or create moral beliefs by rewards (Boyce and Jensen 1978, 143).

A more important question, however, is whether expressed beliefs convert to behavior. Kohlberg believed that only when there is an internalization of all the cognitions and values associated with a moral stage is there consistency between beliefs and behavior. For instance, schoolchildren who are ranked higher on moral stages are less likely to cheat when given the opportunity, and people who hold higher beliefs are more likely to protest injustice. There is also some evidence to indicate that compliance gained from external rewards is not stable until it becomes internalized, which involves adaptation to existing personality structures (Borchert and Stewart 1986, 133–45). The question of when and why beliefs and values are internalized is not as easy to research. If we could ensure ethical behavior, it would probably be contingent on continuing rewards. Providing rewards will not necessarily develop moral character unless beliefs somehow become internalized.

In summary, both Kohlberg's theory of moral stages and learning theory explain how individuals develop moral beliefs. Kohlberg's moral stages would seem to place egoism and utilitarianism in the lower levels of moral reasoning because of the concern for personal welfare and nonuniversalist reasoning. An alternative view is that

Bentham's utilitarianism might actually be stage 6 because of the concern with general welfare and universal laws regarding utility (Boyce and Jensen 1978, 182). However, it is clear that according to a theory of moral stages some ethical systems are more advanced than others. Learning theory, on the other hand, is completely relativistic and postulates that humans learn morality through reinforcement. It holds that morality is completely subjective and that humans do not discover moral laws through reason but can only be taught morality or immorality through rewards and punishment.

ETHICS, BEHAVIOR, AND CRIMINALITY

Many people believe that the general morality of this nation is declining. One of the reasons given for this perceived decline is that we have eliminated many of the opportunities for the teaching of morals. The community is not a cohesive force any longer, the authority of religion is not as pervasive as it once was, the family is weakening as a socializing force, and educators have abdicated their responsibility for moral instruction in favor of scientific knowledge. It was not always this way.

In most colleges in the 1800s a course in moral philosophy was required of all graduates. This class, often taught by the college president, was designed to help the college student develop into a good citizen. The goal of college was not only to educate but also to help students attain the moral sensibility that would make them productive, ideal citizens. As it was taught, ethics involved not only the history of philosophical thought but also a system of beliefs and values and the skills to decide moral or ethical dilemmas for oneself. Gradually, the general field of social science became more and more specialized. Each discipline carved out for itself an area of behavior or part of society to study, so that today we have, among others, sociology, psychology, economics, history, and philosophy. The increasing empiricism of these disciplines crowded out the earlier emphasis on moral decision making. Science was considered ethically neutral although, of course, it is not.

Criminology typically avoids moral definitions, although this area of study is directly concerned with issues of right and wrong, deviance and conformity. We limit our interest to legally defined criminality, rather than looking at crime in terms of evil or immorality, preferring to leave those questions to philosophers. We discuss deviance as a sociological concept. Very rarely in criminology classes do we ask philosophical questions such as "What is evil?" and "What is moral?" An exception might be radical criminology, which challenges the definition of crime itself. We will discuss the radical or conflict perspective more fully in Chapter 5.

If the science of criminology now avoids questions of morality, there was no such hesitation in early corrections. Historically, criminality and sin were associated, and punishment and corrections were primarily concerned with reformation in a religious sense. Hence, early prisons were built to help the individual achieve redemption. There was a heavy dose of moral instruction in society's treatment of criminals; those who were said to lead dissolute and immoral lives were also targeted for reform. Society was much more tolerant of governmental intervention in individuals' lives to help them become moral and productive citizens. For instance, the juvenile court system was given the mission to reform and educate youth in a manner consistent with moral beliefs (Platt 1977). The orientation of corrections in the latter part of this century became more scientific than religious, and intervention adopted the aim of psychological readjustment rather than personal redemption. Today, however, the debate in corrections regarding the rationale to punish may be described as moving back to a moral orientation. Advocates of deterrence versus treatment set up arguments using distinctly moral terms and asking relevant moral questions such as "Does society have the right to treat/punish?" and "What are the limits of punishment/treatment?" The "just-deserts" position, covered in Chapter 8, is probably the clearest example of a moral perspective in criminal justice literature.

Two current attempts to explain criminality seem to indicate that theorists are moving back to developmental rather than social force theories of delinquency and crime. Tonry, Ohlin, and Farrington (1991) report on a long-term study of delinquency in which a cohort sample will be followed from birth to age twenty-five. Variables associated with delinquency will be studied. They include sex (males are more likely to be delinquent), low verbal intelligence, hyperactivity, unpopularity among peers, family history of crime and delinquency, discordant families (marital instability and harsh and erratic disciplinary practices), economic adversity, and living in a socially disorganized community. The authors cite three major theoretical perspectives that address the origins of delinquency—temperament, attachment, and social learning. After exploring the relative merits of these approaches, the authors postulate that temperament and attachment are interrelated in that the personality of the child may affect parental interaction, which, in turn, affects attachment. Alternatively, parents themselves may be poor or inconsistent care givers, in which case attachment will be weak. Not rejecting any of the three perspectives, the researchers state that while parental child-rearing methods (attachment) may affect age of onset of delinquency, peer influence (social learning) may affect continuation or intensity of delinquency. These and many other hypotheses will be tested, but the general findings of the study thus far are that attachment and parental discipline are extremely important factors in delinquency.

In a similar vein, Gottfredson and Hirschi (1990) postulate that low self-control can explain deviance in general, and self-control, in turn, is learned primarily through family and school. If there is no one to care for the child, to identify wrongdoing and to discipline the child, then he or she will not develop self-control and will display a variety of deviant behaviors, including poor impulse control, aggression, alcohol and drug abuse, poor career motivation, and delinquency.

Both of these approaches reject the subcultural deviance theory that delinquent or criminal behavior is learned along with a different moral code that justifies it. Rather, they view deviance as the absence of learning or incomplete socialization. In fact, when the individual does not develop self-control, he or she will not make correct decisions when faced with opportunities to indulge in immediate gratification. Thus, criminals do not have different moral codes; rather, they know what is right, but simply are unwilling to conform their behavior to it because they were not taught to do so at a very early stage of development.

Teaching Ethics

There is one small area in education in which moral instruction has reemerged and that is in the teaching of professional ethics. As mentioned before, we commonly use *ethics* to describe good and bad behavior within the context of a profession or organization. Most professional schools today (law, medical, and business schools) offer at least one class in professional ethics. Typically these classes present the opportunity to examine the moral dilemmas individuals may encounter as members of that profession and help students discover the best way to decide moral issues. Usually, there is a combination of moral discussion and moral teaching. While some class time is devoted to letting the students discuss their views, certainly part of the task is to train new members in what has been determined to be correct behavior. The alternative, of course, would be to ignore ethics in the learning phase of an occupation, and let the person encounter moral questions when he or she is faced with behavioral decisions—for instance, when a prosecutor is tempted to ignore evidence to ensure an easy conviction, when a doctor must choose between two people who both need a heart transplant, or when a business executive is asked to accept a bribe to award a contract. In the rushed, pressure-filled real world, ethical decisions will be made in haste, with emotional overtones, and with peer and situational pressures heavily influencing the decision.

Many believe it is much more effective to present moral or ethical questions to new members of a profession in a neutral arena, such as in a school or academy. Of course, what happens is that once students leave this setting, they are usually told to forget what they've learned. This happens often in police academies, where cadets are taught "the book" and learn "the street" when they are paired with an older officer. This also happens when lawyers realize that the high ideals of justice they learned in law school have little to do with the bargaining and bureaucratic law of the courthouse.

It is often the case that the informal subculture in the workplace is at odds with the formal value system. For instance, the medical profession upholds the value of life, and the highest duty of those in the profession is the preservation of life. One realizes, however, that in the real world, issues of financial reward, convenience, and personal success are just as important in decision making. In the criminal justice system, police are sworn to uphold the law and protect and serve the public, yet the informal subculture supports a degree of violence and a callousness to certain types of service calls considered "garbage calls." The occupational subculture, then, may have a set of ethics different from the official code of that profession. We will see that this is indeed the case with the criminal justice system. One enters a profession or occupation, becomes aware of the occupational ethics, then must adapt to them or change them.

People respond to the discrepancies between official and subcultural ethics in a number of ways. They may ignore, participate in, or confront activities of their peers they feel are wrong. It is difficult to ignore actions that run contrary to one's own value system, but very often employees establish complicated rationalizations to explain why it is not their business that others around them steal, perform less than adequately, or conduct illicit business during working hours. People often do not feel it is right to confront the immoral behavior of others even when their own behavior is consistent with accepted standards of morality.

Others are able to redefine their moral beliefs to accept the type of behavior practiced and approved of in the subculture. A later chapter discusses how police officers develop their "moral careers," which may include many types of otherwise immoral and unethical behavior. Finally, confronting the activities of one's peers typically involves a greater moral strength than most of us possess. An individual who confronts the indiscretions of others risks ostracism and even more serious sanctions. One must also resist the seductive rationalizations for the behavior that the subculture creates. Plea bargaining is completely incorporated into the system of courtroom procedure; lawyers who refuse to go along with this behavior must also be able to resist the rationalization that it is necessary to courtroom efficiency. In another setting, if the office practice is to start ending the work day thirty minutes before 5:00 P.M., then one must also be able to argue against the rationalization that the company doesn't pay enough anyway and is getting all the work it deserves.

One must also often sacrifice other values, such as loyalty or friendship, to confront wrongdoing. A dilemma faces individuals confronted with the choice of saying nothing and allowing corruption to continue or risking ostracism and censure from peers. *Serpico* (Maas 1973) and *Prince of the City* (Daley 1984) are the stories of two police officers who chose to challenge the "blue curtain" of secrecy and testify against their fellow officers in corruption hearings. In *Prince of the City*, the officer who decided he could no longer live with the graft and corruption in the police department nevertheless agreed to testify only if he could protect his partners. Ultimately, he was unable to do so and had to live with the hatred, betrayal, and even suicide of those he had called his friends.

If one were interested in changing unethical behavior in an organization, the primary target might be new recruits since those who have been engaging in unethical activities have built up comprehensive rationales for their behavior. At least, if given a chance to explore moral questions ahead of time, new recruits might have the opportunity to decide their views on moral issues before being influenced. On the other hand, it is difficult, if not impossible, for a new worker to stand alone against a corrupt organizational subculture. Others point out that administrators and managers exert the strongest influence on the ethical climate of an agency. If leaders are honest, ethical, and caring, there is a good chance that those who work for these managers are also ethical. If administrators and/or managers are hypocritical, untruthful, and use their positions for personal gain, then often workers march in these same footsteps.

Learning theorists might say that the most effective way to change the ethics of a profession is to make sure behavior changes. The theory is that if it became absolutely impossible to accept bribes without being caught and punished, then the subcultural supports for this behavior and the moral apologia for it would disappear. In a study examining racism and housing, it was found that when people were forced to live in integrated neighborhoods, their attitudes toward other races became more positive (Brehm and Cohen 1982). The question remains, however, as to what is the most effective way to teach ethics. Other than some behaviorists, most believe that mere monitoring and supervision do not result in consistent ethical behavior. In order for behavior to be predictably correct without monitoring and for people to agree with common principles of right and wrong, they must internalize an ethical system.

Research studies illustrate ways people's values and ethics might be changed. There is support for the direct method of punishment and reward, at least for small children. For instance, in one experiment, children were told a hypothetical story in which an adult punished a neutral act, such as a child practicing a musical instrument; the children later defined that act as bad despite the intrinsic neutrality of the action. This indicates the power of adult definitions and punishment in the child's moral development. What is likely to be more effective in changing adult and older children's moral beliefs is a more indirect method, such as group discussions on the morality of certain actions. This encourages people to think about their beliefs and provides exposure to other views (Boyce and Jensen 1978, 133-70).

According to Kohlberg's theory, people develop at different rates of moral growth. He described the following criteria as necessary for moral growth (Kohlberg 1976):

1. Being in a situation where seeing things from other points of view is encouraged. This is important because upward stage movement is a process of getting better at reconciling conflicting perspectives on a moral problem.
2. Engaging in logical thinking, such as reasoned argument and consideration of alternatives. This is important because one cannot attain a given stage of moral reasoning before attaining the supporting Piagetian stage of logical reasoning.
3. Having the responsibility to make moral decisions and to influence one's moral world. This response is necessary for developing a sense of moral agency and for learning to apply one's moral reasoning to life's situations.
4. Exposure to moral controversy and to conflict in moral reasoning that challenges the structure of one's present stage. This is important for questioning one's moral beliefs and forcing one to look at alternatives.
5. Exposure to the reasoning of individuals whose thinking is one stage higher than one's own. The importance here is in offering a new moral structure for resolving the disequilibrium caused by moral conflict.
6. Participation in creating and maintaining a just community whose members pursue common goals and resolve conflict in accordance with the ideals of mutual respect and fairness.

People may become stuck at a certain point in moral development for several reasons, including not having sufficiently developed cognitive skills and living in a social environment that does not allow for role-taking opportunities or personal growth. For instance, a child growing up in a family that repeats basic moral views with little attempt to explain or defend them will learn to be closed to other viewpoints. A child who is never given responsibility nor forced to take responsibility for his or her own actions will have difficulty developing moral reasoning. Such children will be, in a sense, stunted at the Kohlberg preconventional level of an infant constantly fed and cared for but not allowed to discover that other people exist and must be considered. As adults, if we surround ourselves only with people who think as we do, then it is very unlikely that we will ever change our moral positions or even consider others.

These principles obviously are based on the view that morality is associated with reasoning and that moral views can be discovered through intellectual development and rational argument. This may be an acceptable viewpoint to the reader, but it must be remembered that learning theory would substitute a different approach—that systematically rewarding desired behaviors and values will achieve the desired result. Learning theory would support the view that a more careful application of rewards would be beneficial. For instance, we should remove many mixed messages in society, such as the emphasis on the value of both peaceful resolution and at the same time military power. We also tend to ignore rather than reward good behavior, and this runs contrary to learning theory. For instance, in a classroom, the child who misbehaves usually gets more attention than the children who are quietly doing their work. Children who fight may be rewarded by special attention from important adults; the message is that adults only pay attention to those children who engage in negative types of behavior.

However, according to Kohlberg and others, moral growth and hence moral teaching involves not necessarily forcing moral principles on individuals, but rather exposing individuals to more advanced beliefs and values that challenge their own moral beliefs.

Teaching Ethics in Criminal Justice

A comparison of moral teaching in general with what is suggested for criminal justice and criminology indicates many similarities. According to Sherman (1982, 17–18), the following elements are necessary for any ethics program relating to criminal justice:

1. Stimulating the moral imagination by posing difficult moral dilemmas
2. Encouraging the recognition of ethical issues and larger questions instead of more immediate issues such as efficiency and goals
3. Helping to develop analytical skills and the tools of ethical analysis
4. Eliciting a sense of moral obligation and personal responsibility to show why ethics should be taken seriously
5. Tolerating disagreement and resisting ambiguity
6. Understanding the morality of coercion, which is intrinsic to criminal justice
7. Integrating technical and moral competence, especially recognizing the difference between what we are capable of doing and what we should do
8. Becoming familiar with the full range of moral issues in criminology and criminal justice

In ethics courses in the college classroom or law school there is time to analyze ethical systems and provide in-depth background in moral analysis. In the training academy or in-service training course, there is a need to cover quite a few issues in a short period of time. It is probably best to limit philosophical analysis to the extent that there is enough material to adequately address other issues. For instance, issues such as absolutism and relativism should be introduced as well as a few of the ethical systems. One problem in both settings is whether to present ethical reasoning as a relativistic concept or present the issues in the context of universalism. The first approach may lead students to leave the course thinking that ethics simply depends on which ethical system you use and how you analyze the issue. The second approach runs the risk of preaching and may chill discussion. The instructor may face an ethical dilemma when presented with a blatantly unethical position—should one define it as unethical in the classroom, discuss the issue with the student privately, or give as much credence to this position as all others? The best solution is to at least label the position as stemming from an egoistic ethical system.

In the study of criminal justice and criminology, many areas are ripe for moral inquiry. Issues include the definitions of justice and crime, the appropriate use of force, the relative importance of due process over efficiency, the ethical use of technology to control the populace, the variables used to determine responsibility and punishment, the right of society to treat, and the limits that should be placed on treatment. The remaining chapters of this book explore these and other issues.

CONCLUSION

An ethical system is a set of principles to help us determine what is moral and ethical. Each individual either believes that morals exist naturally and humans only discover their existence and are then able to define morality correctly, or, alternatively, morals are simply whatever we define to be so. The two scientific or psychological approaches in this chapter explain how humans come to develop (or discover) moral principles. Cognitive capacity and the proper environment are necessary to moral development in both approaches. Kohlberg indicates that there is a hierarchy of moral principles and the highest is the one true moral theory, yet not everyone has the cognitive capacity nor the proper exposure to discover it. According to Kohlberg, in the higher stages of moral development ethical relativism must give way to universalism, and all those who reach the highest stages have discovered the true moral principles, which are absolute and exist apart from humans. Kohlberg's theory is consistent with religious ethics, ethical formalism, and perhaps even utilitarianism, but probably not egoism since that theory is completely relativistic in what is considered good. It is also inconsistent with the ethics of care and probably the ethics of virtue.

Learning theory is a completely relativistic theory, in that it postulates human learning as neutral. There is no one true moral theory to discover; rather, the individual will adopt whatever moral theory has been rewarded. This is very consistent with egoism, in that individuals are seen as engaging in behavior that provides maximum utility to the self.

DISCUSSION QUESTIONS

1. Do you believe Kohlberg's theory makes sense? Why or why not?
2. Talk to a child (four to eight years old). Give her a moral dilemma relevant to her world. How does she respond? Can you identify any moral principles? Can you identify which of Kohlberg's stages seems to describe her reasoning?

3. Who has been the greatest influence in your moral development? Why? How?
4. Do you believe the morals of criminals are different from yours? In what way? If you answered yes, do you believe their morals can change? How would you go about it?

ETHICAL DILEMMAS

Please read and respond to the following situations. Be prepared to discuss your ideas.

Situation 1

You are a new probation officer and are excited about the opportunity to help people. After a week on the job you have realized that most other probation officers in your office are lazy and could care less about doing a good job. They sit for two or three hours in the morning complaining about all the work they have to do, they laugh about doing personal shopping when they are supposed to be on home visits, they sneak in late in the morning and leave early in the afternoon, some even close their office doors and do schoolwork or take naps during the workday. The supervisor has been recently promoted and seems to either not notice or not care what is going on. You have already been jokingly told that you'd better "slow down" or you're going to burn yourself out, which you interpret as a warning to stop working so hard because it makes them look bad. What would you do?

Situation 2

You are a judge about to determine whether a juvenile offender should be waived over to adult court. The individual comes from a terrible home environment. Both parents are addicts and his mother evidently took him to various crack houses while she used the drug. He was also taught by his older brothers how to sell crack on the street and has been doing so since the age of five. He has been beaten and neglected for so long that he is distrustful, hostile, and aggressive. He was arrested for committing armed robbery against a fellow high school student. In the incident, he used a gun to rob the other student of his car stereo and then shot him. The student didn't die so it isn't murder, but obviously it is a very serious crime. What would you do?

Situation 3

You are a police officer and enjoy your job. One day you overhear a sergeant talking to a female officer and making very graphic jokes about her anatomy. He is also trying to put his arm around her although she is pushing him away. The conversation you overhear indicates this is not the first time he has done this, since he says, "Why are you always so unfriendly? You know you want me." You also know through the grapevine that this sergeant makes a practice of hitting on all the attractive female officers. The next day the same female officer asks if you would be a witness for her if she reported him for sexual harassment. You know that neither of you would be popular if a report is made; if fact, you may be ostracized by other officers and management since the sergeant is well liked and otherwise a good police officer. What would you do?

4

The Principles
of Justice

A group of people asked to define the word *justice* gave the following definitions: "equal treatment and basic human rights," "right to fairness in the criminal justice system," "an ideology of equality and due process under the law," "reward and punishment for one's actions," and "equal treatment under the law for all individuals regardless of race, sex, creed, or religion." These definitions are similar to standard dictionary definitions of the word: "the maintenance or administration of what is just especially by the impartial adjustment of conflicting claims or the assignment of merited rewards or punishments," "the administration of law; especially the establishment or determination of rights according to the rules of law or equity," "the quality of being just, impartial or fair," and "the principle or ideal of just dealing or right action" (*Webster's Ninth New Collegiate Dictionary* 1991). These definitions include the concepts of *fairness, equality, impartiality,* and *appropriate rewards or punishments.* As we shall see in this chapter, all of these elements are important to the definition of justice.

Another way to define justice is to determine what it is not. Justice "differs from benevolence, generosity, gratitude, friendship and compassion," according to one writer (Lucas 1980, 3). It is not something we should feel grateful for, but rather something we have a right to insist on. Justice should not be confused with "good." Some actions may be considered good but not necessarily just (that is, giving mercy). By the same token, some actions may be considered bad but not necessarily unjust. Justice concerns rights and interests rather than needs. Although the idea of need is important in some discussions of justice, it is not the major component of the concept. It is important to understand that the idea of justice can be separated from a discussion of what is good. For instance, to give to charity is considered good but not necessarily just. We know this because someone who is not inclined to contribute cannot be defined as unjust. Furthermore, if I contributed $100 to the American Heart Association and $1 to the Republican party, I could not be considered as acting unjustly even though I did not contribute equally to both of them. Even if the Republican party needed the money more than the American Heart Association, it would not be an injustice to contribute less money to the Republicans, because they have no right to expect anything from me at all. In other relationships, however, equity may be an important element of justice. The concept of fairness and how it relates to justice will be discussed in more detail later.

People can often be described as displaying unique combinations of generosity and selfishness, fairness and self-interest. Some writers insist that the need for justice arises from the nature of human beings and the fact that they are not naturally generous, openhearted, and fair. If we behaved all the time in accordance with those characteristics, we would have no need for justice. On the other hand, if humans were to act in selfish, grasping, and unfair ways all the time, then we would be unable to follow the rules and principles of justice. Therefore, we uphold and cherish the concept of justice in our society because it is the mediator between people's essential selfishness and generosity; in other words, it is the result of a logical and rational acceptance of the concept of fairness in human relations (Hume in Feinberg and Gross 1977, 75).

Justice does not ordinarily regulate the sphere of private relations but rather is only concerned with rights and interests in public interactions and in the interface between the individual and the government. Justice does not dictate a perfect world, but one in which people live up to agreements and are treated fairly. Justice may be described as "more than voluntary agreement, [but] . . . less than perfect community. It allows us to retain our separate existences and our self-regard; it does not ask us to share the pleasures, pains, and sentiments of others. Justice is intelligent self-regard, modified by the requirements of rational consistency" (Galston 1980, 282).

COMPONENTS OF JUSTICE

Many people have attempted to define and analyze the concept of justice by breaking it down into component parts. For instance, justice can be broken down into distributive, corrective, and commutative justice. *Distributive justice* is concerned with the allocation of the goods and burdens of society to its respective members. Rewards and benefits from society include wealth, education, entitlement programs, health care, and so on. Because some people get less than others, some of us may feel that the goods are not distributed fairly. Burdens and responsibilities must also be distributed among the members of society; decisions must be made about, for instance, who should fight in war, who should take care of the elderly and infirm, who should pay taxes, and how much each should pay. The difficulty in deciding how to divide these goods and burdens is one issue of distributive justice. We are concerned with everyone getting what he or she deserves, by virtue of entitlement, merit, or need.

Corrective justice concerns the determination and methods of punishment. Again, the concept of desert emerges. In corrective justice we speak of offenders getting what they deserve, only this time the desert is punishment rather than goods. The difficulty, of course, is in determining what are "just deserts." Finally, *commutative justice* is associated with transactions and interchanges in society where one person feels unfairly treated. The process of determining a fair resolution—for example, when one is cheated in a business deal or when a contract is not completed—calls into play the concept of commutative justice. The method for determining a fair and just resolution to the conflict depends on particular concepts such as rights and interests.

A continuing theme in any discussion of justice is the concept of *fairness*. In the earlier example, giving a greater amount of money to the Heart Association than the Republican party was not considered unjust because neither group had a right to expect anything. Other distributions, however, are scrutinized under a fairness doctrine. For instance, parents ordinarily give each child the same allowance unless differences between the children, such as age or duties, warrant different amounts. In fact, children are sensitive to issues of fairness long before they grasp more abstract ideas of justice. No doubt every parent has heard the plaintive cry "It's not fair—Johnny got more than I did!" or "It's not fair—she always gets to sit in the front seat!" What children are sensing is unequal and therefore unfair treatment. Obviously, the concept of fairness is inextricably tied to equality and impartiality.

One of the prevalent themes of justice is the concept of *equality*. There is a predisposition to demand equity or equal shares for all. In contrast to the concept of equal shares is the idea of needs or deserts; in other words, we should get what we need, or alternatively, what we deserve because of status, merit, or other reasons. The concept of equality is also present in retributive justice in the belief that similar cases should be treated equally—for instance, that all individuals who commit a similar crime should be similarly punished. Again, the alternative argument is that sometimes it serves the purpose of justice to sentence similar crimes differently because of mediating or aggravating circumstances of the crime.

Beccaria (1738–1794) and Bentham (1748–1832) provided the standard argument for equality in retributive punishment, even though their reasoning was utilitarian. Punishment should be based on the seriousness of the crime; the more serious the crime (or the greater the reward the crime offered the criminal), the more serious and severe the punishment should be. Because everyone responds equally to the threat of punishment, the argument goes, this is fair and effective. The positivists, on the other hand, view men and women as individually motivated toward crime, either through biology or temptation and circumstance. According to this line of reasoning, because each individual engages in criminal acts for different reasons, the punishment due them should also be different. This is the *treatment ethic* in criminal justice: the amount of punishment and even whether there should be any punishment at all depends on the individual culpability and vulnerability of each offender.

The concept of *impartiality* is the core of many systems of criminal justice. Our symbol of justice represents, with her blindfold, impartiality toward special groups and, with her scales, proportionally just punishments. Impartiality implies fair and equal treatment of all without discrimination and bias. It is hard to reconcile the ideal of "blind justice" with the individualized justice of the treatment ethic, since one can hardly look at individual circumstance if one is blind to the particulars of the case. We will explore these inconsistencies later in the chapter, but first, it is useful to look at the earliest roots of the concept of justice.

ORIGINS OF THE CONCEPT OF JUSTICE

One of the earliest origins of our concept of justice is in the Greek word *dike*, which is associated with the concept of everything staying in its assigned place or natural role (Feinberg and Gross 1977, i). This idea was closely associated with Plato's and Aristotle's definitions of justice. Even today, some writers describe justice as "the demand for order: everything in its proper place or relation" (Feibleman 1985, 23).

According to Plato, justice consists of maintaining the societal status quo. Justice is one of four civic virtues, the others being wisdom, temperance, and courage (Feibleman 1985, 173). In an ordered state, everyone performs his or her role and does not interfere with others. Each person's role is the one for which the individual is best fitted by nature; thus, *natural law* is upheld. Moreover, it is in everyone's self-interest to have this ordered existence continue because it provides the means to the good life—appropriate human happiness. Plato's society is a class system, based on innate abilities, rather than a caste system, which differentiates by accidents of birth.

Aristotle believed that justice exists in the law and that the law is "the unwritten custom of all or the majority of men which draws a distinction between what is honorable and what is base" (Feibleman 1985, 174). Aristotle distinguished *distributive justice* from *rectificatory* (or *corrective*) *justice*. Distributive justice, as described earlier, determines what measurement should be used to allocate shares. Aristotle believed in the idea of proportionality along with equality. Aristotle's conception of justice included the idea that there could be free men and slaves, rulers and ruled, men and women (who had very little status or power in Aristotle's society), and these status differentials would not conflict with a principle of justice as long as the individual was in the role in which, by nature, she belonged. In other words, unequal people should get unequal shares. In Aristotle's theory, using proportionality and merit, some who have more merit deserve more from society, because they have greater responsibilities (Frankena in Feinberg and Gross 1977, 46).

This "formal principle of justice" in which like should be treated alike and unequals should be treated unequally was the starting point for all subsequent theories of justice. One problem with the formal system of justice, however, is the measurement of equality. What should be taken into account to determine if two people are equal? For instance, if you have two people who want a promotion and each has similar qualifications but one is a member of a minority, are they equal or not? Should the factor of membership in a minority group make the person more qualified if there has never been a minority member in the position? What about punishment issues? What factors should distinguish two offenders when determining punishment? Are two burglars always equal, and if not, what factors should distinguish them?

Rectificatory justice, which we have previously referred to as commutative justice, concerns business deals where unfair advantage was taken or undeserved harm occurred. Justice demands remedies or compensations to the injured party. Aristotle's notions of justice, according to one writer, were primarily concerned with preserving an existing order of rights and possessions (Raphael 1980, 80).

DISTRIBUTIVE JUSTICE

The concept of the appropriate and just allocation of society's goods and interests is one of the central themes in all discussions of justice. According to one writer, justice always involves "rightful possession" (Galston 1980, 117–19). The goods that one might possess include economic goods (income or property), opportunities for development (education or citizenship), and recognition (honor or status). Obviously, if these items are in plentiful supply and everyone has enough of them, the concept of justice is not relevant. It is only in a condition of scarcity that a problem arises with the allocation of goods. What is a just distribution of societal goods, given a condition of scarcity? Two valid claims to possession are *need* and *desert*. The principles of justice involve the application of these claims to specific entitlements. These situations usually involve cases where individuals' entitlements conflict with one another. The following questions proposed by Galston (1980, 92) bear on these cases:

- Would A's possessing Y exclude any others from possessing Y (or something similar to Y)?
- Would possessing Y be beneficial to A or to anyone else?
- Does A or anyone else have a rational claim on Y?

Different writers have presented various proposals for deciding issues of entitlement. Lucas (1980, 164–65) lists several different distribution theories. One proposed by Ross would distribute goods to everyone according to merit; to everyone according to performance; to everyone according to need; to everyone according to ability; and to everyone according to rank and station. Vlastos proposes the following distribution: to each according to his need; to each according to his worth; to each according to his merit; to each according to his work; and to each according to agreements he has made. Rescher's theory would distribute goods to each as equals; to each according to her needs; to each according to efforts and sacrifices; to each according to her actual productive contribution; to each according to the requirements of the common good; and to each according to a valuation of her socially useful services in terms of their scarcity in the essentially economic terms of supply and demand. Chaim Perelman's principles of distributive justice dictate: to each the same thing; to each according to his merits; to each according to his needs; to each according to his rank; and to each according to his legal entitlement (Raphael 1980, 90).

The difficulty, of course, is determining the weight of each of the factors in a just allocation of benefits. The various theories can be categorized as egalitarian, Marxist, libertarian, or utilitarian, depending on which factors are emphasized (Beauchamp 1982). Egalitarian theories start with the basic premise of equality or equal shares for all. Marxist theories focus on need over desert or entitlement. Libertarian theories promote freedom from interference by government in social and economic spheres; therefore merit, entitlement, and productive contributions are given weight over need or equal shares. Utilitarian theories attempt to maximize benefits for individuals and society in a mixed emphasis on entitlements and needs.

How do the theories apply to the wide disparities in salaries found in this country? For instance, a professional athlete's salary is sometimes one hundred times greater than a police officer's salary. Which principle might justify this discrepancy? While libertarian theories would support such disparity, Marxist theories would not. Of the few distribution systems mentioned above, only the one proposed by Ross might support such a wide salary differential. Obviously, few would agree that workers in all jobs and all professions should be paid the same amount of money. First, not many people would be willing to put up with the long hours and many years of schooling needed in some professions if there were no incentives. Second, some types of jobs demand a greater degree of responsibility and involve greater stress than others. On the other hand, we can readily see that some remuneration is entirely out of proportion to an analysis of worth; for instance, it is hard to see how any corporate executive could deserve $10 million for one year's work. The same argument applies to athletes, rock music stars, and movie stars.

If we are primarily concerned with performance and ability, why do we not pay individual workers in the same job category differently if one works harder than the other? Although some production jobs pay according to how much is produced (the piecework payment method), most of us are paid according to a step-grade position, earning roughly what others in the same position earn. Which is the fairer system of payment? What about people who produce less on the piecework system because they are helping their coworkers or taking more time to produce higher quality products? Is it fair for them to earn less? If all work were paid according to production, how would one pay secretaries, teachers, or lawyers, whose production is more difficult to measure?

Should we pay people according to need, as Marxist distribution systems propose? This sounds fair in one sense since people would get only what they needed to survive at some predetermined level. In that case, a person with two children would earn more than a person with no children. In the past, this was the argument used by employers to explain why they would hire, promote, and pay more to men than women—because men had families to support and women did not. Two arguments were used against this type of discriminatory treatment: the first was that women deserve as much as men if they are of equal ability and performance; the second was that women have equal needs because they also, more often than not, have families to support. These two arguments emphasize different principles of justice. The first is based on an equal-deserts argument; the second on an equal-needs argument.

Pregnancy or family leave is one current issue in the area of employment rights. The principle of justice that is being used to support the right to leave (whether it be the unpaid leave now mandated by Congress or paid leave) is not worth, merit, ability, or performance; rather, it is need. Does justice dictate an employee's right to family leave? This is certainly not equal treatment (since we're discriminating against people who are not pregnant and do not fit other categories of the family leave bill, but who would like leave for other reasons). This may, in fact, be a question of goodness rather than justice. That is, while it would be a social good if companies gave leave (good for society, good for the individual), it cannot be defined as an injustice if it is denied.

Looking at other goods distributed to members of a society, we continue to encounter difficulties in determining a just distribution. Welfare is one example of this difficulty. Obviously, we are using the principle of need to redistribute goods; we take from the financially solvent, through taxes, and give to those who have little or nothing. But what about those who have nothing because they do not work, such as the so-called lazy poor, who are said to sponge off the rich. If there are such people, justice may dictate that they be dropped from welfare rolls. Self-induced need is controversial when scarce resources are allocated. Few would argue that single mothers with children need assistance, but if a young woman has had several children with no visible means of support, depending on welfare for the birth and continued support of each child, when does need end and abuse begin? Does justice dictate we continue to give aid or does it justify punishing her for taking advantage of the system? And if we decide that she does not deserve our help, how do we view her innocent children?

Another good or benefit society distributes to its members is opportunity. Many people would argue that education is a privilege that should be reserved for those few who have the ability and the drive to succeed. The educational system of this country, however, is fundamentally democratic. Not only do we have guaranteed, in fact compulsory, education at lower elementary and secondary levels, we also have open admission to some universities. Also, remedial courses are available to help those without the skills to meet college standards. In fact, massive amounts of time and money are devoted to helping some students improve their skills and ultimately graduate from college. What quantity of scarce resources should be expended to help the marginally capable? Further, if a decision must be made to allocate resources to remedial courses or honor courses, where should the money go?

It is difficult to reconcile the concepts of opportunity and ability. Affirmative action attempts to provide opportunities to groups that historically have been discriminated against—blacks, women, Hispanics. Now those groups that have been favored in the past—whites, males—feel that they are the new victims of discrimination. Some feel that taking affirmative steps to increase opportunities for minority groups has simply transferred unfair treatment to another group. The difficult question is: "What is acceptable to overcome previous discrimination?" Unfortunately, a promise to hire "the best person for the job" is not enough, because historical and institutionalized discrimination will take many years to overcome. For instance, educational differences result in some students who have fewer skills and are less qualified than those from better schools. To assume one is eliminating discrimination by hiring on the basis of individual ability, then, does not solve the problem of blocked access; it merely perpetuates it in a more subtle way.

This controversy only points out the extreme difficulty of determining just distribution of goods. The fact that everyone is not equal, in terms of ability, performance, motivation, need, or any other measure, is easy enough to agree on. Very few people would argue that everyone should receive the same salary, get the same education, and achieve the same status in society. On the other hand, to acknowledge inequality puts us in the position of distributing goods and other interests on the basis of other criteria, and it is here that problems arise. When injustice occurs, we sense it on the basis of fairness. We feel somehow that it is not fair that there are starving children and conspicuous wealth in the same country or the same world. We sense unfairness when people work hard yet still struggle to get along on poverty wages, while star actors or athletes make millions of dollars largely through luck and for contributions to societal welfare that seem trivial.

The final good to be distributed is status or recognition. Should a person who struggles to achieve a certain skill be rewarded more than a person who achieves the same skill with little effort? Should a person who struggled through a terrible childhood and achieved a measure of success be more highly regarded than a person who was born to status and privilege? Should we expect more from certain people than from others? In criminal justice, should we expect less from those we have every reason to believe will fail? Should we congratulate probationers or prison releases for mediocre adjustment as opposed to failure? It doesn't seem unfair in some instances to judge performances unequally if efforts or abilities are not equal. This is consistent with Aristotle's formal system of justice—treat likes alike and unequals unequally—yet to what extent should this difference be allowed? Would students be content to know that the grades they received were influenced by the teacher's expectations of their abilities? Would you be happy if your salary were dependent not solely on your performance but also on a perception of your ability to perform? In some instances, then, we demand equality in allocating recognition regardless of ability. The student who receives the highest test score feels he or she deserves that score even if he or she didn't work as hard as another student who only received a C.

The various distributional theories outlined earlier include everything from status to societal needs as bases for distributional equations. Some are obviously contradictory; for instance, how would one reconcile distribution according to equality and legal entitlement? Obviously, some people have much more than others and are entitled to these goods, perhaps not morally, but legally through inheritance or contract. Supply and demand might explain some extreme differences in economic rewards (such as those given athletes, rock music stars, and movie stars), but should they outweigh other factors such as merit or common good? Although rank and status certainly were part of Aristotle's and Plato's distributional equation, should we continue to include them as legitimate and fair criteria for distribution? On the other hand, even in the most egalitarian and democratic societies, individual differences in status and rank are accepted.

John Rawls's theory of justice proposes a basically equal distribution unless a different distribution would benefit the disadvantaged. Rawls believes that any inequalities of society should be to the benefit of those who are least advantaged (Rawls 1971, 15). He proposes the following (cited in Kaplan 1976, 114):

1. Each person is to have an equal right to the most extensive total system of basic liberties compatible with a similar system of liberty for all.
2. Social and economic inequalities are to be arranged so that they are both reasonably expected to be to everyone's advantage; and attached to positions and offices open to all (except when inequality is to the advantage of those least well off).

Of course, Rawls has his critics. First, Rawls uses a heuristic device he calls the *veil of ignorance* to explain the idea that people will act unselfishly and according to objective principles of distribution if they are ignorant of their position in society, since they may just as easily be "have-nots" as "haves" (Rawls 1971, 12). Thus, justice and fairness are in everyone's rational self-interest since, under the veil of ignorance, one's own situation is unknown, and the best and most rational distribution is the one most equal to all. Critics argue, however, that the veil of ignorance is not sufficient to counteract humanity's basic selfishness: given the chance, people would still seek to maximize their own gain even if it involved a risk (Kaplan 1976, 199). Second, critics argue that Rawls's preference toward those least well off is contrary to the good of society. Rawls states that "all social values—liberty and opportunity, income and wealth and the bases of self-respect—are to be distributed equally unless an unequal distribution of any, or all, of these values is to the advantage of the least favored" (cited in Sterba 1980, 32). Critics believe this preference is ultimately dysfunctional for society since if those least well off have the advantages of society preferentially, there will be no incentive for others to excel. Some also argue that Rawls is wrong to ignore desert in his distribution of goods (Galston 1980, 3).

In contrast to Rawls, Sterba (1980, 55) offers these principles to follow in distributive justice:

1. *Principle of need.* Each person is guaranteed the primary social goods that are necessary to meet the normal costs of satisfying basic needs in the society in which he or she lives.
2. *Principle of appropriation and exchange.* Additional primary goods are to be distributed on the basis of private appropriation and voluntary agreement and exchange.
3. *Principle of minimal contribution.* A minimal contribution to society is required of those who are capable of contributing when social and economic resources are insufficient to provide the guaranteed minimum to everyone in society without requiring that contribution or when the incentive to contribute to society would otherwise be adversely affected, so that persons would not maximize their contribution to society.
4. *Principle of saving.* The rate of saving for each generation should represent its fair contribution toward realizing and maintaining a society in which all the members can fully enjoy the benefit of its just institution.

If we apply Sterba's distribution principles to health care in this country, we must agree that every citizen deserves a basic standard of health care necessary to survival (principle of need). Further, if an individual has enough resources to purchase additional care over this basic level, then that should be allowed to benefit both the purchaser, who would receive superior care, and the supplier, who would earn profit (principle of appropriation and exchange). Basic health care should be paid for by everyone according to ability to pay—that is, citizens should pay taxes and medical professionals should be required to provide some level of basic services at cost (principle of minimal contribution). Finally, there should be an upper limit on how much can be charged above cost by surgeons, hospitals, and other medical care providers. The expense of such services has increased so astronomically that it cannot be justified by fair profit principles and it endangers all citizens' ability to apportion their income in a way that ensures financial solvency (principle of saving).

An Aristotelian conception of distributive justice would encompass differential status. Libertarian systems emphasize entitlements and merit. Marxist theories emphasize need, as does an ethic of care perspective. Rights to consume and to accumulate great wealth are inconsistent with an ethic of care if the right to wealth exists concomitantly with great need. Remember, this ethical system is concerned with needs and not rights. In the same way that a mother would sacrifice for a child, this moral system assumes that humans naturally would sacrifice their wealth for others, and that this would be the moral thing to do. Utilitarian theories try to maximize individual and societal concerns. John Rawls's theory is both utilitarian and Kantian since it demands a basic level of individual rights but also attempts to establish a preference toward those who have less, for the good of all society. Interestingly, how one resolves these questions concerning distributive justice has some relevance to the discussion of retributive justice.

CORRECTIVE JUSTICE

As mentioned before, corrective justice is concerned with dispensing punishment. As with distributive justice, the concepts of equality and desert, fairness and impartiality are important. Two components of corrective justice should be differentiated. *Substantive justice* involves the concept of just deserts or how one determines a fair punishment for a particular offense, and *procedural justice* concerns the steps we must take before administering punishment.

Substantive Justice

What is a fair punishment for the crime of murder? Many believe the only just punishment is death, since that is the only punishment of a degree equal to the harm caused by the offender. Others might say life imprisonment is equitable and fair. One's beliefs about what is fair punishment are usually related to one's perception of the seriousness of the crime. More serious crimes deserve more serious punishments.

Since the beginning of codified law, just punishment has always been perceived as punishment set in relation to the degree of harm incurred. This was a natural outcome of the early, remedial forms of justice, which provided remedies for wrongs. For instance, the response to a theft of a slave or killing of a horse involved compensation. The only just solution was the return or replacement of the slave or horse. This remedial or compensatory system of justice contrasts with a punishment system: the first system forces the offender to provide compensation to the victim or the victim's family, and the second apportions punishment based on the degree of seriousness of the crime suffered by the victim. They both involve a measurement of the harm, but in the first case measurement is to adequately compensate the victim, and in the second it is to punish the offender. In a punishment-based system, the victim is a peripheral figure. The state, rather than the victim, becomes the central figure (Karmen 1984).

Retributive justice   The concept of retributive justice is one of balance. The criminal must suffer pain or loss proportional to what the victim was forced to suffer. In an extreme form, this retribution takes the form of *lex talionis,* a vengeance-oriented justice concerned with equal retaliation ("an eye for an eye; a tooth for a tooth"). A milder form is *lex salica,* which allows compensation; the harm can be repaired by payment or atonement (Allen and Simonsen 1986, 4). A punishment equal to a harm is sometimes hard to determine. A life for a life might be easy to measure but very seldom is it required for retribution, even in those systems that use capital punishment. In other types of victimizations, how does one determine the amount of physical or mental pain suffered by the victim, or financial loss that involves lost income or future loss? And if the offender cannot pay back financial losses, how does one equate imprisonment with fines or restitution?

Historically, corporal and capital punishment were used for both crimes against property and violent crimes. With the development of the penitentiary system in the early 1800s, punishment became equated with terms of imprisonment rather than amounts of physical pain. In fact, the greater ease of measuring out prison sentences probably contributed to its success and rapid acceptance. One can sentence an offender to one, two, or five years, depending on the seriousness of the crime. Imprisonment not only was considered more humane than corporal punishment, it was also incapacitating, allowing the offender to reflect on his crime and repent; further, it did not elicit sympathy for the offender from the populace. On the other hand, a term of imprisonment is much harder to equate to a particular crime. While one can intuitively understand the natural balance of a life for a life, $10 for $10, or even a beating for an assault, it is much harder to argue that a burglary of $100 is equal to a year in prison or an assault is equal to a term of two years. A year in prison is hard to define. Research on prison adjustment indicates that a year means different things to different people. For some, it may be no more than mildly inconvenient; for others, it may lead to suicide or mental illness (Toch 1977).

In addition to retribution, imprisonment was tied to reform of the criminal offender. Reform or rehabilitation may be a laudable goal, but it has no place in a retributive scheme of justice. Retributive punishment is based on balancing the victim's harm with the offender's pain or suffering; treatment involves no such balance; therefore, there is no retributive rationale for its existence. Philosophical support for treatment of criminal offenders is found in utilitarianism. This discussion will continue in a later chapter.

Retributive justice is not a simple equation, since other factors are taken into account in addition to the seriousness of the crime. For instance, *mens rea* (intent) has long been considered a necessary element in determining culpability. Those who are incapable of rational thought—the insane and the young—are said to be incapable of committing wrong morally or legally; therefore, to punish them would be an injustice under a retributive framework. Other situations might prove to involve partial responsibility—

for example, the presence of compulsion, coercion, or irresistible impulse. In these cases, most people feel justice is not compromised by a lesser amount of punishment, even though the harm to the victim is obviously the same as if the offender had acted deliberately and intentionally. In this sense, we see that the amount of punishment is not solely measured by the amount of harm to the victim but involves characteristics of the offender as well.

Just punishment may also involve considering the participation of the victim. *Victim precipitation* refers to the victim's role in the criminal event. Some people fear that this examination has the potential to "blame the victim" rather than the offender for the crime. Nevertheless, some research indicates that the victim plays a significant part in some types of crime (Karmen 1984, 78). Retributive justice would consider instances where the victim "caused" victimization by enraging or threatening the offender, or precipitated victimization by engaging in careless or dangerous behavior. This does not mean that individuals who go out late at night deserve to be robbed or women who are drinking alone deserve to be raped. Victim precipitation refers to those situations where, for instance, batterers taunt their victims to shoot them and they do. In this case, the batterer is ostensibly the victim because he has been shot, but an examination of his conduct would reveal that the so-called offender is also a victim and the batterer's own behavior largely contributed to his victimization. In barroom brawls, often pure luck determines who becomes the injured and who becomes the offender. In these situations, the victim actually participates in the criminal event. We might allow for partial culpability, since the responsibility for the crime must be shared by both the offender and the victim. We see, then, that in a retributive justice system we must look not only at the seriousness of the crime to determine punishment, but also at the actions and mental states of both the offender and the victim.

Of course, other factors may play a part in determining the punishment. Some would not be consistent with retributive justice. In earlier justice systems, the status of the victim was important in determining the level of harm and thus the punishment. Nobles were more important than freemen, who were more important than slaves. Men were more important than women. Punishment for offenders was weighted according to these designations of the worth of the victim. Although we have no formal system for weighting punishment in this way and have rejected the worth of the victim as a rationale for punishment, many feel that our justice system still follows this practice. People argue that harsher sentences are given when the victim is white than when the victim is black and when the victim is rich as opposed to poor. In a similar manner, many argue that the justice system discriminates unfairly and unjustly against characteristics of the offender. Many believe that offenders receive harsher sentences because of their race, background, or income.

Whether or not these charges are true, it is important to recognize that earlier systems of justice, including the Greek and Roman, approved of and rationalized these discriminations as perfectly fair and just. Our system of justice has rejected these discriminations even while holding on to others; specifically, intent, partial responsibility, and to some extent, victim precipitation. It is difficult, if not impossible, for everyone to agree upon a fair and equitable measurement of punishment when one allows for exceptions, mediating factors, and partial responsibility. That is why there is so little agreement on what is fair punishment. Even when two defendants are involved in a single crime, our system of justice can support different punishments under a retributive rationale.

In Rawls's theory of justice, retributive punishment is limited in the following way (cited in Hickey and Scharf 1980, 168):

> The liberties of a person . . . may only be reduced, compared with the liberties of other people, when it is for the good of the least advantaged, considered from the "veil of ignorance" assumption of not knowing what role one will occupy.

This means that only when punishment can be shown to benefit the least advantaged (the victim) can it be justified; and when the advantage changes (when the victim has been repaid), then punishment must cease. Hickey and Scharf (1980, 169) point out that this limitation is similar to that proposed by Norval Morris:

1. We must punish only to the extent that the loss of liberty would be agreeable were one not to know whether one were to be the criminal, the victim, or a member of the general public, and
2. The loss of liberty must be justified as the minimal loss consistent with the maintenance of the same liberty among others.

In both these propositions the moral limit to punishment is reached when what is done to the criminal goes beyond what is considered equal to the extent of his or her forfeiture, as determined by the crime.

One other issue that must be addressed here is the concept of *mercy*. Seemingly inconsistent with any definition of justice, mercy is nevertheless always associated with the concept. From the earliest beginnings of law, there was the element of forgiveness. Even tribal societies had special allowances and clemencies for offenders, usually granted by the king or chief. The concept of sanctuary, for instance, allowed a person respite from punishment as long as she or he was within the confines of church grounds. Benefit of clergy, dispensation, and even probation are examples of mercy by the court. It must be clear, however, that mercy is different from just deserts. If, because of the circumstances of the crime, the criminal, or the victim, the offender deserves little or no punishment, then that is what he or she deserves, and it is not mercy to give a suspended sentence or probation. On the other hand, if an offender truly deserves a period of imprisonment, and the court forgives the offense and releases the offender with only a warning, then the individual is not getting what is deserved and this is mercy. Mercy is connected with repentance. It may be given if the offender regrets the wrongdoing and probably will not be given if the offender is defiant.

Utilitarian justice   We have been discussing retributive justice as a rationale for and means to determine punishment. However, other rationales also support punishment. The alternative to retribution is utilitarianism. While the goal of a retributive framework of justice is to restore a natural balance by righting a wrong or neutralizing criminal gain with an equal amount of loss or pain, the goal of a utilitarian framework is to benefit society by administering punishment to deter offenders from future crime.

A utilitarian framework of justice would determine punishment on the basis of deterrence. Bentham's *hedonistic calculus,* for instance, is concerned with measuring the gain of the crime, so that the amount of threatened pain can be set to deter people from committing that crime; the goal is not to restore some natural balance undone by the criminal act. Measurement is important in both retributive and utilitarian rationales of justice. In a retributive system, we measure to determine the proportional amount of punishment to right the wrong; in a utilitarian system, we measure to determine the amount of punishment needed to deter. We see that under the utilitarian framework, there is no necessity for perfect balance. In fact, one must threaten a slightly higher degree of pain or punishment than the gain or pleasure that comes from the criminal act; otherwise there would be no deterrent value in the punishment.

When one argues for capital punishment on the basis of protection for society, one is arguing from a utilitarian framework. When one argues for longer punishments for repeat offenders, one is arguing the utilitarian philosophy. These punishments have little to do with retribution in the sense of matching punishment with criminal harm, but they are perfectly acceptable and just under utilitarianism since what is just is what contributes to the well being and continued protection of society.

In some cases, retributive notions of justice and utilitarian notions of justice may conflict. If a criminal is sure to commit more crime, the utilitarian could justify holding him in prison as a means of incapacitation, but to hold him past the time "equal" to his crime would be seen as an injustice under a retributive system. Treatment, as mentioned before, is acceptable under a utilitarian justice system and irrelevant and unsupported by a retributive one. While deterrence is the primary determinant of justice under a utilitarian system, desert is the only determinant of a retributive system of justice.

Other systems   Other ethical systems also support punishment. A religious ethical system, especially under some religions such as Christianity, supports proportional punishments—or at least most people believe that they can find evidence of the righteousness of punishment in the Bible. An ethics of care would support treatment. We will discuss more thoroughly how an ethics of care might be applied to the correctional system in a later chapter. It seems clear that an ethics of care would not be concerned with apportioning punishment for the sake of punishment, as in the retributive system. Because the ethics of care is based on human relationships and caring for each other, the concern would be to discover what the victim needs and what the offender needs. The problem would not be resolved through an application of rights, but rather an application of care—toward both the offender and the victim.

Procedural Justice

We turn now to the procedure of administering punishment— our legal system. Justice and law are not synonymous: most writers describe law as objective and justice as subjective. Law is the procedure used to determine punishment or resolve disputes, a system of rules for relations—the "whole field of the principles laid down, the decisions reached in accordance with them, and the procedures whereby the principles are applied to individual cases" (Raphael 1980, 74). There is, then, a difference between justice and law. Justice is a concept or judgment of fairness; law is a system of rules.

The law is an imperfect system. Fuller (1969, 39) explores the weaknesses of law and describes ways that the procedure of law may fail to achieve justice. Possible failures include a failure to achieve rules at all, so that every decision must be made on its own; a failure to publicize rules; retroactive application of law, which abuses the concept of justice; the existence of contradictory rules; too-frequent changes in rules; and a lack of consistency between the rules and their actual administration. These failures weaken the law's ability to resolve disputes or control conflict in an objective and fair manner.

Some argue that because of the legal system's inability to determine what is just, justice derives not from the application of legal rules but rather from deciding each case on its merits without regard to rule or precedent. Wasserman argues that legal precedent is an unsatisfactory way of determining justice since the particularity of each case is important; however, individual intuitive decisions are no better since then justice becomes "unsteady" and "wavering" (quoted in Feinberg and Gross 1977, 28–34). Some have argued that property and interest cases can be decided by legal rule, while cases involving conflicts of human conduct cannot. Even this bifurcation is criticized, however, since the most straightforward contract disagreements may involve human action, misinterpretation, and interest (Wasserman in Feinberg and Gross 1977, 34).

We are left to assume that although a system of law is necessary for the ordered existence of society, it is not necessarily helpful in determining what is just. In fact, "moral rights" may differ from "legal rights," and "legal interests" may not be moral. On the other hand, legal rules very often specify the procedures and steps taken in judicial decision making, and if these rules and procedures are broken we believe an injustice has occurred.

In our system of justice, *due process* exemplifies procedural justice. Our constitutional rights of due process require careful inquiry and investigation before punishment or forfeiture of any protected right can be carried out by the state. One has the right to due process whenever the state seeks to deprive an individual of protected rights of life, liberty, or property. Due process is the sequence of steps taken by the state that are designed to eliminate or at least minimize error. Procedural protections such as a neutral hearing body, trial by a jury of peers, cross-examination, presentation of evidence, and counsel do not eliminate deprivation or punishment, but they improve the possibility of accurate and "just" deprivation. Thus, if due process has been violated—by use of coercion to obtain a confession, use of "tainted evidence," or use of improper police procedure—we say that an injustice has occurred. The injustice does not arise because the offender does not deserve to be punished but because the state does not deserve to do the punishing, having relied on unfair or unjust procedures.

The *exclusionary rule* is supposed to ensure that the state follows the correct procedural steps before exacting punishment by excluding illegal evidence from the trial. There is debate as to whether the exclusionary rule is a mere legal protective device created by the court or a natural inherent right embedded in the Constitution. The exclusionary rule has been subject to a great deal of criticism because it is perceived as a rule that lets criminals go free. Obviously, a utilitarian framework might support punishment even if the procedural rules were broken, since the net utility of punishment may outweigh the violation of due process. Under utilitarianism, the justice of the punishment comes from its utility to society, primarily through its deterrence value. On the other hand, even a utilitarian may argue against punishment when the procedural protections have been broken if the damage to general respect for the law is greater than the deterrent utility of punishment. In fact, one of the rationales for the exclusionary rule is that it serves as a judicial "slap" at police departments and a deterrent against improper investigation procedures. This is clearly a utilitarian argument.

Would a retributive system of punishment accept a violation of due process if the offender were clearly guilty? It would seem that in this case, justice is violated whether one is punished or not. If we allow the offender to go free, then the crime has not been balanced by punishment. If we punish the offender, we violate our system of procedural justice.

Supreme Court decisions have shown reduced support for the exclusionary rule. Exceptions have been created that some say threaten to undermine the rule itself. For instance, the "inevitable discovery exception" indicates that if the tainted evidence would have been discovered without the improper procedure, then it can be admitted anyway (*Nix v. Williams*, 104 S. Ct. 250 [1984]). The good will exception was recognized by the Court in a case where the law enforcement officers thought they had a legal warrant even though the warrant and therefore their search was actually unlawful (*United States v. Leon*, 104 S. Ct. 3405 [1984]). Another exception to the exclusionary rule was recognized in *New York v. Quarles* (104 S. Ct. 2626 [1984]). In this case, since the officer's goal was public safety and not collection of evidence, his failure to give Miranda warnings did not result in excluding the evidence he obtained by questioning a suspect without Miranda warnings. The presence of such exceptions and other holdings imply that the Court is taking a more utilitarian stance. The majority displayed distinctly utilitarian reasoning in their cost/benefit arguments to support the holdings of the previously mentioned cases. It may be that the Supreme Court will become reluctant to uphold sanctions against any but the most extreme misconduct by police. *Rochin v. California* (343 U.S. 165 [1952]) is a case often cited as the bottom line of improper police procedure. The "shocking to the conscience" test is one where the common observer is appalled by the police procedure. In *Rochin*, the procedure found "shocking to the conscience" was forcing a suspect to regurgitate drugs. In other applications it appears that conduct must be this extreme before the utilitarian scale tips against the police.

Plea bargaining will be addressed more thoroughly in a later chapter, but here it must be recognized as a circumvention of due process. In plea bargaining, the end of efficiency is substituted for due process. Supporters point to the fact that defendants freely choose to plead guilty in return for sentence reductions or other rewards. Opponents point to the cynical assumption of guilt in contradiction to the basic principle of "innocent until proven guilty" of our justice system and question the voluntariness of any plea with the ever-present possibility of coercion inherent when the state "negotiates" with a powerless defendant. Hypocrisy reigns when the judge questions the suspect before the plea is taken, asking, "Have you been offered anything in exchange for your plea?" The defendant is coached to say no so everyone can continue the charade of impartial justice.

We have been discussing legal procedures for determining punishment, but in some cases legal procedures may be followed completely and injustice still occur. It is unlikely that anyone would argue, for instance, that Nelson Mandela, when he was imprisoned in South Africa, or André Sakharov, a Soviet dissident, received just punishment even though the legal procedures of their respective countries were followed scrupulously. One can see that a legal system can contribute to injustice if procedural justice enforces unjust laws. Justice, then, is a concept tied to but distinct from a system of laws.

JUSTICE AND VICTIMS' RIGHTS

It is often heard that the criminal justice system is concerned with the rights of the offender and not those of the victim. In many respects this is true. As discussed previously, retributive justice is concerned with what the offender deserves, not what the victim deserves. Procedural justice is concerned with protections against error in the deprivation of the suspect's life, liberty, and property; the victim in most states has no recognized procedural rights. In ancient codes of law, the focus was on the victim and compensation. This focus changed to the state and punishment instead of compensation in English common law around the time of the Magna Carta (1215). Eventually two systems of law developed, one to deal with private wrongs (civil law) and one to deal with so-called public wrongs (criminal law). The two may overlap, as in the case where a rape victim may sue her attacker in civil court concomitantly with a state prosecution. In the civil system, the victim is the plaintiff, but in the criminal law system, the victim is only a witness.

The legal theory of the state as opponent is that the harm done in any crime is only incidentally to an individual. The more important harm is the crime against the state. Obviously, this is not true in reality. It is the individual who bleeds, loses property, and is buried. It is the individual's family who grieves. Thus, we need to examine some concepts and issues relevant to whether the victim is treated justly in the criminal justice system.

Victimology has emerged as a separate discipline in criminology. One of the most startling findings is that the individuals who most fear crime are those who have least to fear, and those who are most likely to be the victims of some types of crime are very similar demographically to those who are most likely to be criminal—young, lower-class, minority males (Karmen 1984). Also, a very small group of people are disproportionately subject to multiple victimization. Elias reports that only 1 percent of the population bears one-quarter of all multiple victimization from violent crime, 2 percent absorb one-third, and 5 percent suffer one-half (1986, 61). This fact reflects the political nature of criminal justice statistics and the distance between the reality and the perception of the "crime problem."

While it is popular for politicians to campaign with a crime control agenda, their message panders to the voting public's fears rather than sheds light on a complex social problem where often there are no distinct lines between victims and offenders. The media, too, contribute to general fears and to the stereotype of the white middle-class victim and the lower-class minority criminal. Actually, minority groups and the poor are much more likely to be victimized. Most victims and offenders come from the same neighborhood. Criminals are often victims themselves of past or current crimes. Also, there are many more victims than those defined as such by the system. Customers of inner city supermarkets that charge higher prices for items because they know their customers do not have transportation to shop competitively are victims of economic exploitation. There are victims of retail credit schemes in which furniture rental stores rent and repossess a single piece of furniture several times for multiple profit. There are victims of employers who pay less than minimum wage or do not pay at all because they know the employees will not protest either because they are illegal aliens or because they desperately need the job. Finally, there are victims of slum landlords who must pay rent or be evicted even though the apartment has a multitude of health and safety hazards. These victims are rarely considered in discussions of the "crime problem."

The media may be most responsible for creating a false perception of crime. While violence occupies up to three-quarters of all television news time, it is a small percentage of actual crime (Elias 1986, 43). The constant barrage of murders, rapes, and robberies in television drama contributes to the public's general fear of crime, as does the local news media's sensationalistic treatment of such crimes even while ignoring more pervasive social problems. In fact, an individual is more likely to die of pneumonia, cancer, heart disease, household fires, auto crashes, or suicide than of homicide (Elias 1986, 48). While this is not to say that violent crime is not a problem, there is disproportionate emphasis on this type of crime relative to other types of victimization.

In the real world, most victims suffer relatively small losses but receive virtually no help at all from the system. Police do not respond at all to many burglary calls because there are so many calls and so little the police can do about them. Assault calls may be handled informally and cavalierly when the combatants are acquaintances or relatives. Victims rarely have much to do with the system unless a suspect is arrested, a rare occurrence in many categories of crime. When there is a prosecution, the victim may feel used by the system since the goal is to get a conviction, not to provide aid or compensation. The prosecutor is more interested in how the jury will perceive the victim than how much the victim lost or suffered from the crime.

Recently there has been a "rediscovery" of victims. Many states have enacted victims' rights bills that enumerate various rights victims have under the law. These rights may include being present at trial (circumventing procedural rules that exclude victim-witnesses from the courtroom during other testimony), being notified of any hearing dates and plea-bargain arrangement, submitting a victim impact statement to be considered during the sentencing decision, being treated courteously and compassionately by all law enforcement and justice system personnel, and so on. Some of these bills have created victim-witness programs in police departments or prosecutors' offices that attend to the needs of victim-witnesses. Duties of program personnel may include keeping victims informed of their case, providing information, accompanying victims in court, and helping them fill out victim compensation forms.

Victim compensation programs are also being created in many states. These programs provide compensation for certain types of crime when the victim is without insurance or other means of reimbursement. Funding comes either through court costs paid into a general fund by all criminal offenders or through the state's general funds. Usually only violent crime and not property crimes are targeted by such programs. They can provide help, however, with such expenses as lost wages, hospital and doctor bills, and even burial expenses, whether or not the offender is arrested. Restitution programs are much more common today than they have been, and these programs do target property victims as well as victims of violent crime. Restitution programs only help victims of criminals who are caught, however, and that is unfortunately not very many for crimes such as burglary and larceny.

Victims have a right to be treated fairly by the system. All people should be accorded the same level of service and treatment regardless of who they are. The "bag lady" should receive the same care as the mayor if both are mugged. Victims should also receive the same consideration in any punishment decision. The amount of punishment inflicted on an offender should not be based on the economic or social status of the victim, any more than it should be based on the economic or social status of the offender.

Other issues are not so simple. For instance, should the victim have equal say in the amount of punishment? What if the prosecutor believes that a plea bargain of probation is sufficient punishment considering the crime and the costs of a trial, but the victim demands imprisonment? Should a burglary victim have the right to veto a plea bargain? What about an assault victim? We spoke of mercy before; would not some argue that the state does not have the power to grant mercy, only the victim? These questions also relate to the decision to parole. Many states now have procedures whereby the victim or the victim's family has the right to address the parole board when the criminal's parole date comes up. Should these victims have the right to veto parole when the board would have otherwise paroled the criminal? We characterize the victim's feelings of vengeance as personal revenge and the state's as retribution or justice, with the implication that one is bad and the other is good. In fact, victims who "take the law into their own hands" become criminals themselves. But why is the state's determination of sufficient punishment any better than the victim's? Supposedly it is because the state has the power to objectively and rationally determine the correct measurement, but if there are other variables at work, such as goals of efficiency and convenience, then where is the objective measurement of punishment? Favoritism, bribery, and incompetence may also affect outcomes. Obviously, in these cases neither the victim nor the offender receives justice.

Some writers mistrust the current interest in victims' rights and believe that this recent concern is really a cynical manipulation of victim-witnesses to advance the goal of making them better witnesses for the state. Also, because the definition of the victim continues to be narrow and limited to stereotypes, obfuscation as to who are victims continues. This serves to blind those most at risk to the realities of their own victimization and protects those who victimize in ways other than street crimes, such as white-collar and social crimes (Elias 1986).

We have a system of punishment and retribution that is oriented completely to the offender. What would a system be like where the emphasis was on the victim's rights, needs, and compensation? In a system with a primary emphasis on the victim rather than the offender, money would be spent on victim services rather than prisons. It would be victims who received job skills training, not offenders. Some of the money that now goes to law enforcement and corrections would be channeled to compensation programs for victims of personal and property crimes. Victims would be helped even if their offenders were not caught. The major goal would not be punishment, but service. Offenders would be peripheral figures; they would be required to pay restitution to victims and the only punishment would occur if they did not fulfill their obligations to their victims. Could such a system work? Would such a system provide more justice?

CONCLUSION

In this chapter we have explored the definitions and components of justice. Distributive justice is concerned with allocating the scarce resources of society, as well as the burdens. Retributive justice is concerned with apportioning punishments. The determination of how much punishment is fair is the focus of substantive justice, and the procedures necessary for a fair administration of punishment are the content of procedural justice. Justice applies to both the offender and the victim. Offenders deserve a system that minimizes error and exacts a fair and equitable punishment. Victims deserve a system that recognizes their needs and acts as an advocate for their interests.

DISCUSSION QUESTIONS

1. Describe your concept of justice.
2. Explain how Aristotle and Plato associated status with justice. Is the status of the victim and the offender important today?
3. Explain the utilitarian argument for punishment and the retributive position. How would each justify prison sentences? Capital punishment? Chemical castration for sex offenders? Restitution?
4. Would you describe our legal system as just? Why or why not?

⊰⊱ ETHICAL DILEMMAS ⊰⊱

Please read and respond to the following situations. Be prepared to discuss your ideas.

Situation 1

Two individuals are being sentenced for the crime of burglary. You are the judge. One of the individuals is a twenty-year-old who has not been in trouble before and only participated because the other individual was his friend. The second person has a history of juvenile delinquency and is now twenty-five. Would you sentence them differently? How do you justify your decision?

Situation 2

You are a police chief in a small town who must select one of two people for a promotion to a sergeant's position. One is a white male and the second is a white female. The male received two points more than the female on a subjective interview by a selection panel. Their other qualifications are substantially equal. There has never been a female in this position. Whom would you choose? Why? Would your answer change if the second person were a member of a minority group? What if you knew the interview panel included members who had expressed sexist views? Racist views?

Situation 3

You are a welfare administrator who is confronted with the following dilemma: a young mother of two on welfare is trying to raise her standard of living by working part-time. Unfortunately, the amount of money she earns, while paltry, is enough to put her over the limit that entitles her to welfare benefits. The difference is only $10. Rules clearly specify that she should be expelled from the program. What would you do?

⤙ 5 ⤚

Ethics and the Law

The law serves as a written embodiment of society's ethics and morals. It is said to be declarative as well as active—it declares correct behavior and serves as a tool for enforcement. Law is both a prohibition and a promise. It cautions against certain types of behavior and warns of the consequences for ignoring the warning. *Natural law* refers to the belief that some law is inherently valid and can be discovered by reason. A corollary of this thought is that some behavior is intrinsically wrong (*male in se*). In contrast, *positive law* refers to those laws written and enforced by society. This type of law is man-made and therefore fallible (Mackie 1977, 232).

We can trace the history of law back to very early codes, such as the code of Hammurabi (c. 2000 B.C.), which mixed secular and religious proscriptions of behavior. These codes also standardized punishments and atonements for wrongdoings. Early codes of law did not differentiate between what we might call public wrongs and private wrongs. Today, two different areas of law can be distinguished. Criminal law is said to be punitive, while civil law is reparative. The first punishes while the second seeks to redress wrong or loss. Of the two, criminal law is more closely associated with the moral standards of society, yet it is by no means comprehensive in its coverage of behavior. Nor is there unanimous agreement about what it should or does cover.

LAW AND SOCIETY

There are two basic paradigms that aid our understanding of the function of law in society. A paradigm, according to Rich (1978, 1), is a "fundamental image of the subject matter within a science. . . . It subsumes, defines, and interrelates the exemplars, theories, and methods/tools that exist within it." The *consensus paradigm* views society as a community consisting of like-minded individuals who agree on goals important for ultimate survival. This view is functionalist since it views law as an aid to the growth and/or survival of society. Under the *conflict paradigm*, society is perceived as being made up of competing and conflicting interests. According to this view, governance is based on power; if some win, others lose, and those who hold power in society follow self-interest, not the greater good. A less extreme view than the conflict paradigm is *pluralism*. Although sharing the perception that society is made up of competing interests, pluralism describes more than two basic interest groups and also recognizes a changing power balance as part of the dynamics of society.

The Consensus Paradigm

According to the consensus paradigm, law functions to unify the whole. Durkheim wrote that there are two types of law: the repressive, criminal law, which serves to enforce universal norms; and the restitutive, civil law, which necessarily developed because of the division of labor in society and resulting social interests. In Durkheim's view, criminal law exists as a manifestation of consensual norms: "We must not say that an action shocks the common conscience because it is criminal, but rather that it is criminal because it shocks the common conscience" (Durkheim 1969, 21). What this statement means is that we define action as criminal because the majority of the populace hold the opinion that it is wrong. To label such an action *crime* is actually redundant because everyone already knows that it is wrong. This "common" or "collective" conscience is referred to as *mechanical solidarity*. Each individual's moral beliefs are indistinguishable from the whole. The type of law that reflects this conscience is *repressive law*. The function of punishment, then, becomes the maintenance of social cohesion; it contributes to the collective conscience by providing examples of deviance.

Although Durkheim recognized individual differences, he believed these differences, resulting from the division of labor in society, only made the individual more dependent on society as a part of a whole. His concept of *organic solidarity* draws the analogy of individuals in society as parts of an organism: all doing different things but as parts of a whole. Individuals exist, but they are tied inextricably to society and its common conscience. *Restitutive law* is said to mediate those differences that may come about because of the division of labor. Even here the law serves an integrative function.

The consensus view would point to evidence that we all agree for the most part on what behaviors are wrong and on the relative seriousness of different types of wrongful behavior. In criminology, the consensus view is represented by classical thinkers such as Bentham and Beccaria who relied on the accepted definitions of crime in their day without questioning the validity of these definitions, only their implementation. Although the positivists virtually ignored societal definitions of crime, Garofalo (1852–1934, a legal anthropologist) had an idea of natural law that might be considered a consensus concept. As defined earlier, natural law is the view that certain behaviors are so inherently heinous that they go against nature, and therefore there are natural proscriptions against such behavior that transcend individual societies or time periods (Kramer 1982, 36). We have recent evidence that there is at least some consensus in people's definitions of what constitutes criminal behavior; studies have shown that not only do individuals in this culture tend to agree on the relative seriousness of different kinds of crime, but there is also substantial agreement cross-culturally as well (Nettler 1978,

215). Law in the consensus paradigm is representative. It is a compilation of the dos and don'ts we all agree on. Furthermore, law serves to reinforce social cohesion. It emphasizes our "we-ness" by illustrating deviance. Finally, law is value-neutral; that is, it resolves conflicts in an objective and neutral manner.

The Conflict Paradigm

A second paradigm of law and society is the conflict paradigm. Rather than perceiving law as representative, this perspective sees law as a tool of power holders, which they use for their own purposes, to maintain and control the status quo. In the conflict paradigm, law is perceived as restrictive or repressive rather than representative, and as an instrument of special interests. Basically, there are three points to the conflict paradigm: first, criminal definitions are relative; second, those who control major social institutions determine how crime is defined; and third, the definition of crime is fundamentally a tool of power (Sheley 1985, 1). Quinney (1969, 17) describes the conflict paradigm as follows:

> By formulating criminal law (including legislative statutes, administrative rulings, and judicial decisions), some segments of society protect and perpetuate their own interests. Criminal definitions exist, therefore, because some segments of society are in conflict with others. By formulating criminal definitions these segments are able to control the behavior of persons in other segments. It follows that the greater the conflict in interests between segments of a society, the greater the probability that the power segments will formulate criminal definitions.

Quinney's description of conflict theory draws heavily from Marxist definitions of power and power holders in capitalism. Quinney (1974, 15–16) outlines the following points as making up the conflict paradigm:

1. American society is based on an advanced capitalistic society.
2. The state is organized to serve the interests of the dominant economic class . . .
3. Criminal law is an instrument of the state and ruling class to maintain and perpetuate the existing social and economic order.
4. Crime control in capitalist society is accomplished through a variety of institutions and agencies established and administered by a governmental elite . . .
5. The contradictions of advanced capitalism . . . require that the subordinate classes remain oppressed by whatever means necessary . . .
6. Only with the collapse of capitalist society and the creation of a new society . . . will there be a solution to the crime problem.

The conflict view would point to laws against gambling, the use of some drugs, prostitution, and pornography as evidence that the ruling class punishes only those activities that are engaged in by other classes. In other words, cultural differences in behavior exist, but only the activities of certain groups (the powerless) are labeled deviant. For instance, only some types of gambling are illegal: numbers running is always illegal, yet some states have legalized horse racing, dog racing, or casinos. Only some drugs are illicit: heroin and cocaine are illegal while Valium and alcohol are not. Conflict theorists believe that these laws exist to protect and benefit the powerful groups in society and their interests.

Recall Jeffrey Reiman's description of the difference between reporting a mining accident and a multiple murder. Despite the same end result (dead victims), the mining company would probably go unprosecuted or receive very minor punishments for its role in the death of the miners. For the conflict theorist, this would be an example of how law has been written differentially to serve the interests of the power holders. The definition of what is criminal often excludes corporate behavior, such as price fixing, toxic waste dumping, or monopolistic trade practices, because these behaviors, although just as harmful to the public good as street crime, are engaged in by those who have the power to define criminality. The regulation of business, instead of the criminalization of harmful business practices, is seen as arising from the ability of those in power positions to redefine their activities to their own advantage. Even though the Occupational Safety Board, the Food and Drug Administration, the Federal Aeronautics Administration, and other similar governmental agencies are charged with the task of enforcing regulations governing business activities in their respective areas, no one seriously believes that the level of enforcement or labeling that results is as stringent as in criminal law. Often relationships between the watched and the watchdog agencies are incestuous: heads of business often are named to governmental agencies, and employees of these agencies may move to the business sector they previously regulated.

Some would even go so far as to parallel corporate crimes and organized crime in the belief that they are from the same spectrum of behavior (Krisberg 1975, 35). Certainly it is fairly well documented that large and small corporations engage in dishonest and even criminal practices. One study reported that from a sample of businesses, 60 percent reported enforcement activity in response to one of the following violations: restraint of trade, financial manipulation, misrepresentation in advertising, income tax evasion, unsafe working conditions, unsafe food or drug distribution, illegal rebates, foreign payoffs, unfair labor practices, illegal political contributions, or environmental pollution (Clinard et al. 1985, 205).

In criminology, the conflict view was represented by early theorists such as Bonger (1876–1940), a Marxist sociologist who explained crime causation as a result of economic power differential and the ability of power holders to label some behavior as criminal. During the 1960s, a small number of criminologists attempted to redefine criminals as political prisoners based on their views that the state used criminal definitions to control minority groups (Reasons 1973). We also see the definitional process of the criminal justice system questioned in labeling theory, which illuminates the fact that only some people are labeled as deviant even though many more commit deviant acts. The conflict theory is represented by theorists such as Platt, the Schwendingers, Krisberg, Quinney, Taylor, Walton, and Young and Chambliss (Kramer 1982, 41). The conflict theorists explain that the myth of justice and equality under the law serves to protect the interests of the ruling class, because as long as there is a perception of fairness, fundamental questions about the distribution of goods will not be raised: "The combination of formal legal equality and extreme economic inequality is the hallmark of the liberal state" (Krisberg 1975, 49). Law functions to depoliticize even the most obviously political actions of the oppressed by defining these actions as crime, but its greatest power is to hide the basic injustice of society itself, according to Krisberg (1975, 54):

> The relationship between the offender's actions and the larger system of economic and political oppression is denied by the ideology of law. Through its denial of the culpability of the privileged in the social reality of the criminal event, the state masks its own crimes and supports the appearance of the moral superiority of the privileged classes.

An incident drawn from current events may help to illustrate how the consensus and conflict paradigms are used to explain reality. The Los Angeles riots in 1992 were sparked by the acquittal of four police officers who were videotaped beating Rodney King, a motorist who had outstanding arrest warrants for traffic violations. The riots were described by some as a political action. According to this view, minorities who were frustrated by economic hopelessness and angered by the criminal justice system's oppressive and brutal treatment retaliated in like form. The riots, seen in this view, were political statements against oppression. Alternatively, others described the same actions as blatant and simple criminality. In this perspective, violent individuals merely took advantage of the incident to exhibit their individual deviance. Conflict theorists would support the first definition, while consensus theorists would propose the second.

Other Paradigms

Distinct from conflict theorists are the pluralists, who also view law as arising from interest groups but decline to identify power as being held by only one group. Roscoe Pound defines the following as interests protected by power holders: security against actions that threaten the social group, security of social institutions, security of morals, conservation of national resources, general progress, and individual life. Power is exercised in the political order, the economic order, the religious order, the kinship order, the educational order, and the public order. Law and social control constitute the public order, and powerful interests affect the law by influencing the writing of laws and enforcement of written laws (Quinney 1974).

This theory does not simply state that rich people make laws to benefit themselves. As mentioned previously, basic interests are always present in the law and must be served. However, some interests may be at odds with other interests, or certainly the interpretation of them may be. For instance, conservation of natural resources is a basic interest necessary for the survival of society, but it may be interpreted by lumber companies as allowing them to harvest trees in national forests as long as they replant, or, alternatively, by conservation groups as mandating more wilderness areas. Which is right? According to the pluralist paradigm, it depends on which group is more powerful at any particular time.

This perspective is more complex than the conflict theory described earlier. Interest groups hold power, but their power may shrink or grow depending on various factors. Since there are many interest groups, coalitions and shared interests may shift the balance of power. The definition of crime may change depending on which interest groups have the power to define criminal behavior and what is perceived to be in the best interests of the most powerful groups.

Another perspective or paradigm is the *social learning view*, which postulates that law is a tool to change behavior. Some writers consider this paradigm conceptually distinct from those just discussed (Hornum and Stavish 1978, 148). Law is seen as a tool of social engineering and a way of changing behavior to a desired state (Aubert 1969, 11). In this view there is little recognition or analysis of who is deciding what ideal behavior should be or what behavior needs to be changed. Law is seen as influencing behavior either indirectly, by changing social institutions, such as the family or education, that in turn influence behavior, or directly, by prohibiting behavior that had previously been accepted, such as polygyny in some countries (Dror 1969, 93). It is questionable whether this paradigm is distinctly different from the others. It would be consistent with any of the three previously mentioned assuming that if there is a change in the perception of a certain behavior, the law will reflect that change and institutionalize it.

We might consider the *social contract theory* of Hobbes and Rousseau another paradigm of law and society. In many ways it is a paradigm that combines conflict and consensus views. According to this idea, members of society freely give up their natural rights of liberty, including the liberty to act selfishly against others, in return for the protections of society. In this idea, the natural inclination of individuals to use power for their own ends is recognized, as is the rational response of conceding power for the mutual benefit of all—in essence a consensus resolution to conflicts of power. According to Hobbes, each individual has chosen to "lay down this right to all things; and be contented with so much liberty against other men, as he would allow other men against himself" (from Hobbes, *Leviathan*, 1651, in Beauchamp 1982, 264). Law is viewed as a mutual contract and transfer of rights.

Ideologies of Liberalism and Conservatism

An *ideology* is "a set of general and abstract beliefs or assumptions about the correct or proper state of things, particularly with respect to the moral order and political arrangements, which serve to shape one's positions on specific issues" (Hornum and Stavish 1978, 143). Two opposing ideologies regarding crime and criminals are the liberal and the conservative. Although these categorizations are drawn with a broad brush, they do illuminate basic values and important issues in social control and crime. Both the liberal and the conservative perspectives operate under the consensus paradigm, in that they accept the basic definitions of crime as given by law.

The liberal perspective   The liberal perspective explains criminal behavior and deviance through reference to psychological, social, or biological causation. Because individuals are seen as influenced by factors outside their control, they are not considered completely culpable for their crimes. Explanations are developed for why criminals commit crime and what can be done to treat the problem. The *rehabilitative ethic*, with its view of crime as a symptom of pathology, is associated with the liberal perspective.

In policing, the liberal perspective is manifested when police departments make themselves more accessible and develop informal means of resolving disputes. Innovations such as neighborhood policing, team policing, and youth athletics help the police understand and empathize with groups that may be predisposed to crime. Police patrol is seen as negative social control in that it is proscriptive and is based on fear and coercive control; the liberal perspective would endorse positive social control such as providing services to the community that would influence prosocial values. For instance, "Officer Friendly" programs in schools not only teach bicycle safety tips but also give the message that police officers are friends, and children should look up to them as role models. Neighborhood policing models also emphasize a proactive positive service role for police officers.

In courts, the liberal perspective is seen in individualized justice—the consideration of the offender rather than the offense. This involves accepting reasons or rationales for unlawful behavior. For instance, a burglar who had lost his job and had bills to pay, an enraged wife who killed her husband because he left her for another woman, or a ghetto youth whose father turned him on to drugs would all have their individual backgrounds considered in determining responsibility and punishment. The liberal perspective would hold that the law is given an impossible task of defining wrongdoing and setting punishments for human behavior that cannot be described and dealt with by categories and definitions. Human behavior is complex and is motivated by causes that the law does not take into account. Thus, the courts, and their human representatives in the legal system, must use discretion and administer justice to each as an individual.

All the correctional programs developed in the last several decades derive from a liberal ideology. Attempts to make criminals more like "us," by vocational training, education, and social skills training, are based on the idea that the criminal can change given a different environment, different influences, or solutions to such problems as illiteracy or addiction. Correctional programs target biological problems (addiction), social problems (negative role models), or psychological problems (weak ego state); these programs assume that if one could correct whatever is wrong, the criminal will no longer commit crime. The *treatment ethic* postulates that crime is a symptom of an underlying pathology that can be treated.

The liberal perspective's ethics dictate that treatment of the offender must take into account individual factors. It would be considered unethical, for instance, to institute zero tolerance enforcement when the policy would capture innocents or minor criminals; to ignore a prisoner's need for special attention or medical care; to prosecute a very young offender in the same way that one would a more culpable older offender; or to ignore evidence that an individual was mentally ill when committing an offense. Basically, the liberal objects when the law is used to uphold some unrealistic standard of objective justice, since that is not possible.

The conservative perspective   The conservative generally agrees with the liberal that the legal code is a true representation of society's morals and values but differs in the perception of the offender. The offender is seen as an evil person who freely chooses actions and must be held accountable for them, not as a person influenced by forces beyond his or her control. The criminal is considered different from the innocent populace; criminals are evil and not worthy of the same protections the law affords the rest of us.

Conservatives see police as enforcers of society's morals; any attempts to weaken that role should be resisted. Court restrictions on police powers or actions should be limited since criminals must be caught and punished in whatever way is most effective. Police are seen as becoming "soft" or bureaucratized in recent years; there may be a wistful element in the popularity of such fictional characters as "Dirty Harry," who bypasses due process to get criminals off the streets.

In the conservative perspective, courts are the worst threat to society because they allow criminals to go free and cost the public money by forcing the state to provide expensive programs and "luxuries" for prisoners. Only the most punitively oriented judge receives the conservative's approval; the majority of judges are seen as do-gooders who do not give criminals the prison sentences they deserve. Probation is considered a slap on the wrist that only teaches the criminal that he or she can commit crime and receive no punishment as a consequence. If a criminal has served a prison sentence and then commits a crime on parole, the sentence should be twice as long because he or she didn't learn a lesson the first time. In this view, the death penalty is used far too seldom and even when it is given, judges are much too likely to accept appeals. Criminals are believed to have too many rights and victims none.

According to the conservative perspective, too many correctional programs coddle criminals rather than give them what they deserve. All correctional programs, from education to group therapy to work release, teach inmates that they will be rewarded and excused for criminal behavior. According to conservatives, we should go back to the old way of punishing, with the whip and the rock pile. In those days criminals knew they were being punished and they learned from it.

Conservative ethics would condemn those criminal justice practitioners who use their powers of discretion too freely. In this view, it is unethical to plea bargain or to let criminals go because of some error in the proceedings. It is seen as unethical for police to ignore wrongdoing by informants and for criminal justice practitioners to give special privileges to rich or powerful criminals. Whenever the system is less than objective in meting out punishment, as in the case of disparate sentencing based on offender characteristics, the conservatives' concern for ethics is aroused. It is seen as unethical, for instance, for one defendant to get more years in prison than another due to different circumstances if they both committed the same crime.

Herbert Packer described a *crime control model* that stresses containment of criminal behavior in the most rapid and efficient way possible. This concept can also be used to represent conservative interests. Objectives of the crime control model are, first, to detect, apprehend, convict, and incarcerate offenders; second, to deter potential law violators; and, third, to create an orderly and stable society (cited in Rich 1978, 92). The *due process model* stresses protecting individual liberties against bureaucratic efficiency. Both of these models, however, have similar goals in that they are fundamentally concerned with the control of crime.

The author of the following quote (Smith 1982, 137) uses the term *right* instead of *conservative*, but the description encapsulates the values and objectives of the conservative viewpoint.

> For the right, the paramount value is order—an ordered society based on a pervasive and binding morality—and the paramount danger is disorder—social, moral and political. For the left, the paramount value is justice—a just society based on a fair and equitable distribution of power, wealth, prestige and privilege—and the paramount evil is injustice.

Although many people would associate the liberal, or left, viewpoint with due process, as in the preceding quotation, it seems more true that the liberal ideology, because of its rehabilitative ethic, does not necessarily or even logically support a due process position. The liberal treatment position is that one should do all one can for an offender, who is considered sick. This position of providing whatever treatment is necessary may go beyond what even conservative, retributive ends would dictate. Therefore, there are three distinct positions here: the treatment position (which here is called the liberal ideology), the crime control model (which is called the conservative position), and the due process model (which does not fit into either).

Retributionists, such as von Hirsch, who postulate a "just-deserts" model, would be easily identified as conservatives. According to his view of justice, the state should be involved in restraint and retribution when the actions of one individual are inconsistent with the liberties of others; however, state intervention should be parsimonious, and extreme constraints must be placed on deterrence not related to crime commission, such as rehabilitation or selective incapacitation (von Hirsch 1976). The rehabilitative ideal is rejected in this framework, not only because it is bankrupt—no treatment programs can be shown to work—but also because it oversteps the authority of the state. This is a Kantian view of retribution and punishment; we will cover this perspective more fully in Chapter 8.

Despite the obvious generalizations of these characterizations, they do illuminate basic positions. We can detect the conservative perspective or the liberal perspective in news coverage or political speech. The conservative position is currently more popular than the liberal perspective, and themes of accountability and punitiveness are pervasive whenever crime and social control are discussed. Our interest in these positions is that each perspective emphasizes different ethical concerns.

MORALITY AND THE LAW

The law restricts individual liberty. Without law, you could engage in any behavior you could get away with; that is, until someone more powerful stopped you. We agree that restricting liberty is necessary. The *social contract theory*, mentioned previously, explains that the law is a contract—each individual gives up some liberties and in return is protected from others who have their liberties restricted as well. How much and what type of liberties the law should restrict are subject to controversy. Rough formulas or guidelines indicate that the law should interfere as little as possible in natural liberties and should step in only when the liberty in question injures or impinges on the interests of another.

One author offers "mediating maxims" to govern the application of restrictive laws. First, risk assessment: Does the behavior involve risk to others? The second maxim is the minimum restriction rule: Is the restriction the minimum necessary to accomplish the end desired. Finally, interest balancing is applied: the individual interest in the activity is measured against society's interest in prevention. Some principles that may justify the limitation of liberty are as follows (Feinberg in Feibleman 1985, xiii):

1. *The harm principle:* to prevent harm to persons other than the actor when probably no other means are equally as effective
2. *The offense principle:* to prevent serious offense to persons other than the actor
3. *Legal paternalism:* to prevent harm—physical, psychological, or economic—to the actor
4. *Legal moralism:* to prohibit conduct that is inherently immoral
5. *Benefit to others:* when the prohibition of the action provides some benefit to persons other than the actor

In the conflict paradigm, the law is seen as a tool of certain powerful interests in society, and the principles just enunciated would be filtered through the egocentric lens of the powerful group. The consensus paradigm, including the liberal and conservative ideologies, encompasses the belief that the law represents the will of the majority and there would be general agreement on how the principles would be applied. After some comments addressing the first two of these principles, we will explore legal paternalism and legal moralism more thoroughly.

How far should the law go in managing citizens' behavior? Obviously, we agree on laws that restrict behavior blatantly harmful to innocent victims—for example, homicide; but there is no agreement on, for instance, the right of the government to regulate the means by which a property owner chooses to protect himself. Is a lethal trap set for a burglar murder or self-protection? Should we pass laws that allow individuals to use deadly force to protect their property? Only fairly recently have laws been rewritten to afford more protection for family members against the violence of other family members. Historically, the law allowed the household head to be the supreme power, even allowing physical violence to be used as long as it remained within the family. The *rule of thumb*, for instance, was the common law rule that allowed a husband to beat his wife if he used a stick no greater in diameter than his thumb. Most of us are repelled by family violence and believe children and spouses have the right to be protected, but even today some people believe that family discipline is a private matter.

Recently, fear of AIDS has engendered debate over the limits of government intervention. Some people want AIDS victims to be registered and be prohibited from many jobs and types of participation in the public sector. Some want mandatory testing in certain occupational groups. Others believe that these proposed laws are discriminatory and only serve to further stigmatize the sufferers. The balance between individual freedom and government control is reached with difficulty when fear and misunderstanding about the potentiality of danger fuel emotions.

Abortion is an example of a behavior that results in harm to another but has been ignored, outlawed, and then allowed by the law. Criminalization of maternal drug abuse is another trend that illustrates the dynamics of law. Maternal drug abuse has been a social problem for a long time, but only fairly recently has there been an effort to prosecute pregnant women who expose their fetuses to harmful drugs. Prosecutors either use existing laws in creative ways or they advocate writing new laws to cover such behavior. The harmful effects of these behaviors have not changed, only the beliefs about the right of the law to interfere. The law is always in flux—some behaviors that result in harm to others are seen as more or less evil over time and the law responds to these beliefs.

Legal Paternalism

Many of our laws are *paternalistic*—they try to protect persons from their own behavior. Examples include seat belt laws, motorcycle helmet laws, speed limits, drug laws, licensing laws, alcohol consumption and sale laws, smoking prohibitions, and laws limiting certain types of sexual behavior. The strict libertarian view would hold that the government has no business interfering in a person's decisions about these behaviors as long as they don't negatively impact on others. The opposing view is that as long as a person is a member of society (and everyone is), he or she has a value to that society, and society is therefore compelled to protect the person with or without his or her cooperation.

It may also be true that there are no harmful or potentially harmful behaviors to oneself that do not also hurt others, however indirectly; so society is protecting others when it controls the individual. Speeding drivers may crash into someone else, drug addicts may commit crime to support their habits, gamblers may neglect their families and cause expense to the state, and so on. You may remember that in the first chapter we limited moral judgments to behavior that influences another. The application of paternalistic laws is consistent with the view that most behaviors one engages in also affect others.

Some believe that government can only justify paternalism with certain restrictions. First, a paternalistic law is only appropriate if the decision-making ability of the actor is somehow impaired, by lack of knowledge or something else. An example of this would be child labor laws, which restrict hiring children for their own protection. Another example is laws that restrict the sale and consumption of alcohol by those under a certain age; again the intent is to save children from themselves, with the presumption that their lack of knowledge prevents them from making rational decisions. The second rule of paternalism is that the restriction should be as limited as possible. For example, laws against drinking and driving define legal intoxication, which is the point where intoxication may affect behavior. Seat belt laws exist in most states, but few, if any, require expensive airbags. When mountain passes are closed due to weather conditions, they are reopened as soon as it is relatively safe to cross them. Finally, the third rule of paternalism states that the laws should only seek to prevent a serious and irreversible error: a death from DWI, an accident on an icy road, and so on. These rules seek to create a balance between an individual's liberty and government control (Thompson 1980).

Paternalistic laws can be supported by an ethics of care. In this framework, remember, morality is viewed as integral to a system of relationships. The individual is seen as having ties to society and every member of society. Relationships involve responsibilities as well as rights. We can expect the minimum level of care necessary for survival from society under the ethics of care. However, the corollary of this is that society also can care for us by restricting harmful behaviors. Rights are not important in this framework; therefore, to ask whether society has a right to intervene or an individual has a right to a liberty is not relevant to an ethics of care. Rights are important under ethical formalism; individuals must be treated with respect and as ends in themselves. This may result in recognizing the rights of individuals to engage in careless or even harmful behavior as long as it is consistent with the universalism principle of the categorical imperative. But under the ethics of care, the individual's rights are not as important as his or her well-being.

Legal Moralism

The law also acts as the moral agent of society, some say in areas where there is no moral agreement. Sexual behavior, gambling, drinking and drug use, pornography, and even suicide and euthanasia are some areas in which the law defines morality and immorality. The laws against behavior in these areas may involve principles of harm or paternalism, but they also exist to reinforce society's definitions of moral behavior.

For example, consensual sexual behavior between adults harms no one, yet the Georgia state law prohibiting sodomy was upheld by the Supreme Court in *Bowers v. Hardwick* (106 S. Ct.. 2841 [1986]). What harm is the state preventing by prohibiting this consensual behavior? The answer may be harm to community standards of morality. Pornography is defined as obscene and prohibited, arguably because of moral standards, not harmful effect. Recently, a governmental commission concluded that pornography contributes to sex crimes (Attorney General's Commission on Pornography 1986), but this commission's findings can be contrasted with those of an earlier Johnson commission that found that pornography does not contribute substantially to sex crimes (Commission on Obscenity and Pornography 1970). Hence, we have a factual issue: does it or does it not contribute to sex crimes? This issue is associated with the harm principle. Yet even if pornography does not prove to be harmful to others, the legal morality principle endorses the government's right to prohibit the sale and purchase of pornographic materials to consenting adults.

If we accepted the fact that laws are the embodiment of society's morals, then legal morality would be less controversial, but in our society there is by no means agreement that these actions are immoral. Personal actions such as homosexuality and the use of pornography can be judged using the ethical frameworks discussed in a previous chapter. An egoist would probably find nothing immoral with homosexuality and pornography since they provide pleasure and thus are good for the individual. Utilitarianism may or may not provide support for the morality of such behavior, depending on a consideration of the utility for the individual versus the total amount of utility for society. A good argument might be made that overall, homosexuality does not provide utility to society since it does not contribute to propagation and, therefore, society's survival; pornography may be considered, on the whole, a negative since its utility to society is hard to define. On the other hand, if one could show that an action does no harm to society and does provide utility to the individual, then that would be sufficient to judge that action as good. Ethical formalism may not condemn such actions if one agrees that everyone should be able to engage in similar behavior. Religious ethics would probably condemn the actions, although this depends on interpretation. The Bible, as has been demonstrated many times, can be used as evidence to condemn or support many behaviors.

According to the ethical formalism framework, drugs can be considered immoral because they abuse the body and deny the individual humanity of the taker. They are immoral in that the individual is using his or her body as a means for transitory pleasure and thus violating a basic principle of respect for the person. Furthermore, a universal law allowing drug taking would probably violate the categorial imperative. Therefore, ethical formalism would probably support drug laws. Even egoism may reject drug taking if one considers that in the long run the body is abused and drug taking may lead to addiction or other negative effects. Similar analyses might be made of gambling, prostitution, drinking, and other behaviors.

The ethics of virtue could be applied as well. Remember that in this ethical system, one determines virtues—kindness, generosity, integrity, courage, and so on—and then determines whether an individual behaves in a manner consistent with such virtues. If he or she does, then that person is a moral individual and will make correct moral decisions. If one does not practice such virtues in daily living, then we cannot expect her or him to make correct moral decisions. One might justify legal moralism as an educational tool for developing moral virtues in members of society. Remember the paradigm that described law as a tool of social learning. In this schema, the legal morality principle ensures that laws can be used as tools for social learning in morality.

In some cases, individuals may agree that a particular action is immoral but at the same time may not believe that the government should have the right to restrict an individual's choice. Some proponents of choice regarding abortion take great care to distinguish the difference between pro-choice and pro-abortion. To them, one does not have to approve of abortion to believe that it is wrong for government to interfere in the private decision of the individual whether to use the procedure. Similarly, some who advocate decriminalization of drugs do so because of cost effectiveness or libertarian reasons, not because they approve of drug use. We do not have a system where the law completely overlaps with the moral code, and some would argue that it would be impossible in a society as heterogeneous as ours for this to occur.

In conclusion, we must allow for the possibility that some laws that are justified under legal morality may not necessarily conform to our personal views of good and bad. Many criminal justice practitioners also feel that some of the so-called gray areas of crime should be decriminalized. These areas of law are where a great deal of discretion is employed by police and court personnel. Police will routinely ignore prostitution, for instance, until the public complains; they routinely let petty drug offenders go, rather than take the trouble to book them; and they may let gamblers go with a warning if no publicity is attached to the arrest. Police use discretion in this way partly because these behaviors are not universally condemned.

IMMORAL LAWS AND THE MORAL PERSON

In the previous section we discussed laws prohibiting behaviors that are judged as immoral, at least by some part of the populace. In this section we will look at laws and governmental edicts that are themselves immoral. Examples might include the laws of the Spanish Inquisition that permitted large numbers of people to be tortured and killed for having different religious beliefs from the crown, or the laws of Nazi Germany that demanded Jews give themselves up to be transported to concentration camps and often death. Examples in this country might include the internment laws during World War II that forced American citizens of Japanese descent to give up land and property and be confined in internment camps until the end of the war, or the segregationist laws that forced blacks to use different building entries and water fountains. These laws are now thought of as immoral, but they were not at the time. It is important to understand why an ethical system might condemn such laws, because only an objective system of ethical analysis would prevent the passage of such laws in the first place.

The example of Japanese-American internment can be used to illustrate how one might use the ethical systems to judge a specific law. The religious ethical framework would not provide any moral support for that action because it runs contrary to some basic Christian principles, such as "Do unto others as you would have them do unto you." Ethical formalism could not be used to support this particular law since it runs counter to the categorical imperative that each person must be treated as an end rather than as a means and to the universalism principle. The principle of forfeiture could not justify the action since these were innocent individuals, many of whom were fiercely loyal to the United States. The only ethical framework that might be used to support this law is utilitarianism. We must be able to show that the total utility derived from the law outweighed the negative effect it had on the Japanese who lost their land and liberty. Did it save the country from a Japanese invasion? Did it allow other Americans to sleep better at night? Did the benefits outweigh the extreme harm to Japanese Americans?

Are there any laws that might be considered immoral today? Some right-to-life advocates believe that laws that allow abortions in the first and second trimesters are immoral. Some say that the laws excluding prayer in public schools are immoral. Could the religious ethical system be used to support or condemn such laws? What about utilitarianism? In other countries the legal climate allows for torture and death squads to be used against political dissidents. If you were in a South American country and knew of assassinations by government police and nighttime kidnappings and disappearances, would you follow a law that required you to turn in political subversives? Or if you lived in South Africa, would you uphold apartheid laws? These issues are at the heart of our next discussion.

Can one be a moral person while enforcing or obeying an immoral law? Martin Luther King, Jr., Gandhi, and Thoreau agreed with St. Augustine that "an unjust law is no law at all." There is a well-known story about Henry David Thoreau, jailed for nonpayment of what he considered unfair taxes. When asked by a friend, "What are you doing in jail?" Thoreau responded, "What are you doing out of jail?" The point of the story is that if a law is wrong, a moral person is honor-bound to disobey that law: as Thoreau put it, "Under a government which imprisons any unjustly, the true place for a just man is also a prison" (in Fink 1977, 109). If this is true, what would happen to the stability of society? Another story concerns Socrates. About to be punished for the crime of teaching youth radical ideas, he had the opportunity to escape and in fact was begged by his friends to leave the country; yet he accepted the drink of hemlock willingly because of a fundamental respect for the law of his country.

While to follow all laws regardless of their intrinsic morality may set up a situation like Nazi Germany, if we agree with the proposition that an unjust law is no law at all, we may set up a situation in which all citizens follow or disobey laws at will depending on their own conscience. If one held a relativist view of morality, specifically the belief that one can intuit morals or decide morality on an individual basis, then two people holding different moral positions could both be right even though one position might be inconsistent with the law. An absolutist view holds that there is only one universal truth, which would mean that if one knew a law to be wrong based on this universal truth, then that person would be morally obliged to disobey the law. Evidentally either position could support civil disobedience.

Civil disobedience is the voluntary disobedience of established laws based on moral beliefs. Rawls defines it as a public, nonviolent, conscientious, yet political act contrary to law and usually done with the aim of bringing about a change in the law or policies of the government (Rawls 1971). Many great social thinkers and leaders have advocated breaking certain laws thought to be wrong. Note how Martin Luther King, Jr., defends his lawbreaking in the following quote (cited in Barry 1985, ii):

> [T]here are two types of laws[:] just and unjust. I would be the first to advocate obeying just laws. One has not only a legal but a moral responsibility to obey just laws. Conversely, one has a moral responsibility to disobey unjust laws.

Many philosophers believe that the moral person follows a higher law of behavior that usually, but not necessarily, conforms to human law. It is an exceptional person, however, who willfully and publicly disobeys laws he or she believes to be wrong. Psychological experiments show us that it is difficult for individuals to resist authority, even when they know that obeying authority is wrong. The Milgram experiments are often used as an example of how easily one can command blind obedience to authority. In these experiments, subjects were told to administer shocks to individuals hooked up to electrical equipment as part of a learning experiment. Unbeknownst to the subjects, the "victims" were really associates of the experimenter and only faked painful reactions when the subjects thought they were administering shocks. In one instance, the subject and "victim" were separated and the subject only heard cries of pain and exclamations of distress, and then silence, indicating the "victim" was unconscious. Even when the subjects thought they were harming the "victims," they continued to administer shocks because the experimenter directed them to do so and reminded them of their duty (Milgram 1963).

Although it is always with caution that one applies laboratory results to the real world, history shows that individual submission to authority, even immoral authority, is not uncommon. Those who turned in Jewish neighbors to Nazis or those who participated in massacres of Native Americans in this country were only following the law or instructions from a superior authority.

To determine what laws are unjust, King used the following guidelines: "A just law is one that is consistent with morality. An unjust law is any that degrades human personality or compels a minority to obey something the majority does not adhere to or is a law that the minority had no part in making" (cited in Barry 1985, 3). Hook offers several principles to guide individuals contemplating civil disobedience (cited in Fink 1977, 126–27):

1. It must be nonviolent in form and actuality.
2. No other means of remedying the evil should be available.
3. Those who resort to civil disobedience must accept the legal sanctions and punishments imposed by law.
4. A major moral issue must be at stake.
5. When intelligent men of good will differ on complex moral issues, discussion is more appropriate than action.
6. There must be some reason for the time, place and target selected.
7. One should adhere to "historical time."

To explore this issue further, one could refer back to the two paradigms of conflict and consensus. The consensus view of society would probably provide a stronger argument for the position of following laws whether one agrees with them or not. The conflict and pluralist perspectives, however, hold that laws may be tools of power and are not the embodiment of the will of the people; therefore, individuals may legitimately disagree with immoral laws and have a duty to disobey. The consensus view, remember, includes liberal and conservative perspectives. Liberals, for instance, typically do not advocate mass noncompliance with laws but may seek to change them through the democratic process. Conflict theory, on the other hand, paints a picture of power struggle and, because of this different perspective, may provide moral support for lawbreaking. From another perspective, Kohlberg might propose that only individuals who have reached higher stages of morality would think to challenge conventional definitions of right and wrong. Most of us struggle to achieve goodness using the definitions of the society we live in; very few reach beyond accepted definitions to meet a higher standard of morality.

Remember that civil disobedience occurs when the individual truly believes the law to be wrong and therefore believes that enforcement of or obedience to it would also be wrong. We are not referring to chronic lawbreaking because of immediate rewards. Indeed, most criminals have a fairly conventional sense of morality. They agree with the laws even though they break them. Even those gray-area laws where there is disagreement over the "wrongness" of the behavior are not proper grounds for disobedience. The laws in these cases are not inherently wrong or do not prescribe inherently immoral action; there is just disagreement over whether the government should restrict the behavior.

One other issue needs to be addressed here; that is the widespread belief that law is synonymous with morality and that as long as one remains inside the law, one can be considered a moral person. Callahan (1982, 64) points out that we live in a society where the borderline between law and ethics often becomes blurred. For many, morality is simply doing that which the law requires; a fear of punishment is the only motivation for behavior in some minimally acceptable way.

Obviously the author is concerned with the false perception that law is the total definition of morality. Many of us feel satisfied that we live up to legal standards of behavior, but fewer of us would be able to say that we live up to ideal moral standards.

LAW AND POLICY

We have, for the most part, assumed that all laws are equal in their symbolic meaning as well as their practical enforcement. This is obviously not true. The enactment of a law is only one element of the impact the law may have on behavior. If there is no enforcement—usually because of less-than-unanimous support for the law in the first place—there is less impact on behavior. Recently, in a major city, a teenage curfew law was passed after much debate over the legal and moral implications of such a law. Several months after the law had taken effect, it was discovered that the police department had instituted a policy of nonenforcement. Not a single arrest had been made or was planned for violators of the law. Obviously, once brought to light, this nonenforcement policy was criticized by those who had originally favored the law, as well as by some who had been opposed. The latter group were upset that the police department had taken it upon themselves to decide the value of such a law despite the fact that those who were elected to enact laws had already made the decision. Realistically, however, this goes on all the time. Police departments create prostitution crackdowns, traffic ticket "blizzards," drug sweeps, and pornography raids with more or less cyclical patterns, sometimes conforming to political happenings, sometimes not. Their policies are independent of legislative intent. In this sense, they are de facto definers of the law.

If we see laws as the "ought" of societal definitions of misbehavior, then enforcement policies must be viewed as the "is" of what is tolerated and what is not tolerated. Many laws on the books are routinely ignored and forgotten, especially in the area of private behavior. One might ask why such laws are not thrown out as irrelevant to the times we live in. The reason they continue to exist, however, is that no politician is going to champion removal of "ought" laws because it would seem that he or she was in favor of the behavior the law defines as immoral. On the other hand, some argue that to have laws that are ignored endangers the credibility of the entire legal system.

Politicians often pass laws for symbolic reasons, with no real intention of backing up the principles expressed with action. For instance, some regulatory agencies have no enforcement powers or so little money their actual impact is negligible. When President Bill Clinton chose Zoë Baird as his nominee for attorney general, it was discovered that she had violated the law prohibiting hiring illegal aliens as well as the tax law that required payment of social security taxes for household employees. The political fallout that resulted caused Baird to withdraw from the confirmation process. But the situation serves to illustrate the wide gulf between law and policy, since it was brought to light that large numbers of Americans violate these same laws and it is well known that the chance of being punished for such a "crime" is extremely small.

Often there is a policy to enforce the law in a particular manner; for example, street prostitutes are arrested but hotel prostitution and massage parlors are ignored; or those who engage in numbers running are arrested but church bingo is ignored even though both activities are illegal. Often policy is created when a law proves to be unsavory to powerful groups. For example, in one county, an ordinance was passed that prohibited all smoking in county buildings, and then a "policy" emerged allowing judges to ignore the law in their courtrooms and chambers.

Policy may be tacitly recognized and approved of by society and political forces, or it may be internal to an agency or department. There may be informal policies that conflict with formal, such as a formal use of force policy and an informal acceptance of unlawful force. It may be a personal policy, as in the case of criminal justice workers who use personal guidelines to make decisions about enforcement or acceptance of gratuities. When policy and law diverge greatly, it is questionable whether the law truly represents the people.

THE CRIMINAL JUSTICE PROFESSIONAL

This discussion of law and morality is not just academic for the criminal justice professionals who must uphold the law. Line staff often face questions of individual morality versus obedience and loyalty. The My Lai incident has passed out of this nation's consciousness, but at the time controversy existed over whether soldiers should follow their superiors' orders blindly or make an independent assessment of the morality of the action. In this case, several officers were prosecuted by a military court for killing women and children in a village during the war in Vietnam without any evidence that they were a threat to the unit's safety. The officers' defense was that their superiors gave the orders to take the village without regard to whether the inhabitants were civilians or guerrillas. The rationale was that often there wasn't time to establish whether a civilian was friendly or not, and in any event civilians often carried grenades and otherwise harmed American troops. There was vociferous discussion in support of and against the soldiers' actions. Movies such as *Platoon* provide dramatic fictional accounts of other actions carried out by officers and the dilemma of soldiers who knew such actions were unethical and illegal. One can either excuse the individual from personal moral decisions when he or she follows orders, or one can condemn the behavior, allowing and supporting disobedience of established laws or orders that don't conform to a personal ethical standard.

A soldier's dilemma is not all that different from a police officer's. If a police officer received orders to storm a hostage situation where there was certainty that many would be killed and other alternatives were available, should he follow the superior's orders or refuse on the basis of his moral judgment? If an officer were told to repeatedly pick up an individual on minor charges as a form of harassment to get the individual to serve as an informant, should she agree to do so or refuse? If an undercover officer were told to get the evidence "at any cost," even if it meant using drugs or sex to gain the trust of dealers, what should the officer do? Does the police officer have the right to make moral decisions and use personal moral judgment, or is obedience to superiors mandatory? If a prosecutor were trying a case in which the judge was obviously biased against the accused and allowed many errors to occur, resulting in a violation of due process, should the prosecutor obey the advice of his or her boss and accept an easy conviction or make a stand against the judge's actions? What about a correctional officer who is ordered to ignore the beating of an inmate who injured another officer; should that person follow orders or not?

Each individual is faced with moral choices in the course of her or his career. Some of these choices are easy to make. Some of the hardest decisions, however, involve choices between values and/or choices that involve going against superiors or colleagues. When the accepted pattern of behavior has the law on its side it becomes extremely difficult to object and take an individual stand.

The final issue to be discussed involves discretion. When discretion is possible, it can be abused, especially in those areas where the practitioners sense that the public does not believe in the validity of the applicable laws. Studies indicate that most corruption and graft occurs in gray areas of crime such as prostitution, gambling, and drugs. It is easy to explain the emergence of unethical behavior in these areas, since laws against these crimes do not have the same moral sentiment behind them as do laws against more serious crimes such as murder and child molestation. Many officers who would have no problem letting a prostitute go free will risk their lives to catch a child-killer.

The moral commitment that professionals have toward the laws they are supposed to uphold influences their actions. Soldiers are more loyal when they believe in the morality of the war they are fighting. Police are more determined when they believe in the laws they are enforcing. Prosecutors and defense attorneys are more committed to due process when they believe in the concept. Corrections officers are less likely to allow prisoners to corrupt them when they have a sense of their goals and a belief in the integrity of the system. And all criminal justice professionals are more likely to operate in an ethical manner when they believe in the validity and justness of the system that employs them. In the following chapters we will look more closely at some of the ethical decisions criminal justice practitioners are forced to make and the moral dilemmas that confront them.

CONCLUSION

In this chapter we have looked at the relationship between law and morality. There is not a perfect overlap between what is considered moral or immoral and what is defined as legal or illegal. This is because there is no unanimous agreement among members of any society in defining illegal behaviors. The consensus and conflict paradigms view law somewhat differently. The consensus view holds that the law more or less does represent majority opinion whereas the conflict view describes law as a tool of power holders. At times there may be conflict between a person's moral code and societal laws. Some individuals will feel compelled to commit civil disobedience. Criminal justice professionals may have a professional duty to enforce laws they personally believe are wrong. In such situations, their professional ethics may conflict with their personal ethics.

DISCUSSION QUESTIONS

1. Would you disobey a law you thought was wrong? Have you? Do you think others would?
2. How restrictive do you think government should be in controlling people's behavior? Do you agree with laws that prohibit gambling? Drinking while driving? Underage drinking? Prostitution? Drugs?
3. What is an example of one type of behavior considered wrong by a majority of people, without a law against it? What is an example of a law proscribing some type of activity that is not considered wrong by the majority of people?
4. Conduct a survey of your classmates to determine how they would rank the seriousness of ten different crimes. Include in your list toxic waste dumping and price fixing, as well as the U.C.R. index crimes. What were the results? Did everyone agree?

⊰⊟ ETHICAL DILEMMAS ⊟⊱

Please read and respond to the following situations. Be prepared to discuss your ideas.

Situation 1

You ride a motorcycle and you think it is much more enjoyable to ride without a helmet. You also believe your vision and hearing are better without one. Your state has just passed a helmet law and you have already received two warnings. What would you do? What if your child was riding on the motorcycle? Do you think your position would be any different if you had had any previous accidents and had been hurt?

Situation 2

You are asked to enforce a law that you believe to be wrong. For instance, you are a police officer and are supposed to protect a member of the Ku Klux Klan while he gives a speech, but your feelings are directly contrary to the views expressed by this individual and you don't believe he should have the right to speak. What would you do? What would you do if you were told to deliberately perform your job in such a way as to ensure that the speaker would be injured by a hostile crowd?

Situation 3

You are a juror in a trial where an individual had been burglarized many times and in frustration had set up a trigger device that subsequently killed a seventeen-year-old youth who was attempting to burglarize this man's home yet another time. Because there are laws in this state prohibiting such devices, the man was charged with involuntary manslaughter and if convicted could spend time in prison. How would you vote during deliberation on guilt or innocence?

Situation 4

You are a legislator and must decide how to vote on a new law that would make it illegal to use animal organs or tissues for transplanting in humans. How would you vote? What if the law outlawed the use of fetal tissue for experimentation or for any medical use? How would you vote on a law prohibiting assisted suicide? Euthanasia? Surrogate motherhood contracts? How would you vote on a new crime control law that mandated long prison terms for drug offenders even on the first offense? Capital punishment for felony drug trafficking?

6

Ethics and
Law Enforcement

The images of the Rodney King beating are indelibly imprinted in the psyche of the American public and will forever shade the image of law enforcement. Fortunately, the use of unlawful force by police is not a pervasive problem in this country, nor is corruption, abuse of authority, or other illegal practices. For every officer involved in the Rodney King episode there are hundreds of others who risk their lives saving hostages, help motorists, reassure frightened homeowners, find lost children, and in a number of other ways dramatic and mundane, epitomize the best of law enforcement. These men and women usually don't appear on the front page of newspapers or on the evening news and they often pay the price for the few who do through decreased public confidence and even public scorn. It is important to keep in mind as we discuss issues of law enforcement ethics that the majority of officers are honest and ethical and spend their careers simply trying to do a good job every day. Harsh scrutiny is often directed at police practices, and officers may feel they are treated unfairly by the public and the media. This chapter will look at the reasons why we may hold police to higher standards of behavior and why some police do not meet even minimum standards of ethical behavior, and will also discuss some specific issues relevant to law enforcement ethics.

Authority, force, discretion—these elements are inherent in the role of a law enforcement officer. No other criminal justice professional wields so much discretion over so many situations as part of everyday duties. No other criminal justice professional comes under so much constant and public scrutiny. This scrutiny is understandable, however, when one realizes that police are power personified. They often have the choice to arrest or not to arrest, to mediate or to charge, and in decisions to use deadly force, they even hold the power of life and death. As Murphy and Moran (1981, 291) write,

> no other public figure, or indeed any other human being, possesses greater authority over personal destiny. A jury, after a lengthy court trial and painful deliberation, may find a defendant guilty of murder and recommend the death penalty; the judge may respond by invoking the death penalty after more painful deliberation within his own conscience; and, finally, then the state may actually carry out that execution—perhaps after a dozen or so

years of experiencing one appeal after another exhausted. But the police officer, in one split second, without the benefit of law school or judicial roles or legal appeals, acting as judge, jury and executioner may accomplish the same final result.

Police officers operate very much in the public eye; they are often criticized for things the public feels they should be doing or perhaps should not be doing. Sometimes police feel denigrated and therefore defensive. Perhaps we do tend to critique police activities with the benefit of hindsight. Yet the scrutiny is warranted if one understands that police represent government's interface with the private lives of individuals. If we expect police to be perfect, it is because they are the guardians of society's "goodness." Obviously police aren't perfect; many examples of corruption and graft have been uncovered by various committees and investigative bodies (Barker and Carter 1991; Murphy and Moran 1981, 87). In one study it was reported that by officers' own accounts, 39 percent of their number engaged in brutality, 22 percent perjured themselves, 31 percent had sex on duty, 8 percent drank on duty, and 39 percent slept on duty (Barker and Carter 1991). Souryal also chronicles the extent of police deviance (1992, 300). Why do some police officers abuse their position? Unethical behavior is largely a matter of abuse of authority, force, or discretionary power.

AUTHORITY AND POWER

Klockars (1984) describes police control as composed of the following elements: authority, power, persuasion, and force. *Authority* is the unquestionable entitlement to be obeyed. Neither persuasion nor force is needed to achieve domination when one possesses authority. *Power* is similar to authority in that it is held by the organization, and the individual merely draws upon it as a representative of that organization; but it is different from authority in that power implies that there might be resistance to overcome. It also implies that if there is resistance it will be crushed—power is the means to achieve domination. *Persuasion* also may be used in response to resistance but seeks to overcome it "by mobilizing signs, symbols, words, and arguments that induce in the mind of the person persuaded the belief that he or she ought to comply." Finally, *force* is different from the previous three means of control in that it is physical, whereas the other three are exercised through mental domination and control. When force is used, "the will of the person coerced is irrelevant" (Klockars 1984, 532).

Police control and coercion, then, involve four different types of domination, from unquestioned authority to physical force. Why does law enforcement have the right to employ these types of control? "We give it to them," is the easy answer. "Police power" is a governmental right invested in federal, state, and local law enforcement agencies. It means that this organization, unlike almost any other except perhaps the military, has the right to control citizens' movements to the point of using physical and even deadly force to do so. Cohen and Feldberg (1991) develop a careful analysis of and justification for police power and propose that it stems from the social contract. As discussed in a previous chapter, Hobbes and Locke developed the concept to explain why people have given up liberties in civilized societies. According to this theory, each citizen gives up complete liberty in return for societal protection against others. The deprivation of complete freedom is in return for guaranteed protection. Police power is part of this quid pro quo—we give the police power to protect us, but we also recognize that this power can be used against us.

There are corollary principles to this general idea. First, each of us should be able to feel protected. If not, then we are not gaining anything from the social contract and may decide to renegotiate the contract by regaining some of the liberties given up, such as use of guns and first-strike options. Second, since the deprivations of freedoms are limited to those necessary to ensure protection against others, police power is circum-scribed to what is necessary to meet the agreed-upon purpose. If police exceed this, then the public rightly objects. Third, police ethics are inextricably linked to their pur-pose. If the social contract is the root of their power, it is also the root of their ethics. Cohen and Feldberg (1991) propose five ethical standards that can be derived from the social contact: fair access, public trust, safety and security, teamwork, and objectivity.

Delattre (1989) approaches police authority and power from a slightly different point of view. As public servants, Delattre asserts police need those qualities one desires in any public servant. He quotes Madison, who stated that wisdom, good character, bal-anced perception, and integrity are essential to any public servant. Only if the person entrusted with public power has these qualities can we be assured that there will be no abuse of such authority and power; "granting authority without expecting public ser-vants to live up to it would be unfair to everyone they are expected to serve" (Delattre 1989, 79). In this proposition, the right to authority lies in the character of the person—if one has those virtues necessary to be a public servant, one has the right to use the authority invested in the role; if one does not have those virtues, then one should not be in that position to begin with.

All the unethical practices discussed in this chapter are abuses of one of the types of control and domination Klockars identified. Abuses of discretion are abuses of author-ity, unlawful use of force is obviously an abuse of force, intrusive and deceptive investi-gation and interrogation practices are abuses of power and persuasion, and so on. If we cannot be sure that we have Madison's public servants—people of wisdom, good char-acter, balanced perception, and integrity—who need no guidance in how to perform in an ethical manner, how can the organization provide the guidance necessary to maxi-mize the possibility of ethical action and minimize the abuses of the four types of con-trol? The formal ethics of an organization attempts to provide such guidance.

FORMAL ETHICS FOR POLICE OFFICERS

Many organizations have either a value system or a code of ethics to educate and guide the behavior of those who work within the organization; some have both. An organi-zational value system identifies the mission and the important objectives of the orga-nization. Just as individual values influence one's ethics, an organizational value sys-tem influences the ethics of the organization's members. For example, if a person's highest value is wealth, integrity may be sacrificed to achieve it; in a similar way, if the value system of an organization promotes profits over all else, customer satisfaction and quality may be sacrificed. A police department with a value system emphasizing crime control may allocate resources differently from one with a value system promoting community-oriented policing. Officers in these two departments may be rewarded differently, and the formal culture of the agency will encourage different behavior patterns.

A code of ethics is more specific to the behavior of the individual officer. A professional code of ethics addresses the unique issues and discretionary practices of that profession. Davis (1991) explains that there are three distinct kinds of codes: the first is an aspiration or ideal describing the perfect professional, the second provides principles or guidelines that relate to the value system of the organization, and the third provides mandatory rules of conduct that can serve as the basis of discipline. The code of ethics promulgated by the International Association of Chiefs of Police, which will be discussed shortly, is the first kind of code. It is an aspiration or ideal that describes the perfect police officer.

All police departments also have an oath of office that is a shorthand version of the value system or code of ethics. For instance, in a typical oath of office (see Box 6-1), duties are described that relate to service to the community and the sacred trust it entails for the officer.

The Law Enforcement Code of Ethics

The International Association of Chiefs of Police promulgated the Law Enforcement Code of Ethics (see Box 6-2) and many departments have used this code or adapted it for their own use. Even though this code has been widely adopted, there is some question as to its relevance to individual police officers (Johnson and Copus 1981, 59–65; Swift, Houston, and Anderson 1993). One argument is that the code specifies such perfect behavior that it is irrelevant to the real lives of most officers. The wide disparity between the code and actual behavior is detrimental to the validity and credibility of the code. For instance, Davis, referring to the code provision "I will never act officiously or permit personal feelings, prejudices, animosities or friendships to influence my decisions" writes, "Any officer who takes this mandatory language seriously will quickly learn that he cannot do what the code seems to require. He will then either have to quit the force or consign its mandates to Code Heaven" (Davis 1991, 18).

The opposing argument is that the code is valuable specifically because it provides an ideal for all officers to aspire to. It is a goal to work toward, not an average of all behaviors. It would be hard to be proud of a professional code that instructed an officer to be unbiased and objective unless there were personal reasons to favor one party or another, or to be courageous unless personal danger were involved, or to be honest in thought and deed only when it served egoistic purposes. Since the code describes the highest standard of policing, all officers can improve because no officer is perfect. Davis (1991) contends, however, that an aspirational code cannot be used to judge or discipline behavior that falls short of it. That is no doubt true; that purpose is served by departmental policies and rule books, which are more objective and enforceable. A code is far more valuable as a motivator than a discipline device, a symbol rather than a stick.

Box 6-1
OATH OF A POLICE OFFICER
_____, USA

I, _____, a police officer for _____,
USA, do solemnly swear (or affirm) that during my continuance in said
office, I will to the best of my skill and ability, faithfully uphold the
Constitution of the United States, the Constitution of the State of
_____, and in all cases conform to and enforce the
laws of the United States, the State of _____, and
the Charter and Ordinances of the Consolidated Government of
_____, USA.

   I will execute the orders of my Superiors and in all cases comply with
the rules and regulations governing the _____ Police
Department and will report any violation thereof to my Superiors. I will
not persecute the innocent, nor shield the guilty from prosecution or
punishment, nor will I be influenced in the discharge of my duty by fear,
favor or affection, reward or the hope thereof; and in all my acts and
doings, I will be governed by the rules and ordinances applicable to the
_____ Police Department.

   So help me God.

(Reprinted by permission. Columbus Police Department, Columbus, Georgia.)

The principle of justice or fairness is the single most dominant theme in the law
enforcement code. Police officers must uphold the law regardless of the offender's identity. They must not single out special groups for different treatment. Police officers
must not use their authority and power to take advantage of people. They must avoid
gratuities because they give the appearance of special treatment. A second theme is that
of service: police officers are fundamentally public servants who exist to serve the community. Another theme is the importance of the law: police are protectors of the Constitution and must not go beyond it or substitute rules of their own. Because the law is
so important, police not only must be concerned with lawbreakers, but also their own
behavior must be totally within the bounds set for them by the law. In investigation,
capture, and collection of evidence, their conduct must conform to the dictates of law.
The final theme is one of behavior: police, at all times, must uphold a standard of behavior consistent with their public position. This involves a higher standard of behavior
in their professional and personal lives than that held out for the general public
(Bossard 1981, 31).

   Why is professional ethics important to law enforcement? First of all, ethics contributes to the image of law enforcement as a profession. Ideally, a set of ethics will help
the officer make decisions in a lawful, humane, and fair manner. A code of ethics also

Box 6-2
LAW ENFORCEMENT CODE OF ETHICS

As a law enforcement officer, my fundamental duty is to serve the community; to safeguard lives and property; to protect the innocent against deception, the weak against oppression or intimidation and the peaceful against violence or disorder; and to respect the constitutional rights of all to liberty, equality and justice.

I will keep my private life unsullied as an example to all and will behave in a manner that does not bring discredit to me or to my agency. I will maintain courageous calm in the face of danger, scorn or ridicule; develop self-restraint; and be constantly mindful of the welfare of others. Honest in thought and deed both in my personal and official life, I will be exemplary in obeying the law and the regulations of my department. Whatever I see or hear of a confidential nature or that is confided to me in my official capacity will be kept ever secret unless revelation is necessary in the performance of my duty.

I will never act officiously or permit personal feelings, prejudices, political beliefs, aspirations, animosities or friendships to influence my decisions. With no compromise for crime and with relentless prosecution of criminals, I will enforce the law courteously and appropriately without fear or favor, malice or ill will, never employing unnecessary force or violence and never accepting gratuities.

I recognize the badge of my office as a symbol of public faith, and I accept it as a public trust to be held so long as I am true to the ethics of police service. I will never engage in acts of corruption or bribery, nor will I condone such acts by other police officers. I will cooperate with all legally authorized agencies and their representatives in the pursuit of justice.

I know that I alone am responsible for my own standard of professional performance and will take every reasonable opportunity to enhance and improve my level of knowledge and competence.

I will constantly strive to achieve these objectives and ideals, dedicating myself before God to my chosen profession . . . law enforcement.

(Copyright by the International Association of Chiefs of Police. Reprinted by permission.)

helps to engender self-respect in individual officers; self-pride comes from knowing one has conducted oneself in a proper and appropriate manner. Further, a code of ethics contributes to mutual respect among police officers and helps in the development of an *esprit de corps* or group feeling toward a common goal. Agreement over methods, means, and aims is important to these feelings. As with any profession, an agreed-upon code of ethics is a unifying element and one that can help define law enforcement as a profession, since it indicates a willingness to uphold certain standards of behavior and promotes the goal of public service, an essential element of any profession.

The Police Subculture and Formal Ethics

One of the forces most resistant to the adoption of and allegiance to a formal code of ethics is the police subculture. One characteristic of any profession or occupation is a special set of standards: certain behaviors may be considered acceptable for a member of that profession to perform, even though the behavior would be wrong if performed by anyone else. For instance, only doctors can ethically and morally cut open a person's chest; only lawyers should withhold information regarding lawbreaking by their clients; and only politicians should withhold information from the public on the basis of national security. Police, too, have professional justifications for certain actions that would be wrong if engaged in by anyone else, such as speeding, using a weapon, wiretapping, and so on. Professional ethics should guide these special privileges, but often the occupational subculture endorses standards of performance that take advantage of professional privileges.

Several writers have described the police and the police subculture; through these sources an image of the police and the police value system emerges that is very different from the value system described by formal ethics. Some research has found police officers to be generally cynical, isolated, and alienated, with a poor self-image, defensive, distrustful, dogmatic, and authoritarian (Johnson and Copus 1981, 52). Some elements of the police value system are inconsistent with the high ideals of the code of ethics. For instance, Sherman (1982, 10–19) describes some common themes running through police attitudes: first, loyalty to colleagues is essential; and second, the public, or most of it, is the enemy. Further, he explains that the values of police officers include the use of force, discretion, and a protective use of the truth (see Box 6-3).

Other writers have also discussed the theme of loyalty. Brown describes police loyalty as arising from a fundamental distrust of superiors and bureaucratic administration (Brown 1981, 82). Muir explains loyalty by reference to the complicity that develops when police engage in individual rulebreaking; once a police officer has violated a standard or rule, he or she is bound to remain silent regarding others' violations, even if they are more serious (Muir 1977, 67, 72).

Scheingold (1984) has emphasized three dominant characteristics of the police subculture. First is the idea of cynicism. Police view all citizens with suspicion. Everyone is a possible problem, but especially those who fit a type. Regional differences exist in the language used to describe these types (such as *goofs*, *turds*, and so on), but the meaning is the same—these individuals are to be dealt with as if they have already committed a crime, because they probably have! Recruits learn this way of looking at others from older officers. Cynicism spills over to their relations with other people, since they have found that friends expect favors and special treatment, and since police routinely witness negative behavior from almost all citizens. Their work life leads them to the conclusion that all people are weak, corrupt, and/or dangerous.

Box 6-3
POLICE VALUES

1. *Discretion A:* Decisions about whether to enforce the law, in any but the most serious cases, should be guided by both what the law says and who the suspect is. Attitude, demeanor, cooperativeness, and even race, age and social class are all important considerations in deciding how to treat people generally, and whether or not to arrest suspects in particular.

2. *Discretion B:* Disrespect for police authority is a serious offense that should always be punished with an arrest or the use of force. The "offense" known as "contempt of cop" or P.O.P.O. (pissing off a police officer) cannot be ignored. Even when the party has committed no violation of the law, a police officer should find a safe way to impose punishment, including an arrest on fake charges.

3. *Force:* Police officers should never hesitate to use physical or deadly force against people who "deserve it," or where it can be an effective way of solving a crime. Only the potential punishments by superior officers, civil litigation, citizen complaints, and so forth should limit the use of force when the situation calls for it. When you can get away with it, use all the force that society should use on people like that—force and punishment which bleeding-heart judges are too soft to impose.

4. *Due Process:* Due process is only a means of protecting criminals at the expense of the law abiding and should be ignored whenever it is safe to do so. Illegal searches and wiretaps, interrogation without advising suspects of their Miranda rights, and if need be (as in the much admired movie, *Dirty Harry*), even physical pain to coerce a confession are all acceptable methods for accomplishing the goal the public wants the police to accomplish: fighting crime. The rules against doing those things merely handcuff the police, making it more difficult for them to do their job.

5. *Truth:* Lying and deception are an essential part of the police job, and even perjury should be used if it is necessary to protect yourself or get a conviction on a "bad guy." Violations of due process cannot be admitted to prosecutors or in court, so perjury (in the serious five per cent of cases that ever go to trial) is necessary and therefore proper. Lying to drug pushers about wanting to buy drugs, to prostitutes about wanting to buy sex, or to congressmen about wanting to buy influence is the only way,

and therefore a proper way, to investigate these crimes without victims. Deceiving muggers into thinking you are an easy mark and deceiving burglars into thinking you are a fence are proper because there are not many other ways of catching predatory criminals in the act.

6. *Time:* You cannot go fast enough to chase a car thief or traffic violator, nor slow enough to get to a "garbage" call; and when there are no calls for service, your time is your own. Hot pursuits are necessary because anyone who tries to escape from the police is challenging police authority, no matter how trivial the initial offense. But calls to nonserious or social-work problems like domestic disputes or kids making noise are unimportant, so you can stop to get coffee on the way or even stop at the cleaner's if you like. And when there are no calls, you can sleep, visit friends, study, or do anything else you can get away with, especially on the midnight shift, when you can get away with a lot.

7. *Rewards:* Police do very dangerous work for low wages, so it is proper to take any extra rewards the public want to give them, like free meals, Christmas gifts, or even regular monthly payments (in some cities) for special treatment. The general rule is: take any reward that doesn't change what you would do anyway, such as eating a meal, but don't take money that would affect your job, like not giving traffic tickets. In many cities, however, especially in the recent past, the rule has been to take even those rewards that do affect your decisions, as long as they are related only to minor offenses—traffic, gambling, prostitution, but not murder.

8. *Loyalty:* The paramount duty is to protect your fellow officers at all costs, as they would protect you, even though you may have to risk your own career or your own life to do it. If your colleagues make a mistake, take a bribe, seriously hurt somebody illegally, or get into other kinds of trouble, you should do everything you can to protect them in the ensuing investigation. If your colleagues are routinely breaking rules, you should never tell supervisors, reporters, or outside investigators about it. If you don't like it, quit—or get transferred to the police academy. But never, ever, blow the whistle.

(Reprinted by permission from "Learning Police Ethics," by L. Sherman, *Criminal Justice Ethics*, 1, no. 1 (1982): 10-19. Copyright 1982 by the John Jay College of Criminal Justice.)

The second value is related to the use of force. The police subculture embraces force for all situations wherein a threat is perceived. Threats may be interpreted as threats against the officer's authority rather than the physical person, so anyone with an "attitude problem" is thought to deserve a lesson in humility. Force is both expressive and instrumental. It is a clear symbol of the police officer's authority and legitimate dominance in any interaction with the public, and it also is believed to be the most effective method of control. It cuts across all social and economic barriers and is the most effective tool for keeping people in line and getting them to do what is required without argument.

Finally, there is the idea that police are victims themselves. They are victims of public misunderstanding and scorn, of low wages and vindictive administrators. This feeling of victimization sets police apart from others and rationalizes a different set of rules for them as opposed to other members of society (Scheingold 1984, 100–4).

Scheingold (1984, 97) describes the police subculture as no more than an extreme of the dominant American culture; it closely resembles the conservative perspective described in the previous chapter.

> If the police subculture is ultimately shaped by American cultural values, does it really make sense to talk about a separate subculture among American police officers? My answer is that the police subculture is not so much separate as an *in extremis* version of the underlying American culture. When Americans in general become preoccupied with crime, we also move in punitive directions, but our preoccupation with crime tends to be abstract and episodic. . . . The real difference between police officers and the rest of us is that coping with crime is their full-time job. There is, in short, reason to believe that they and we share the same values but that the police are distanced from us primarily by the nature of their work.

In other words, we all agree with certain elements of the police value system; if the general public is less extreme in its views, it is only because citizens have not had a steady diet of dealing with crime and criminal behavior as have the police. Furthermore, citizens are not too upset when the civil rights of "criminal types" are violated, but are upset only when police misbehavior is directed at "good" people.

Scheingold goes on to describe the factors that lead to the extreme nature of the police subculture. They include the fact that police typically form a homogenous social group; they have a uniquely stressful work environment; and they participate in a basically closed social system. Historically, police in the United States have always come from the white middle and lower classes; they are similar racially, culturally, and economically. Because of these similarities, police feel themselves to be more similar to each other than to the public they encounter as a part of their job. Homogenous social groups lead to *group think*; everyone agrees with the group value or belief because to do otherwise would ostracize the individual. Police are further set apart by their work life. The job of a police officer entails a great deal of stress caused by danger and unpleasant experiences. Again, this results in the feeling that police are special and different from everyone else. Finally, because of strange working hours and social stigmatism, their social life tends to be totally centered around other police officers. This leads to closed viewpoints and legitimation of subcultural values (Scheingold 1984, 97–100).

This subculture and the values just described above might be breaking down among police departments today. Several factors contribute to the possible weakening of the subculture. The increasing diversity of police recruits has eliminated the social homogeneity of the work force. Many diverse groups are now represented in police departments, including African-Americans, Hispanics, women, and the college-educated, even if only in token numbers. These different groups bring elements of their own cultural backgrounds and value systems into the police environment. Also, police unions with their increasing power formalize relationships between the line staff and the administration, and subcultural methods for coping with perceived administrative unfairness are becoming more formal than informal. Increasingly, individual officers, especially those who come from other backgrounds and are not tied in as strongly to police tradition, may challenge the informal system rather than ignore or go along with obvious misconduct or corruption. Finally, civil litigation has increased the risk of covering for another officer. Although police officers may lie to Internal Affairs or even on a witness stand to save a fellow officer from sanctions, they are less likely to do so when large money damages may be leveled against them because of negligence and perjury. Yet, it is still safe to say that the police, like any occupational group, maintain an informal subterranean value system that guides and provides a rationale for decision making. This value system is more influential than the police rule book or code of ethics.

It is apparent that the formal code of ethics or the organizational value system is quite different from subcultural values. Violations of formal ethical standards such as in the use of force, acceptance of preferential or discriminatory treatment, use of illegal investigation tactics, and differential enforcement of laws are all supported by the subculture. The police subculture has an ethical code of its own. Muir describes some elements of the informal police code: "You cover your men: don't let any officer take a job alone," "Keep a cool head," and "Don't backdoor it," a prohibition against certain gratuities (Muir 1977, 191).

The reason these differences exist may be related to the mixed goals police are forced to operate under. They are given the task of protecting society and catching criminals, yet this is sometimes impossible to do if they follow legal guidelines. For some crimes, it seems that one must act like a criminal to catch a criminal. To catch a prostitute or a drug dealer necessarily involves undercover work, which in turn involves methods that may violate legal guidelines. Very few arrests would be made if police depended on observation and chase alone to catch criminals; yet the most expedient methods to uncover crime may also directly violate ethical and legal standards.

Another reason subcultural values are not consistent with the code of ethics is related to the social isolation and feeling of victimization characteristic of the police subculture. When a group feels it is special for any reason, this perception may justify different rules or may be used to justify excusing the group from rules that apply to everyone else. This is true for other professions as well; for instance, representatives and senators in Congress may feel it is appropriate to take trips and receive services at public expense because they could earn more money in the private sector than their government salary. In similar ways, some police officers are able to justify behavior that would be wrong if engaged in by others because of their unique position. For instance, police may feel that use of force in some situations results in quick justice that the courts are unable to deliver. Police may feel justified in accepting gratuities because their pay is less than they feel they deserve.

Police also hear mixed messages from the public regarding certain types of crime. They are asked to enforce laws against gambling, pornography, and prostitution, but not too stringently. They are expected to enforce laws against drunk driving but also to be tolerant of individuals who aren't really "criminal." They are expected to uphold laws regarding assault, unless it is a family or interpersonal dispute that the disputants want to settle privately. In other words, we want the police to enforce the law unless they enforce it against us.

We also ask the police to take care of social problems such as the homeless or transients without a great deal of concern as to whether or not they step outside the law to do so. Extralegal means are acceptable as long as they are used when implementing desirable social goals. Citizens who want police to move the transients away from a street corner or get the crack dealers out of the neighborhood aren't concerned with the fact that the police have the power to control individuals' behavior only when a law has been broken. If a little "informal" justice is needed to accomplish the task, then that is fine. Yet when we accept police power that exceeds the bounds of legality in those situations, then we must also be responsible for police use of power exceeding legality in other situations.

The police role as enforcer in a pluralistic society is problematic. The justification for police power is that police represent the public: "The police officer can only validly use coercive force when he or she in fact represents the body politic" (Malloy 1982, 12). But if they do not represent all groups, then their power is defined as oppressive. It should be no surprise that police were seen as an invading army in the ghettos of the 1960s. They were not seen as representing the interests of the people who were the target of their force. More recently, the Los Angeles riots illustrate the tension between minority communities and police departments that are perceived as brutal and racist. Police encounter resistance from those groups that feel alienated and thus resent and do not accept police power; on an individual level, some police officers may themselves have personal difficulties enforcing laws against the interests of certain groups: "The conflicting moral choices patrolmen are called on to make derive from deeply rooted conflicts over the use of police power within American society" (Brown 1981, 78).

———◆◆◆———

DISCRETION AND DUTY

Discretion can be defined as the ability to choose between two or more courses of behavior. Law enforcement professionals have a great deal of discretion regarding when to enforce a law, how to enforce it, how to handle disputes, when to use force, and so on. Every day is filled with decisions—some minor, some major. An inherent element of all professions is discretion. Discretion is a necessary element in law enforcement; there is no one who would advocate full enforcement of all laws, but the need for discretion also leads to a greater dependence on individual ethical codes in place of rules and laws. Most ethical dilemmas police officers face derive from their powers of discretion. These ethical dilemmas are part and parcel of the job. Muir describes moral dilemmas of the police officer as frequent and unavoidable; not academic; always unpopular with some groups; usually resolved quickly; dealt with alone; and involving complex criteria (Muir 1977, 211).

Ethical dilemmas may differ depending on police function. Patrol officers are the most visible members of the police force and have a duty to patrol, monitor, and intervene in matters of crime, conflict, accident, and welfare. Investigating officers are primarily concerned with collecting evidence to be used in court. The ethical decisions these two groups encounter are sometimes different. Patrol officers may have to make ethical decisions relevant to their decision-making power in defining crime and initiating the formal legal process, and they are subject to the temptations of gratuities. Undercover officers must make decisions regarding informants, deception, and target selection. Managers and administrators have ethical dilemmas of their own unique to the role of being responsible for others (Bossard 1981, 25). We should also note that since most police departments in this country are small, many officers fulfill two or more functions, so that their ethical dilemmas cross the boundaries designated above. Officers also face many common ethical dilemmas regarding the way they perform their job and interactions with fellow police officers and the public. Many of these dilemmas involve values of honesty, loyalty, and duty. In the following sections, we will discuss two categories of ethical dilemmas officers may encounter. The first deals with those situations where the officer has the discretion to choose between alternatives. The officer's ethics often determine how that decision is made. The second section addresses those situations involving the definition of the officer's duty.

Use of Discretion

Police possess a great deal of discretion in defining criminal behavior and their reaction to it. When police stop people for minor traffic violations, they can write tickets or give warnings. When they pick up teenagers for drinking or other delinquent acts, they can bring them in for formal processing or take them home. After stopping a fight on the street, they can arrest both parties or allow the combatants to work out their problems. In many day-to-day decisions, police hold a great deal of decision-making power over people's lives because of their power to decide when to enforce the law.

One study found that police do not make arrests in 43 percent of all felony cases and 52 percent of all misdemeanor cases (Williams 1984, 4). The amount of discretion depends on the style of policing characteristic of a certain area. For instance, the "legalistic" style of policing is described as the least amenable to discretionary policing, since full enforcement and established procedures are emphasized. The "watchman" and the "caretaker" styles, however, are characterized by discretionary enforcement. In the "watchman" style, police define situations as threatening or serious depending on the groups or individuals involved, and act accordingly. The "caretaker" style treats citizens differentially depending on their relative power and position in society (Wilson 1976).

The new "professional police" are said to be increasingly bureaucratic in their decision making. However, old values die hard, and even in departments that emphasize a professional orientation, one finds individual adaptations. For instance, Brown describes four types: the "old style crime fighter," who is only concerned with action that might be considered crime control; the "clean beat officer," who seeks to control all behavior in his or her jurisdiction; the "service style," which emphasizes public order and peace officer tasks; and the "professional style," which is the epitome of bureaucratic, by-the-book policing (Brown 1981, 224). Muir describes the following types: the "professional," who balances coercion with compassion; the "reciprocating officer," who allows citizens to solve problems and may engage in deals to keep the peace; the "enforcer," who uses coercion exclusively; and the "avoider," who either cannot handle the power he or she must use or fears it and so avoids situations where he or she may be challenged (Muir 1977, 145).

The very nature of policing necessarily involves some amount of discretion. Cohen (1985) describes discretion as balancing justice for the individual against justice for the group and points out that full enforcement would be unfair at times to individuals. Even courts have seemed to support police discretion over full enforcement (Williams 1984, 26). This opens the door, however, for unethical decisions. The power to make a decision regarding arrest creates the power to make that decision using unethical criteria, such as a bribe in return for not arresting. The power to decide how best to conduct an investigation also creates the power to entrap and select suspects in a biased or otherwise unfair manner. Selective enforcement may not necessarily be crime control, but rather, harassment to get an undesired person to leave an area (Brown 1981, 160).

Perhaps one effective way to encourage using discretion in an ethical manner is to delineate ethical versus unethical criteria for decision making. For instance, the decision to ticket a motorist stopped for speeding or to let him or her go with a warning can be made using ethical or unethical criteria. Those criteria that might be considered appropriate are miles over the speed limit, danger posed by the speeding (school zone or open road?), excuse used (emergency or late to work?), and probably others. Unethical criteria might be sexual attraction, the identity of the motorist (fellow police officer, political figure, or entertainment figure), the race of the motorist, a bribe, and so on. Other factors are less clear: Is the fact of a quota an ethical or unethical criterion? What about attitude? Many officers explain that a person may get a ticket, even for a minor violation, if she or he displays a hostile or unrepentant attitude. Is this merely an egoistic use of power on the part of an officer or a utilitarian use of the ticket as a tool of social learning. After all, if the individual does not display any remorse, there is little guarantee that the person won't commit the same violation as soon as the officer is out of sight.

Many officers defend the use of professional courtesy to other officers stopped for speeding. Justifications for different treatment are diverse and creative. For instance, some honest justifications are purely egoist: "If I do it for him, he will do it for me one day." Other justifications are under the guise of utilitarianism—"It's best for all of us not to get tickets and the public isn't hurt because we are trained to drive faster." If the officer would let another person go with a warning in the same situation, it is not an unethical use of discretion. However, if any other person would have received a ticket, but the officer did not issue one because the motorist was a fellow officer, then that is a violation of the code of ethics (. . . enforce the law . . . without fear or favor). It is a violation of deontological universalism as well as utilitarianism: the fact that the speeding officer can cause an accident just as easily as a civilian motorist means that the utility for society is greater if the ticket is issued, because it might make officers slow down.

Discretion also comes into play when the officer is faced with situations with no good solutions. Many officers agonize over family disturbance calls where there are allegations of abuse, or when one family member wants the police to remove another family member; other calls involve elderly persons who want police to do something about the "hoodlums" in the neighborhood, homeless persons with small children who are turned away from full shelters, and victims of crime who are left without resources to survive. In response to all of these calls, officers must decide what course of action to take and can decide to do nothing at all. We will deal with these issues again in the next section.

Discretion is by no means limited to law enforcement. In each of the subsequent chapters, we will see that discretion is an important element in the criminal justice practitioner's role and plays a part in the creation of ethical dilemmas. Discretion in criminal justice has been attacked as contributing to injustice. McAnany (1981) chronicles disillusionment with discretion, citing such works as Davis's *Discretionary Justice* (1973) and the American Friends Service Committee's *Struggle for Justice* (1971). An argument might be made that solutions that attempt to put guidelines on discretion are unsatisfactory since the suggested rules and standards either limit decision making to mechanistic applications of given rules or provide only rhetorical ideals with little or no enforcement capability. Dissatisfaction with discretion is caused by the misuse of discretion. When it is used wisely, objectively, and ethically, discretion is a necessary element in tempering law with humanity.

The Limits of Duty

Another ethical concern in general police practice involves the use of discretion in the performance of duty. It is now clearly established that most of police work is *order maintenance;* police are called into situations that do not involve crime control and are often termed "social work" calls. Many police officers do not feel these are legitimate calls for their time and either give them superficial attention or do not respond at all. Brown calls the skill police develop in avoiding these calls "engineering" (Brown 1981, 142).

Police may respond to a domestic dispute and find a wife bruised, upset, and without money or resources to help herself or her children. The officer may ascertain that departmental policy or law does not dictate any action and the woman is afraid to press charges, so the officer can leave with a clear conscience that official duties have been completed. The officer might, however, take the woman to a shelter or otherwise help her get out of a bad situation. What is the ethical choice? It is difficult to determine the extent of the officer's responsibility in cases such as this.

The formal code of ethics gives no clear guidelines as to how much consideration police should give a citizen in distress. The caretaker style of policing found in small cities and suburbs, where police departments are community oriented, emphasizes service and encourages police assistance to victims or citizens who need it. Our traditional image of police and fire departments getting cats out of trees has a basis in reality, but only in certain areas with certain types of policing. In major cities, however, if police spent their time in service roles, they would have precious little left to spend on crime control. Matthews and Marshall (1981) discuss the lack of departmental support for any action beyond the minimal obligations of duty. Those officers who become personally involved or commit the resources of the department beyond the necessary requirements are not rewarded, but viewed as troublemakers. Structural support for this ethical action does not exist. Officers who attempt to do what they believe is right often do so on their own, risking formal or informal censure. Yet beyond the departmental policies concerning service actions, what is the individual responsibility of the police officer to a fellow human being in distress?

If a young boy, upset over a lost bicycle, approaches two police officers during their dinner, what do the strict guidelines of their job dictate? What is the ethical thing to do? Should they immediately interrupt their dinner and go search for the missing bicycle? Should they take a report to make the boy feel better, knowing they won't or can't do anything about it? Should they tell the boy to go away because they've had a hard night and are looking forward to a hot meal? Very often police encounter travelers who have been robbed during their passage through the city. Should they leave such victims on the street to fend for themselves? What does law or policy say they must do? What should they do?

In all of these situations we face three questions. First, what must police do under the law? Second, what does departmental policy dictate? Third, what do individual ethics dictate? A very altruistic, involved style of interaction where the police officer would be compelled to help the victims in any way possible is supported by the ethics of care, the ethics of virtue, utilitarianism, religious ethics, and ethical formalism. But a more self-protective standard, where the actions mandated would be only those necessary to maintain a self-image consistent with the police role, might also be justified using utilitarianism or ethical formalism. If police became personally involved in every case and went out of their way to help all victims, they would probably exhaust their emotional reserves in a very short time. As a matter of survival, police develop an emotional barrier between themselves and the victims they encounter. It is virtually impossible to observe suffering on a consistent basis if one does not protect oneself in such a way. Unfortunately, the result is often perceived as callousness and because of the extreme personal resources needed to remain sensitive to individual pain, emotional deadening may result in unethical behavior toward individual victims.

When asked to share ethical dilemmas, police officers often raise the concept of duty. Officers are faced with the choice of responding to certain situations or not, leading to tempting opportunities to ignore duty.

> It is 10 minutes to OD time. You on-view an accident. Do you work the accident even though you want to go home, or do you avoid the accident by sneaking around it?

You have received the same 911 call at the same location at least 20 times. Each and every time it has been unfounded. You have just been dispatched to that 911 again. Should you check it or just clear it as unfounded without driving by?

Neither of these are dilemmas in the true sense of the word, which implies a difficult decision where both choices are equally valid and supported by ethical theory. In both cases, the officer's clear duty is to serve the public. On the other hand, these mundane, some might say trivial, decisions are faced by all officers, and their repeated decisions in such situations form the fabric of their moral character. How officers use their discretion to file a report or not, to answer a call or not, to stop and investigate or not, are just as relevant to an ethical inquiry as the decision to accept a gratuity or report the use of excessive force.

In the types of instances previously mentioned, officers must decide how much to get involved in any particular incident. Another issue of duty is raised by the nature of police work and how easy it is for officers to abuse their freedoms. Officers may report they are on a call, when in reality they are doing nothing or performing personal tasks such as shopping or standing in line at the post office. Some officers have been known to attend college classes during duty hours by informing the dispatcher that they are out on a call. Officers may turn in overtime slips for surveillance when in fact they were at home. They may misrepresent times they started and finished the day. Finally, the way court appearances can be used to increase one's monthly salary is part of the socialization of every rookie. That these actions are wrong is not in question; however, many officers rationalize them in a variety of ways, such as by pointing out their low pay, the fact that they sometimes do "police work" when off duty, and so on. The general acceptance of such behavior leads to an environment where each individual sets personal limits on the extent to which he or she will deviate from formal ethics. Even those who stop at minor transgressions must cover their actions by lying, which is another layer of deception added to the first.

GRAFT AND GRATUITIES

Corruption, graft, theft, and accepting bribes and gratuities are all examples of unethical law enforcement practices. Cohen refers to these behaviors as exploitation and describes exploitation as "acting on opportunities, created by virtue of one's authority, for personal gain at the expense of the public one is authorized to serve" (Cohen 1986, 23). Most people would agree that taking bribes, participating in shakedowns, or "shopping" at a burglary scene are wrong, even illegal. Police are often tempted with "fringe benefits" that some may rationalize are merely compensation for the less desirable aspects of the job. One should understand that for a few officers, life is not always black and white, but rather shades of gray. To accept protection money from a prostitute may be rationalized by the relative lack of concern the public shows for this type of lawbreaking. The same argument could be made about gambling or even drugs. We often formally expect the police to enforce laws while we informally encourage them to ignore the same laws. Would we even want the police to fully enforce every law? Many laws are outdated and exist only on paper. Other laws, if enforced against the general populace, would lead to ridiculous scenarios—for instance, laws restricting certain sexual behaviors or other private matters. As long as the public gives such clear indications that it is willing to overlook many crimes, it is no surprise that the police are able to rationalize nonenforcement.

The Incidence of Graft

Muir described a small-town police department as relatively free from corruption, but even in this department, widespread patronage and petty bribery occurred because of the functional and beneficial aspects of this type of graft. For instance, a "security" firm was more or less given carte blanche to operate in legal and illegal ways to control burglaries in particular areas of the city. The police also overlooked gambling, after-hour liquor violations, and other minor infractions in exchange for information and cooperation. This behavior was seen as useful; in fact, it would be very difficult to convince the involved police officers that the behavior was at all wrong or unethical. Muir (1977, 76) writes:

> The point is that any police department, even one as free from graft as Laconia's, had a great deal of potential illegal patronage to dispense, giving it the power to purchase cooperation and social repression. Such a patronage system required complicity because it was outside the law. . . . Its utility was so obvious and its initial cost so modest that even the most scrupulous of policemen found it difficult to speak out against it.

Police routinely deal with the seamier side of society—not only drug addicts and muggers, but middle-class people who are involved in dishonesty and corruption. The constant displays of lying, hiding, cheating, and theft create cynicism. The following are some rationales that might easily be used by police to justify unethical behavior (Murphy and Moran 1981, 93):

- The public thinks every cop is a crook—so why try to be honest?
- The money is out there—if I don't take it, someone else will.
- I'm only taking what's rightfully mine; if the city paid me a decent wage, I wouldn't have to get it on my own.
- I can use it—it's for a good cause—my son needs an operation, or dental work, or tuition for medical school, or a new bicycle . . .

Given constant exposure to others' misdeeds, peer pressure, and vague ideas of right and wrong in these situations, the question is not why some officers engage in corrupt practices but rather why more don't. Although research indicates the lack of an affinity argument for police corruption—that is, that deviant individuals are attracted to police work—an affiliation theory is persuasive, arguing that police learn from each other. Sherman believes in the importance of a signification factor, or labeling an individual action acceptable under a personal rationale (Sherman 1985a, 253). Many police develop along what Sherman (1982) called a "moral career" as they pass through various stages of rationalization to more serious misdeeds in a graduated and systematic way. Once an individual is able to get past the first "moral crisis," it becomes less difficult to rationalize new and more unethical behaviors. The previous behaviors serve as an underpinning to a different ethical standard, since one must explain and justify one's own behaviors for psychological well-being (Sherman 1982).

Several books, such as *Serpico* (Maas 1973) and *Prince of the City* (Daley 1984) detail the pervasiveness of this type of behavior in some departments and the relative ease with which individual officers may develop rationales to justify greater and greater infractions. For instance, the main character in *Prince of the City* progresses from relatively minor rulebreaking to fairly serious infractions and unethical conduct, such as supplying drugs to an addicted informant, without having to make major decisions regarding his morality. It is only when the totality of his actions becomes apparent that he realizes the extent of his deviance. Taking bribes from prostitutes may lead to taking bribes from drug pushers and organized crime figures. Justifying stealing a few things from a store that has been burglarized and adding them to the list of stolen goods may lead to greater and more blatant thefts.

When one accepts gradations of behavior, the line between right and wrong can more easily be moved farther and farther away from an absolute standard of morality. Many believe that gratuities are only the first step in a spiral downward. "For police, the passage from free coffee at the all-night diner and Christmas gifts to participation in drug-dealing and organized burglary is normally a slow if steady one" (Malloy 1982, 33). Malloy describes a passage from "perks" to "shopping" (taking items from a burglary scene before the victim arrives) to premeditated theft (Malloy 1982, 36).

Others dispute this view that after the first cup of coffee, every police officer inevitably ends up performing more serious ethical violations. Many police officers have clear personal guidelines as to what is acceptable and not acceptable. While many, perhaps even the majority, of police see nothing wrong with accepting minor gratuities, fewer police would accept outright cash, and fewer still would not actively condemn the thefts and bribes described earlier. The problematic element is that the gradations between what is acceptable or not can vary from officer to officer and department to department. If two officers differ on what is an acceptable gratuity, who is right?

Most misdeeds of police officers are only marginally different from the unethical behaviors of other professionals—for instance, doctors may prescribe unneeded surgery or experiment with unknown drugs, businesspeople cheat on their expense accounts, lawyers overcharge clients, and contract bidders and purchase agents offer and accept bribes. It is an unfortunate fact of life that people in any profession or occupation will find ways to exploit their position for personal gain. This is not to excuse these actions but rather to show that police are no more deviant than other professional groups. In all of these occupational areas, there are some who exploit their position blatantly and perform extremely unethical behaviors, some who violate the ethical code in medium to minor ways, and many who attempt to uphold the profession's code of ethics and their own personal moral code.

The Ethics of Gratuities

While there is no question that bribery and "shopping" are unethical and even illegal behaviors, there is more controversy over the practice of giving and receiving gratuities. Although the formal code of ethics prohibits accepting gratuities, many officers feel there is nothing wrong with businesses giving "freebies" to a police officer, such as free admission or gifts. Many officers believe these are small rewards indeed for the difficulties they endure in police work. Many businesspeople offer gratuities, such as half-price meals, as a token of sincere appreciation for the police officer's work. So what could possibly be wrong with them? One author writes that gratuities "erode public confidence in law enforcement and undermine our quest for professionalism" (Stefanic 1981, 63). How do gratuities undermine public confidence? Cohen believes that gratuities are dangerous because what might start without intent on the part of the officer may become a patterned expectation. It is the taking in an official capacity that is wrong, since the social contract is violated when citizens give up their liberty to exploit only to be exploited, in turn, by the enforcement agency that prevents them from engaging in similar behavior (Cohen 1986, 26).

Kania, on the other hand, writes that police "should be encouraged to accept freely offered minor gratuities and . . . such gratuities should be perceived as the building blocks of positive social relationships between our police and the public" (1988, 37). He rejects the slippery slope argument (that it leads to future deviance) and the unjust enrichment argument (that the only honest remuneration for police officers is the paycheck) and proposes that gratuities actually help cement relations between the police department and the public. Officers who stay and drink coffee with store owners and businesspeople are better informed than those officers who don't, according to Kania. A gift freely given ties the giver and receiver together in a bond of social reciprocity. This should not be viewed negatively but rather as part of the neighborhood-oriented policing concept currently popular in law enforcement. He also points out that those who offer gratuities tend to be more frequent users of police services, justifying more payment than the average citizen. The only problem, according to Kania, is when the intent of the giver is to give in exchange for something in return and not as reward for past services rendered, or the intent of the taker is not to receive unsolicited but appreciated gifts, but rather to use the position of police officer to extort goods from business owners, or alternatively, if in response to an unethical giver who expects special favors, the officer has the intent to perform them.

Another issue that Kania alludes to but doesn't clearly articulate is that a pattern of gratuities changes what would have been a formal relationship into a personal, informal one. This moves the storekeeper-giver into a role more similar to a friend, relative, or fellow officer, in which case there are personal loyalty issues involved when the law needs to be administered. In the same way that an officer encounters ethical dilemmas when a best friend is stopped for speeding, the officer now has a similar situation when he or she stops the store owner who has been providing him or her with free coffee for the past year. They have become, if not friends, at least personally involved with each other to the extent that duty becomes complicated.

Where should one draw the line between harmless rewards and inappropriate gifts? Is a discount on a meal OK, but not a free meal? Is a meal OK, but not any other item like groceries or tires or car stereos? Do the store or restaurant owners expect anything for their money, such as more frequent patrols or overlooking sales of alcohol to under-age juveniles? Should they expect different treatment from officers than the treatment given to those who do not offer gratuities? For instance, suppose an officer is told by a convenience store owner that he can help himself to anything in the store—free coffee, candy, cigarettes, chips, magazines, and such. In the same conversation, the store owner asks the officer for his personal pager number "in case something happens and I need to get in contact with you . . ." Is this a free gift or an exchange? Should the officer accept or not? Many merchants give free or discount food to officers because they like to have them around, especially late at night. The question then becomes the one asked fre-quently by citizens: Why are two or three police cars always at a certain place and not patrolling? Police response to this complaint is that they deserve to take their breaks wherever they want within their patrol area. If it happens that they choose the same place, that should not be a concern of the public. However, an impression of unequal protection occurs when officers make a habit of eating at certain restaurants or congre-gating at certain convenience stores.

Free meals or even coffee may influence the pattern of police patrol and thus may be wrong because some citizens are not receiving equal protection. What happens when all surrounding businesses give gratuities to officers and a new business moves in? Do officers come to expect special favors? Do merchants feel pressured to offer them? Many nightclubs allow off-duty officers to enter without paying cover charges. Does this lead to resentment and a feeling of discrimination by paying customers? Does it lead to the officer's thinking he or she is special and different from everyone else? Other examples of gratuities are when police accept movie tickets, tickets to ballgames and other events, free dry cleaning, free or discounted merchandise, and so on.

The extent of gratuities varies from city to city. In cities where rules against gratu-ities are loosely enforced, "dragging the sack" may be developed to an art form by some police officers who go out of their way to collect free meals and other gifts. One story is told of a large midwestern city where officers from various divisions were upset because the merchants from some areas provided Christmas "gifts," such as liquor, food, ciga-rettes, and other merchandise, while merchants in other divisions either gave nothing or gave less attractive gifts. The commander, finally tired of the bickering, ordered that no individual officer could receive any gifts and instead sent a patrol car to all the mer-chants in every district. Laden with all the things the merchants would have given to individual officers, the patrol car returned and the commander then parceled out the gifts to the whole department based on rank and seniority.

Officers in some departments are known for their skill in soliciting free food and liquor for after-hours parties. In the same vein, officers solicit merchants for free food and beverages for charity events sponsored by police, such as youth softball leagues. While the first is similar to an individual officer's receipt of a gratuity, the second situa-tion is harder to criticize. Repeatedly, when asked about gratuities, officers bring up the seeming hypocrisy of a departmental prohibition against individual officers accepting gratuities, yet at the same time an administrative policy of actively soliciting and receiving donations from merchants, such as doughnuts, coffee, and even more expensive fare, for departmental events.

It might be instructive to look at other occupations. Do judges or teachers receive any types of gratuities? Obviously, any attempt to give these professionals gifts would be perceived as an attempt to influence their decisions in matters involving the gift giver. Professional ethics always discourages gratuities in these situations, where the profession involves discretionary judgments about a clientele. Certainly, teachers cannot receive gifts from students and expect to maintain the appearance of neutrality. Judges are usually very careful to distance themselves from the participants in any proceeding. If there is a conflict of interest, if the judge is compromised by a relationship with or knowledge of the participants, then he or she will ordinarily pass the case on to a neutral colleague. To receive a gift from either side would surely result in a mistrial. The receipt of gifts or campaign contributions by politicians is a frequent news item. When members of Congress receive large amounts of money from special interest groups, the public is concerned with the neutrality of their voting. Many companies routinely distribute complimentary gifts to members of Congress. Although they would argue that these gifts do no harm and are only tokens of esteem, the perception is that some special favor is expected and such favors are against the public interest.

However, it does not seem unusual or particularly unethical for a doctor, a lawyer, a mechanic, or a mail carrier to receive gifts from grateful clients. Whether gifts are unethical relates to whether one's occupation or profession involves judgments that affect the gift givers. The police obviously have discretionary authority and make judgments that impact on store owners and other gift givers. This may explain why some feel it is wrong for police to accept gifts or favors. It also explains the difference between gratuities as discussed and "gifts" such as a citizen paying for a police officer's meal as he leaves the restaurant. In this case, because the police officer did not know of the reward, nor did the gift giver make his gift known, no judgment can be affected.

The ethical systems from Chapter 2 can be used to examine the ethics of gratuities. Religious ethics is not much help: no clear guidelines can be gleaned from religious proscriptions of behavior. Ethical formalism is more useful since the categorical imperative when applied to gratuities would indicate that we must be comfortable with a universal law allowing all businesses to give all police officers certain favors or gratuities, such as free meals, free merchandise, or special consideration. Such a blanket endorsement of this behavior would not be desirable. The second principle of ethical formalism indicates that each should treat every other with respect as an individual and not as a means to an end. In this regard also we would have to condemn gratuities since the police officer would be using the businesspeople to obtain goods or services more cheaply. We'd also have to wonder about the ethics of the businesspeople in giving the gratuities to police officers. If they were expecting anything in return, even the good will of the officers involved, then they would be using the police officers as a means to their own end and thus violating the second principle of ethical formalism themselves.

If utilitarian ethics were used, one would have to formulate the relative good or utility of the interaction. On one hand, harmless gratuities may create good feelings in the community toward the officers and among the officers toward the community (Kania's argument). On the other hand, gratuities often lead to perceptions of unfairness by shopkeepers who feel discriminated against, by police who feel that they deserve rewards and don't get them, and so on. In fact, the overall negative results of gratuities, even "harmless" ones, might lead a utilitarian to conclude that gratuities are unethical. There would be some differences in the argument if one used act utilitarianism versus rule utilitarianism. Act utilitarianism would be more likely to allow some gratuities and not others. Each individual act would be judged on its own merits—a cup of coffee or a meal from a well-meaning citizen to a police officer who was unlikely to take advantage of the generosity would be acceptable, but gifts given with the intent to elicit special favors would not. Rule utilitarianism would look to the long-term utility of the rule created by the precedent of the action. In this perspective, even the most innocuous of gratuities may be deemed unethical because of the precedent set by the rule and the long-term disutility for society of that type of behavior.

An ethics of care would be concerned with the content of the relationship. If the relationship between the giver and the receiver was already established, a gift between the two would not be seen as harmful. If there was no relationship—that is, if the store owner gave the gratuity to anyone in a blue uniform—then there may be cause for concern. A preexisting relationship would create ties between the two parties so that one would want to help the other with or without the gift. Kania's theory of social networking is appropriate to apply here. If there is not an existing relationship, then the gratuity may indicate an exchange relationship that is based on rights and duties, not care. Does the gift or gratuity harm the relationship or turn it into an exchange relationship? Officers can usually recite stories of store owners who gave gifts with an expressed purpose of good will, only to remind the officers of their generosity at the point where a judgment was made against them, such as a traffic ticket or parking violation. In this situation, the type of relationship isn't clear until the "chit comes in."

The ethics of virtue would be concerned with the individual qualities or virtues of the officer. A virtuous officer could take free coffee and not let it affect his or her judgment. In fact, no gift or gratuity would bias the judgment of the virtuous officer. On the other hand, if the officer does not possess those qualities of virtue, such as honesty, integrity, and fairness, then even free coffee may lead to special treatment. Further, these officers would seek out gifts and gratuities and abuse their authority by pursuing them.

An egoistic framework provides easy justification for the taking or giving of gratuities. It obviously makes police officers feel good to receive such favors, especially if they feel that they deserve them or that the favors are a measure of esteem or appreciation. Even if the person giving the gift had ulterior motives, the police officer could accept and be ethically justified in doing so under the egoistic ethical framework if the officer gained more from the transaction than he or she lost. In other words, if one could keep a positive self-image intact and obtain the gratuity at the same time, then one would be justified in doing so, and it would be a moral action. This discussion parallels very closely the police subcultural value of accepting bribes for doing something the police officer might have done anyway.

DECEPTION IN INVESTIGATION AND INTERROGATION

According to one author, "deception is considered by police—and courts as well—to be as natural to detecting as pouncing is to a cat" (Skolnick 1982, 40). Offenses involving drugs, vice, and stolen property are covert activities that are not easily detected. Investigations often involve the use of informants, decoys, "covers," and so on. One possible result of these procedures is entrapment.

In legal terms, entrapment occurs when an otherwise innocent person commits an illegal act because of police encouragement or enticement. Two approaches have been used to determine whether entrapment has occurred. The subjective approach looks at the defendant's background, character, and predisposition toward crime. The other, more objective, approach examines the government's participation and whether it has exceeded accepted legal standards. For instance, if the state provides an "essential element" that made the crime possible, or there was extensive and coercive pressure on the defendant to engage in the actions, then a court might rule that entrapment had occurred (Kamisar, LeFave, and Israel 1980, 510).

Stitt and James (1985) criticize the subjective test: it allows the police to entrap people with criminal records who might not otherwise have been tempted; it allows hearsay and rumor to establish predisposition; it forces the individual charged to admit factual guilt, which may stigmatize him or her; it provides a free rein for police discretion in choice of targets; and it degrades the criminal justice system by allowing the police to use misrepresentation and deceit. On the other hand, supporters say that the subjective test allows police to go after those most likely to harm society. The objective test would punish the police and let the criminal go free, forcing police to perjure themselves to save a case (Stitt and James 1985, 133–36).

Legal standards, as we have discussed earlier, are very often useful guidelines for determining ethical standards, but not always. One might disagree with legal standards as being too restrictive, for instance, if one believed that police should be able to do anything necessary to trap criminals. Alternatively, legal guidelines may not be sufficient to eliminate unethical behavior. For example, does a situation where police acting as drug buyers encourage a targeted individual to get them connections raise any legal problems? Probably not, as long as the police didn't entice or coerce the individual. Does it raise any ethical problems? One might look at the methods police use for selecting an individual target. Earlier we discussed discretion in police work. Selection of targets on any other basis than probable cause is a questionable use of discretion. Members of Congress convicted in the Abscam operation alleged improper conduct in the FBI's selection of targets; Marian Barry alleged he was "set up" because of his race after he was videotaped using drugs with a girlfriend in a hotel room. How targets are selected is a serious question; the selection should be based on probable cause. Sherman (1985b) reports that "tips" are notoriously inaccurate as a reason to focus on a certain person. Fundamentally, police operations that provide opportunities for crime change the police role from discovering who has committed a crime to one of discovering who might commit a crime if given a chance (Elliston and Feldberg

1985, 137). This role expansion is dangerous, undesirable, and inconsistent with the social contract basis of policing.

Police also undertake various "stings" where they set up fencing operations to buy stolen goods. This action has been criticized as contributing to burglary. The opposing argument is that burglaries would occur regardless and the good of catching criminals outweighs the negative possibility that burglars steal because they know the fence (police) will take their goods. Both of these arguments exist under a utilitarian framework. One sees that even using the same ethical system, a particular action may be supported as ethical or unethical. Other stings are even more creative, such as sending party invitations to those with outstanding warrants, or staging a murder and then arresting for outstanding warrants those who come out to see what is happening . The utility of such stings is undeniable. Arguments against them point to the deception, which may lead to undermining public confidence in police when they tell the truth.

There are a number of ethical issues in the relationship between the police and the media. Should the police intentionally lie to the media for a valuable end? An example might be lying about the stage of an investigation or to lie about the travel path of a public figure for security reasons. Should the media have complete power to publish or report crime activities regardless of the negative effect on the level of public fear or the possibility of receiving an unbiased trial? Should the media become so involved in hostage situations that they become the news rather than just reporting it? The situation involving David Koresh and his cult of Branch Davidians in Waco, Texas, in the spring of 1993 raised a number of questions concerning the relationship between the police and the media. For instance, the media were banished to a distance far away from the cult compound. Is this an acceptable use of police power or does it infringe on the public's right to know? Could police have ethically used the media to deceive Koresh into giving up by feeding false information to them in response to his stated wish for a sign? Should the media have been better informed during the course of the final assault? These questions can all be analyzed using the ethical systems already described.

Use of Undercover Officers

Undercover officers may have to observe or even participate in illegal activities to protect their cover. Undercover work is said to be a difficult role for the individual officer, who may play the part so well that the officer loses his or her previous identity. If the cover involves illegal or immoral action, the individual may have to sacrifice personal integrity to get an arrest. Marx cites examples of officers who have become addicted to drugs or alcohol and destroyed their marriages or careers because of an undercover assignment (1985b, 109). Kim Wozencraft (1990), an ex-undercover narcotics officer, describes how she and her partner used drugs and became friends with some of the pushers they were collecting evidence against. In her book *Rush*, she alleges that officials in the federal Drug Enforcement Agency (DEA), as well as local law enforcement, knew that undercover officers sometimes used and even became addicted to drugs during the course of an investigation, yet they ignored or covered up such behavior in order to get successful convictions.

Policemen routinely pretend they are "johns," and policewomen dress up as prostitutes. Do we want our police officers to engage in this type of activity? One important element of this debate is the type of relationship involved in the police deception. The two extremes of intimacy are, on one hand, a brief buy-bust incident where the officer pretends to be a drug pusher and buys from a street dealer and moments later an arrest is effected. At the other extreme would be a situation where an undercover officer has an affair with a target of an investigation to maintain his or her cover. The second situation violates our sense of privacy to a much greater degree, yet there have been instances of detectives engaging in such relationships to gain confessions or other information. In one particular case, a private detective (not a police detective) engaged in this type of relationship over a period of months and even agreed to an engagement with the suspect in order to get a confession on tape (Schoeman 1986, 21). In another case, an officer acted as a friend to a target of an investigation, to the extent of looking after his child and living in his house for six months. The purpose of the investigation was to get any evidence on the man so that the topless bar he owned could be shut down. Eventually, the officer found some white powder on a desk in the home that tested positive for cocaine and a conviction was secured. The Supreme Court denied a writ of certiorari in this case (*United States v. Baldwin*, 621 F.2d 251 [1980]).

One of the reasons why some disagree with deceptive practices that involve personal relationships is that they betray trust, an essential element in social life. As Schoeman (1985, 144) explains, intimate relationships are different from public exchanges and should be protected:

> Intimacy involves bringing another person within one's soul or being, not for any independently personal or instrumental objective, but for the sake of the other person or for the sake of the bond and attachment between the persons. . . . There is an expression of vulnerability and unenforceable trust within intimate relationships not present in business or social relationships. . . . Exploitation of trust and intimacy is also degrading to all persons who have respect for intimate relationships. Intimate relationships involve potential transformations of moral duties. Morally, an intimate relationship may take precedence over a concern for social well-being generally.

Note that he is probably arguing from an ethics of care position. In this ethical system, the relationship of two people is more important than rights, duties, or laws. There is no forfeiture in the ethics of care position; thus, one can't say the suspect deserves to be deceived. The harm to the relationship goes in both directions. If the target is hurt by the deception, so too is the deceiver. Schoeman goes on to suggest some guidelines to be used when police interact with others in a deceptive manner. First, he believes that no interaction should go on longer than twenty-four hours without a warrant with probable cause. During this twenty-four-hour period, the officer may not enter any private area, even if invited, unless it is specifically to undertake some illegal activity. Second, although an undercover officer may engage in business and social relationships deceptively during the course of an investigation, he or she may not engage in intimate relationships. Finally, any evidence obtained in violation of the first two principles should be excluded from criminal trials against the targets (1985, 140). These guidelines sound more utilitarian. Recognizing that deception in intimate relationships is harmful, how best can police minimize the harm, yet still obtain some utility from the action? This balancing is characteristic of utilitarian ethics.

Police engage in investigative deception because it is the best (or easiest?) way to investigate drug sales, prostitution, organized crime, illegal alien smuggling, and so on. It is almost necessary in undercover work, especially in the area of vice, to employ deception and techniques that might be considered entrapment. The police have a fairly clear goal: to catch criminals. The ethical question is: What kinds of activities are justified to achieve that goal—lying? stealing? deceiving? tempting? Does the goal justify the means in these cases?

Marx (1985b, 106–7) proposes that before engaging in undercover operations, police investigators should ask the following questions:

1. How serious is the crime being investigated?
2. How clear is the definition of the crime—that is, would the target know that what he or she is doing is clearly illegal?
3. Are there any alternatives to deceptive practices?
4. Is the undercover operation consistent with the spirit as well as the letter of the law?
5. Is it public knowledge that the police may engage in such practices, and is the decision to do so a result of democratic decision making?
6. Is the goal prosecution as opposed to general intelligence gathering or harassment?
7. Is there a likelihood that the crime would occur regardless of the government's involvement?
8. Are there reasonable grounds to suspect the target?
9. Will the practice prevent a serious crime from occurring?

Use of Informants

Police also use informants who often continue to commit crimes while helping police by providing information on other criminal activities. The following describes an informant who had police protection withdrawn (Scheingold 1984, 122):

> The problem is that by the time Detective Tumulty decided to bury Carranza, the informant had already committed, by his own count, two hundred crimes, and he had confessed over one hundred of them to the police. It is not surprising that business persons victimized by Carranza were not particularly pleased when they learned the police had failed to prosecute him.

Protection is sometimes carried to extreme limits. The federal witness protection plan has provided new identities several times to witnesses after they have accumulated bad debts or otherwise victimized an unwary public. The rationale for informant protection, of course, is that greater benefit is derived from using them to catch other criminals than their punishment would bring. This also extends to overlooking any minor crime that they engage in during the period of time they provide information, or afterward if that is part of the deal (Marx 1985b, 109). However, the ethical soundness of this judgment may be seriously questioned. Police use informants partly to avoid problems that undercover police officers would encounter if they attempted to accomplish the task, but also because informants are under fewer restrictions. Reports Marx (1985b, 111):

> Informers and, to an even greater extent, middlemen are much less formally accountable than are sworn law officers and are not as constrained by legal or departmental restrictions. As an experienced undercover agent candidly put it, "unwitting informers are desirable precisely because they can do what we can't—legally entrap."

A recent incident in Houston where an informant was killed in a drug buy brought to light the many ethical issues raised by using informants. This individual came to the police to help them identify pushers. He was married and had small children. He engaged in drug deals and after they occurred, the police would arrest the drug sellers. In one such incident, the informant was in a motel room with the pushers and he was evidently identified as an informant and killed before police could enter the room. The informant was not wearing a wire, and he had no weapon or means of protecting himself. Unlike the families of undercover officers killed in the line of duty, this family is without benefits or compensation for his death (*Houston Post*, January 24, 1993, A20). Some question the use of civilians in such dangerous operations. One might point out the fact that this informant freely volunteered his services, unlike some informants who are threatened with prosecution if they do not cooperate.

Some officers candidly admit that they could not do their job without informants. Some develop close working relationships with informants, while others maintain that you can't trust them no matter how long you've known them. There are disturbing questions one might ask relevant to the use of private citizens for police means. It may be true that narcotics investigations are difficult, if not impossible, without the use of informants. Then one might ask for guidelines and standards to govern the utilization of informants. In the next section, some general justifications are discussed that relate to all undercover and deceptive investigative tactics.

Justifications for Undercover Operations

Undercover operations have been criticized for the following reasons (Marx 1985a, 117–18):

1. They may generate a market for the purchase or sale of illegal goods and services.
2. They may generate the idea for the crime.
3. They may generate the motive.
4. They may provide a missing resource.
5. They may entail coercion or intimidation of a person otherwise not predisposed to commit the offense.
6. They may generate a covert opportunity structure for illegal actions on the part of the undercover agent or informant.
7. They may lead to retaliatory violence against informers.

8. They may stimulate a variety of crimes on the part of those who are not targets of the under-cover operation (for example, impersonation of a police officer, crimes committed against undercover officers).

Ethical systems may or may not support undercover operations. The *principle of double effect* holds that when one does an action to achieve a good end, and an inevi-table but unintended effect is negative, then it might be justified. For instance, if a woman having an operation to save her life loses her fetus, this is not immoral because under the principle of double effect, the death of the fetus was an unintended conse-quence of the good effect of saving the life of the woman. Abortion, of course, would not be an appropriate example of the principle because the death of the fetus is in-tended. We might justify police action in a similar way if the unethical consequence, such as the deception of an innocent, was not the intended consequence of the action, and the goal was an ethical one. However, deceiving the suspect could not be justified under the principle of double effect because that is an intended effect, not an unin-tended effect.

Religious ethics would probably condemn many kinds of police actions because of the deceptions involved. Ethical formalism would condemn such actions because one could not justify them under the categorical imperative. Further, the suspect's being used as a means to his own conviction would also violate the categorical imperative. Utilitarian ethics might justify police deception and deceptive techniques if one could make the argument that catching criminals provides greater benefit to society than al-lowing them to go free by refusing to engage in such practices. Act utilitarianism would probably support deceptive practices, but rule utilitarianism would not, because the ac-tions, although beneficial under certain circumstances, might in the long run under-mine and threaten our system of law. Finally, egoism might or might not justify such actions depending on the particular officer involved and what his or her maximum gain and loss was determined to be.

Under act utilitarianism, one would measure the harm of the criminal activity against the methods used to control it. Deceptive practices, then, might be justified in the case of drug offenses but not of business misdeeds or for finding a murderer but not for trapping a prostitute, and so on. The weakness of this line of reasoning, of course, is that once rules are abandoned, it is more difficult to identify ethical and unethical be-havior. Once again one becomes mired in the quicksand of relativism. Whose standard of seriousness are we using, for instance? I might decide drugs are serious enough to justify otherwise unethical practices, but you might not. Pornography and prostitution raise the same questions.

Marx (1985a) presents a table of ethical justifications for and arguments against undercover work that is replicated in Box 6-4 .

Cohen (1991) proposes a test to determine the ethical justification for police prac-tices (his focus is the use of coercive power to stop and search, but we might apply the same test to analyze undercover or other deceptive practices). First, the end must be justified as a good (conviction of a serious criminal rather than general intelligence gathering). Second, the means must be a plausible way to achieve the end; for instance, choosing a target with no probable cause is not a plausible way to reduce any type of

---

Box 6-4
ETHICAL JUSTIFICATIONS FOR AND
ARGUMENTS AGAINST UNDERCOVER WORK

For

1. Citizens grant to government the right to use means which they individually forsake.
2. Undercover work is ethical when its targets are persons who freely choose to commit crimes which they know may call forth deceptive police practices.
3. Undercover work is ethical when used for a good and important end.
4. Undercover work is ethical when there are reasonably specific grounds to suspect that a serious crime is planned or has been carried out.
5. Undercover work is ethical when it is directed against persons whom there are reasonable grounds to suspect.

Against

1. Truth telling is moral, lying is immoral.
2. The government should not make deals with criminals.
3. The government should neither participate in, nor be a party to crime, nor break laws in order to enforce them.
4. The government through its actions should reduce, not increase, crime.
5. The government should not create an intention to commit a crime which is impossible to carry out.
6. The government should neither tempt the weak, nor offer temptations indiscriminately, nor offer unrealistically attractive temptations.

---

crime. Third, there must be no better alternative means to achieve the same end; no less intrusive means or methods of collecting evidence must exist. Finally, the means must not undermine some other equal or greater end; that is, if the means results in loss of trust or faith in the legal system, it fails the test.

Many people see nothing wrong—certainly nothing illegal—in using any methods necessary to catch criminals. But we are concerned with methods in use before individuals are proved to be criminal. Can an innocent person, such as you, be entrapped into crime? Perhaps not, but are we comfortable in a society where the person who offers you drugs or sex or a cheap television turns out to be an undercover police officer? Are we content to assume that our telephone may be tapped or our best friend could be reporting our conversations to someone else? When we encounter police behavior in these areas, very often the practices have been used to catch a person that we know, after the fact, had engaged in wrongdoing, and thus we feel police are justified in performing in slightly unethical ways. What protectors of due process and critics of police

For	Against
6. When citizens use questionable means, government agents are justified in using equivalent means.	7. Do no harm to the innocent.
	8. Respect the sanctity of private places.
7. Special risks justify special precautions.	9. Respect the sanctity of intimate relations.
8. Undercover work is ethical when it is the best means.	10. Respect the right to freedom of expression and action.
9. Enforce the law equally.	11. The government should not do by stealth what it is prohibited from doing openly.
10. Convict the guilty.	
11. An investigation should be as non-intrusive and non-coercive as possible.	
12. Undercover work is ethical when it is undertaken with the intention of eventually being made public and literally judged in court.	
13. Undercover work is ethical when it is carried out by persons of upright character in accountable organizations.	

(From "Police Undercover Work: Ethical Deception or Deceptive Ethics?" by Gary Marx. In *Police Ethics: Hard Choices in Law Enforcement*, ed. William Heffernan and Timothy Stroup. New York: John Jay Press. All rights reserved. Reprinted by permission.)

investigative practices help us to remember is that those practices, if not curbed, may just as easily be used on the innocent as well as the guilty.

It is clear that norms support police deception during the investigative phase. Laws are vague and contradictory; therefore, police view them as a hindrance to their mission of crime control. If their norms support deception during investigation, it is not surprising that they may protect themselves with deception when their methods are legally questioned. In fact, one of the problems with deceptive practices is that they may lead to more deception to cover up illegal methods. Skolnick (1982) argues, for instance, that weak or nonexistent standards during the investigation phase of policing lead directly to lying on the witness stand because that is the only way an officer can save his or her case.

It is unlikely that these investigative techniques will ever be eliminated; perhaps they should not be, since they are effective in catching a number of people who should be punished. Even if one has doubts about the ethics of these practices, it is entirely possible that there is no other way to accomplish the goal of crime control. However one decides these difficult questions, clearly there are no easy answers. Also, it is important to realize that although for us these questions are academic, for thousands of police officers they are very real.

Deceptive Interrogation

Deception often takes a different form in the interrogation phase of a case. Several court cases document the use of mental coercion, either through threat or promise. The use of the "father confessor" approach (a sympathetic paternal figure for the defendant to confide in) or "Mutt and Jeff" partners (a "nice guy" and a seemingly brutal, threatening officer) are other ways to induce confessions and/or obtain information (Kamisar, LeFave, and Israel 1980, 543).

Skolnick and Leo (1992) present a typology of deceptive interrogation techniques. The following is a brief summary of their descriptions of these types of interrogation practices:

- Calling the questioning an interview rather than an interrogation by questioning in a noncustodial setting and telling the suspect that he is free to leave, thus eliminating the need for Miranda warnings.
- Presenting Miranda warnings in a way designed to negate their effect, by mumbling or by using a tone suggesting that the offender better not exercise the rights delineated or that they are unnecessary.
- Misrepresenting the nature or seriousness of the offense by, for instance, not telling the suspect that the victim has died.
- Using manipulative appeals to conscience through role playing or other means.
- Misrepresenting the moral seriousness of the offense, for instance, by pretending that the rape victim "deserved" to be raped to get a confession.
- Using promises of lesser sentences or nonprosecution beyond the power of the police to offer.
- Misrepresenting identity by pretending to be lawyers or priests.
- Using fabricated evidence like polygraph results or fingerprint findings that don't really exist.

Skolnick writes that because physical means of coercion are no longer used—the infamous third degree—mental deception is the only means left for police officers to gain information or confessions from suspects. How does one get a killer to admit to where he left the murder weapon? If police are imaginative, they may be able to get the defendant to confess by encouraging him or her to think about what would happen if children found the gun. Or police may discover the location of a body by convincing the killer that the victim deserves a Christian burial. Courts have ruled that police who use these methods are unconstitutionally infringing on the defendant's right to counsel because the conversations, even if not direct questioning, constitute an interrogation. Another question one might ask is whether tricking someone into confessing is ethical police behavior or not.

It is certainly much easier to justify deceptive interrogation than physical coercion and intimidation, but their justifications are the same—that is, one uses means that are effective and perhaps necessary to get needed information from a resisting subject. However, most countries have refused to accept this justification for physical coercion and formally condemn the practice. Unfortunately, other countries still endorse physical coercion as acceptable police practice. Reports from Amnesty International document abuses in Chile, Argentina, and many other countries around the world. It is important to note that very often in these situations police are used as the means of control by the dominant political power. They operate, therefore, not under the law, as the code of ethics dictates, but above the law. Codes of ethics, adopted by many police departments that have recognized the danger of police power being misused, are very clear in directing police to abide by the law and not allow themselves to be used by people or political parties for other purposes (Bossard 1981).

Many would argue that whatever information is gained from an individual who is physically coerced into confessing or giving information is not worth the sacrifice of moral standards. The court is primarily concerned with prohibiting methods that would bring the truth of the confession into question. The original legal proscriptions against torture, in fact, come not from an ethical rationale, but from a legal rationale that torture endangered the veracity of the confession. In other words, tortured victims might confess to stop their suffering; thus the court would not get truthful information. Our concern is with the ethical nature of the action itself. If we agree that it is wrong to use physical force or coercion to obtain a confession, do we also agree that deception is an acceptable alternative? If we agree that some deception is acceptable, what are the limits on its use? Again, there is room in this discussion for reasonable people to disagree.

COERCION AND THE USE OF FORCE

Klockars (1983) describes the inevitability of certain unethical or immoral police behaviors as the "Dirty Harry problem," after the movie character who did not let the law get in his way when pursuing criminals. In Klockars's view, using immoral means to reach a desired moral end is an unresolvable problem because there are situations where one knows the "dirty act" will result in a good end, there are no other means to achieve the good end, and the "dirty act" will not be in vain. Klockars's example of this type of problem, taken from a movie, is a situation where a captured criminal refuses to tell the location of a kidnapped victim. Because the victim is sure to die without help, the police officer (played by Clint Eastwood) tortures the criminal by stepping on his injured leg until he admits the location. Obviously, this is an immoral act, but Klockars's point is that there is no solution to the situation. If the police officer behaved in a professional manner, the victim would surely die; if he behaved in an immoral manner, there would be a chance he could save a life. Academic literature does not generally present this dilemma, but in detective and police fiction, it is a dominant theme.

Klockars's conclusion is that by engaging in "dirty" means for good ends, the officer has tainted his innocence and must be punished, because there is always a danger that dirty means will be redefined by those who use them as neutral or even good. Police may lose their sense of moral proportion if the action is not punished, even though the individual police officer involved may have had no other way out of the moral dilemma.

Delattre (1989) also discusses the use of coercive power. He disagrees with Klockars that the officer must inevitably be tainted in the Dirty Harry situation. Delattre points out that if one chooses physical coercion, regardless of temptation, this leads to perjury and lying about the activity and perhaps other tactics to ensure the offender does not go free due to the illegal behavior of the police officer. However, he also excuses the actions of those who succumb to temptation in extreme situations and perform an illegal act (Delattre 1989, 211):

> Police officials are not tainted by refusing to step onto the slope of illegal action, neither are officials of demonstrated probity necessarily tainted by a last-ditch illegal step. Such an act may be unjustifiable by an unconditional principle, but it also may be excusable. . . . Still less does it follow that those who commit such acts are bad, that their character is besmirched, or that their honor is tainted.

One might argue that if officers commit an illegal and unethical act it is hard for their character not to be affected or their honor tainted. To understand an action is not to excuse it. One understands that anger or frustration may lead to violence, but that is not to excuse it. Delattre presents a virtue-based ethical system and evidently believes that an officer can have all the virtues of a good officer and still commit a bad action—in this case, the illegal use of force. His point is well taken that one act of violence does not necessarily mean that the officer is unethical in other ways. The reaction of the officer to his or her mistake is the true test of character. Does the officer cover up and/or ask his or her partner to cover up the action? Does the officer lie to protect himself or herself? Or does the officer admit wrongdoing?

Muir discusses this necessity for the use of coercion: a good policeman, he writes, "has to resolve the contradiction of achieving just ends with coercive means" (Muir 1977, 3). According to Muir, the successful police officer is able to balance willingness to use coercion with an understanding of humankind, which includes such traits as empathy and sympathy toward the weaknesses of human nature. If officers overemphasize coercion, they become cynical and brutal; if they overemphasize understanding, they become ineffectual. Writes Muir (1977, 224):

> Under certain conditions, a youthful policeman was likely to come upon solutions to the paradoxes of coercive power which enabled him to accept the use of coercion as legitimate. However, if his solution to his moral problems required him to blind himself to the tragedy of the human condition, then he became an enforcer. Under other circumstances, a young policeman's choice of responses to paradox left him in conflict about the morality of coercion. Then he would be transfixed by feelings of guilt, would tend to evade situations which aroused those feelings, and would develop a perspective to justify his evasions. This kind of

officer became either a reciprocator or an avoider. Finally, some young officers found ways to exercise coercion legitimately without having to deny their "common sense" of the oneness of the human condition. These men became professionals.

Up to this point we have been discussing the use of instrumental force—force used to achieve an end. Probably more unlawful-use-of-force incidents involve expressive force—force used in anger, frustration, or fear. The use of force by Los Angeles police against Rodney King mentioned before is an example of force used for instrumental or expressive ends, depending on who you believe. This case represents a situation where policy, law, and ethics present different answers to the question: "Did the officers do anything wrong?" The legal question of unlawful use of force is contingent on whether the Los Angeles Police Department's use-of-force policy was legal and whether the officers conformed to departmental policy. The policy stated that the officers could use escalating force if a suspect exhibited "offensive" behavior. The reason that two use-of-force experts—one for the prosecution, one for the defense—disagreed was that the policy, like many other policies in policing, depends on the ethical use of discretion. The defense use-of-force expert analyzed the video and identified offensive movements in every attempt to rise and every arm movement. The prosecution expert, who wrote the policy, testified that a suspect lying on the ground was not in a position to present offensive movements to officers. If an officer perceives offensiveness in every movement of every suspect, the policy justifies his or her use of force. If an officer gets shot at, that obviously would justify use of force under the policy, but if the officer decides that he or she is safe enough behind his or her patrol car to talk the suspect out of shooting again and into giving up the weapon, then the use-of-force policy would support that nonviolent response as well. If an officer is hit in the face by a drunk, the policy would support use of force since that is an offensive action; however, the officer who accepts the fact that the drunk is irrational, allows for it, and simply puts the person in the back of the patrol car is also supported by the policy.

Some officers seem to get involved in use-of-force situations repeatedly, while others, even with similar patrol neighborhoods, rarely get involved in such altercations. Thus, even if every use of force meets the guidelines of the policy, there are lingering questions as to why some officers seem to need to enforce the policy more often than others and why some interpret actions more often as offensive. According to Souryal (1992, 242), the *Report by the Independent Commission of the Los Angeles Police Department* (1991) reveals that the top 5 percent of officers ranked by number of reports of the use of force accounted for more than 20 percent of all reports; and that of approximately 1,800 officers who had been reported for excessive use of force from 1986 to 1990, most had only one or two allegations, but 44 had six or more, 16 had eight or more, and 1 had sixteen allegations.

The most common explanations for police officer use of force are similar to those used to explain correctional officer use of excessive force—that force is the only thing "these people" understand or that "officers are only human" and consequently get mad or frightened or angry, just like anyone else would in that situation. The weakness of such arguments is obvious. If other people get mad and use force, it is called assault and battery and they are punished. If the only thing these people understand is force, it removes the differences that we like to think exist between us to use reactive force against them. As stated before, the use of excessive force is probably not a pervasive problem in this country. It seems that there are a few officers in every department who are truly abusers of power, and a larger number of officers and an organizational culture that protect these officers from sanctions. The more common ethical issue concerning the use of force is that of the officer who observes an unlawful use of force by another officer. This issue is addressed next.

LOYALTY AND WHISTLE BLOWING

Do officers owe their primary loyalty to the department, society, or their fellow officers? One of the most frequent and difficult ethical choices officers confront is what to do when faced with the wrongdoing of another officer. Informing on one's peers has always been negatively perceived by a large contingent of any group, whether that group is lawyers, doctors, students, prisoners, or police officers. The "code of silence" discussed in relation to police work is present in other occupations and groups as well. Why we look away or do not come forward when others do wrong may be egoistic: we don't want to get involved, we don't want to face the scorn of others, we feel it's not our job to come forward when there are others who are supposed to look out for and punish wrongdoing, we don't want to alienate the peer who committed the wrong by reporting him or her. Of course, coming forward may be egoistic as well: we are afraid we will be blamed if the perpetrator is not correctly identified, we will tell the truth to avoid punishment ourselves.

Loyalty in police work is explained by the fact that police depend on each other, sometimes in life-or-death situations. Loyalty to one's fellows is part of the *esprit de corps* of policing and an absolutely essential element for a healthy department. Ewin (1990) writes that something is wrong if a police officer doesn't feel loyalty to fellow officers. Loyalty is a personal relationship, not a judgment. Therefore, loyalty is uncalculating—we do not extend loyalty in a rational way or based on contingencies. Loyalty to groups or persons is emotional, grounded in affection rather than reflection. Wren (1985) also writes of loyalty as an internal moral position, as opposed to external reasoning, such as utilitarianism and deontological arguments. He points out that utilitarianism may defend or condemn informing on other police officers. Arguments for informing are that the harm from a scandal caused by the individual's coming forward would be less than the good of the public's believing that the department was finally free from corruption and that individual corruption would come to a halt. Arguments against informing are that some activities labeled corrupt actually may further the ends of justice and complete adherence to regulations would undermine detection and enforcement. Also, the loss of a skilled police officer, even though that officer may be moderately corrupt, is a loss to society.

In a similar manner, deontological arguments may either support informing or not. Arguments for informing include the fact that a police officer has a sworn duty to uphold the law. Also, one cannot remain silent in one situation unless one could approve of silence in all situations (Kant's categorical imperative), and one must do one's duty. Arguments against informing include the idea that discretion and secrecy are obligations one assumes by joining a police force and that it would be unjust to subject an otherwise good and heroic police officer to the punishment of exposure (Wren 1985, 32–33).

These arguments are what Wren calls external moral arguments, which he contrasts with the internal, such as loyalty. When one considers whether to come forward about the wrongdoing of others, external moral philosophies are rarely very well articulated. What often is the prime motivator is personal integrity. Yet the individual often feels great anguish and self-doubt over turning in friends and colleagues, and that is understandable since "a person's character is defined by his commitments, the more basic of which reveal to a person what his life is all about and give him a reason for going on" (Wren 1985, 35). Thus, the issue of whistle blowing comes down to loyalty to persons or groups versus loyalty to one's principles of integrity and honesty.

Ewin (1990, 13) also points out that loyalty always refers to a preference for one group over another:

> Loyalty always involves some exclusion: one is loyal to X rather than to Y, with Y thus being excluded. At times, the reverse can also be true: that a group of people is excluded (whether or not they are properly excluded) can make them feel a common cause in response to what they see as oppression and can result in the growth of loyalty amongst them. That loyalty, provoked by a dislike and perhaps distrust of the other group, is likely to be marked by behavior that ignores legitimate interests and concerns of the other group.

The application to policing is obvious. If police feel isolated from the community, their loyalty is to other police officers and not to the community at large. To address abuses of loyalty, one would not want to attack the loyalty itself because it is necessary for the health of the organization. Rather, one would want to extend the loyalty beyond other officers to the community. Permeability rather than isolation promotes community loyalty, just as the movement toward professionalism promotes loyalty to the principles of ethical policing as opposed to individuals in a particular department.

Wren believes that police departments can resolve the dilemma of the individual officer who knows of wrongdoing by making the consequences more palatable—that is, by having a fair system of investigation and punishment, by instituting helping programs for those with alcohol and drug problems, and by using more moderate punishments than dismissal or public exposure for other sorts of misbehavior. This is consistent with the ethics of care, which is concerned with needs and relationships. If the relationship can be saved and the need for honesty and change met, then that is the best alternative to the dilemma of wrongdoing.

Delattre (1989) handles the problem differently but comes to somewhat similar conclusions. He turns to Aristotle to support the idea that when a friend becomes a "scoundrel," the moral individual cannot stand by and do nothing. Rather, one has a moral duty to bring the wrongdoing to the friend's attention and urge her or him to change. If the friend will not, then she or he is more scoundrel than friend, and the individual's duty shifts to those who might be victimized by the officer's behavior. One sees here not the ethics of care, but a combination of virtue-based and deontological duty-based ethics.

TRAINING AND MANAGEMENT ISSUES

Malloy (1982, 37–40) discusses several explanations of police corruption, including the rotten apple theory, which ascribes deviance to the individual; the political context theory, which points to structural supports for deviance; the unenforceable law ratio-nale, which notes that certain crimes are more likely to be involved than others; the informal code theory, which blames the police subculture for individual deviance; and the moral career theory, which explains deviance as a gradual movement from lesser to more serious deviant acts. Malloy also offers some possible solutions to police corrup-tion: increase the salary of police, eliminate unenforceable laws, establish civilian review boards, and improve training. One might add to these: improve leadership. Metz (1990) suggests several ways that police administrators can encourage ethical conduct among officers. He suggests setting realistic goals and objectives for the department and providing ethical leadership, a written code of ethics, a whistle-blowing procedure that ensures fair treatment of all parties, and training in law enforcement ethics.

Souryal (1992, 307) also offers advice to ethical leaders. He suggests that they:

- Create an environment that is conducive to dignified treatment on the job.
- Increase ethical awareness among the ranks through formal and informal socialization.
- Avoid deception and manipulation in the way officers are assigned, rewarded, or promoted.
- Allow for openness and the free flow of unclassified information.
- Foster a sense of shared values and incorporate such values in the subculture of the agency.
- Demonstrate an obligation to honesty, fairness, and decency by example.
- Discuss the issue of corruption publicly, expose corrupt behavior, and reward ethical behavior.

Training and Other Change Efforts

Because so much of police work is unpredictable and encounters such a wide range of situations, it is impossible to fashion rules for all possible occurrences. What should take the place of extensive rules are strong ethical standards. As discussed before, police departments have formal ethical codes that are no doubt presented in the academy. The internalization of these standards by individual police officers, however, is at best tenuous; once out in the field, the police officer encounters challenges and threats to the formal ethical code. The informal police subculture is the most obvious threat to the internalization of ethical standards. In the day-to-day interactions of the individual police officer, the informal subculture is much more powerful than any academic discussions of ethics.

Some writers believe the ethical standards themselves are at fault. They are so far removed from reality that they are worse than ignored—they encourage officers to believe there are no relevant ethical guides to behavior (Johnson and Copus 1981, 78). On the other hand, if ethical standards are the highest aspiration of law enforcement, it is necessary that they be set at a level that is higher than an average of real behavior. The fact remains, however, that there is a vast difference between the formal code of ethics and actual police behavior.

The common administrative reaction to unethical police practices is to institute even more rules covering a greater range of behavior. As discussed in previous chapters, extensive rules seem to be present in inverse proportion to high ethical standards; what often occurs is as more rules are written, more creative ways are found to get around them. Rules are not ethical standards, and without a commitment and belief in the legitimacy of the rules, there is no way that more rules will affect the ethics of an organization.

The subculture could endorse desirable ethical standards instead of contrary standards of behavior, but this may involve a change in subcultural values. One example will serve to illustrate how this might occur. The police value of force endorses the use of violence and gives only vague guidelines for when force should not be used. The consequence of this is that some police officers view their uniform as a license to use force against anyone considered a threat. Police use of unreasonable force is an individual problem, but it is also a value problem, because the police subculture does not condemn but rather protects police officers with aggressive tendencies. One attempt to change this situation involved a small group of Oakland, California, police officers and social scientists who were asked to deal with the problem. In this experiment the police officers, who were chosen partly because of their inappropriate use of violence, confronted the issues of aggression and police authority and arrived at methods of coping with them. Police officers were asked to participate in a group created to deal with the problem of citizen complaints against police violence. The following describes the goals of the project (Toch, Grant, and Galvin 1975, 13):

> We would start (in the tradition of "organizational development" teams) with a small group of men who would (1) inform themselves about parameters of the problem and devise an initial set of problem-solving strategies; in this context (2) we would prepare the men to take on roles as leaders for a larger problem-solving group, who would extend the effort further. This second group (or its sub-groups) could then expand the first team's effort, while engaged in both objective and self-directed inquiry. Ultimately, the larger group was expected to set up institutional arrangements in the form of a permanent problem-solving body within the department. Our first group was to be composed of officers defined as "strong" problem solvers; only some of these men were to be derived from the violence-experienced pool. The second generation was to be composed exclusively of violence-prone officers.

The early sessions defined the problem and developed projects designed to help resolve the problem. One of the projects was a panel of peer officers that reviewed violent incidents. Later, individual change was observed to occur even in some of the officers who had many citizen complaints against them. The primary motivation for change seemed to be a change in role perceptions and a comparison of one's own activities to those of others (Toch, Grant, and Galvin 1975, 248–57).

Very probably, these officers at the same time were developing different values regarding violence and its use. Notice the similarity between these techniques and the indirect methods of teaching morals discussed in Chapter 3. In both situations there is an opportunity to explore moral issues and alternative moral positions. This may, in turn, lead to the development of different and perhaps more advanced ethical standards. An alternative explanation, however, is more consistent with learning theory. The officers in the experimental group were rewarded for negative expressions about violence. They were further rewarded when they developed methods for dealing with violent police officers. Their value system thus matured after their behavior, and their behavior was influenced by the reward system, which became one that rewarded nonviolent behavior. Whichever explanation one prefers for the mechanism of change, it seems clear that involving police officers in such change efforts is a valuable and productive way to address problems such as the use of excessive force. There is no reason why similar methods cannot be applied to other ethical problems (Toch and Grant 1991). These methods may, in fact, be more valuable than more traditional types of training.

Ethics training in the academy as well as during in-service courses is common and recommended for all police departments today. However, what these courses might be able to accomplish is more questionable. Most ethics courses use a moral reasoning approach, much as this book does, where various scenarios are examined in light of ethical perspectives such as utilitarianism to determine the right course of behavior. Implicit in this approach is the assumption that once what is right is determined, most officers will conform their behavior and/or make the right decision. This is naive. A different perspective is offered by Delattre (1989) and Delaney (1990) that emphasizes the importance of character. In Chapter 2 we discussed the ethics of virtue, which answers the question, "How does one live a good life?" by the answer, "Developing and forming good habits of character." This is the approach that Delattre and Delaney apply to police ethics. If one has a bad character, ethical analysis is irrelevant since that individual will continue to behave in conformance to his or her traits of avarice, deceptiveness, cowardice, and so on. An individual who has good character possesses those virtues necessary for moral and ethical decision making. Training may help one by reinforcing appropriate values, but one's character is already formed. What are the virtues necessary for a good police officer? Delattre discusses justice, courage, temperance, and compassion. Delaney discusses sagacity, sincerity, and persistence.

This approach would seem to negate the relevance of any attempts to improve the ethics of officers, since character is fairly well formed by the time one is an adult. Yet we might say that ethics training at this point serves to delineate those situations that may not be recognized as questions of ethics. Also, discussions of such dilemmas point out egoistic rationalizations for unethical behavior, making them harder to use by those who would try. Those who do have habits of greed, dishonesty, and so forth, at least must face up to their behavior without disguising it as something else. It must be realized that to know the right course of action does not necessarily mean that any individual will follow it. Many times, more immediate rewards, convenience, or lack of courage will overcome the knowledge of what is right. That is not to say that these officers have a bad character, unless they habitually and consistently choose actions that are contrary to the virtues discussed earlier. None of us are perfect and, furthermore, there are no discrete categorizations of ethical and unethical people. Some of us are more honest than others, some more courageous, some more generous, and so on. Moral analysis, however, develops an individual's ability to recognize decisions as ethical choices and to know which alternative is the more ethical one.

Swift, Houston, and Anderson (1993) present one such training course based on rule utilitarianism, which they believe is the best and most accepted basis for law enforcement ethics. The course they outline discusses the scope of the problem, identifies different problems (brutality, corruption, theft, misuse of authority), discusses how to decide what to do about them (resolving ethical dilemmas, ethical systems), presents rule utilitarianism, and discusses how to apply it. Other training options may involve a more balanced treatment of other ethical systems. All must resolve the issues of relativism versus absolutism, duty versus personal needs, and the issue of when minor transgressions become major.

Ethical Leadership

Most people agree that employee behavior is influenced directly by the behavior of superiors rather than the stated directives or ethics of the organization. Executives engaged in price fixing and overcharging should not be surprised that their employees steal company supplies or time. One cannot espouse ethical ideals, act unethically, and then expect employees to act ethically. Thus, regardless of formal ethical codes, police are influenced by the standards of behavior they observe in their superiors. One may note that most large-scale corruption that has been exposed has implicated very high officials. Alternatively, police departments that have remained relatively free of corruption have administrators who practice ethical behavior on a day-to-day basis.

Besides developing procedures and values in a police department that might maximize the ethical behavior of their officers and making sure their own behavior serves as an example, administrators have their own unique ethical dilemmas to face. Budget allocations, the use of drug testing, affirmative action, sexual harassment, and decisions about corrupt officers all present ethical dilemmas for administrators and supervisors. For instance, some supervisors face problems when they are promoted from the ranks and have friends who now become their subordinates. Such friends may expect special consideration, leaving the supervisor to decide how to respond to such expectations. Supervisors also report ethical dilemmas over how they should allocate resources, such as a new patrol car or overtime. Should seniority take precedence over competence? Friendship over seniority? What should be done with officers who have drug or alcohol problems is another issue. If the administrator decides to counsel or suggest treatment without any change in duty status and the officer endangers the life of someone or actually harms a citizen or other officer due to the problem, is the administrator to blame?

Administrators have duties to the department that are slightly different from those of an officer. They are responsible not only for personal conduct, but also for the actions of those they supervise. In other countries and cultures, this seems to be more pronounced than in the United States. For instance, when the Falkland War occurred, the foreign minister in Great Britain resigned. He did so because the situation happened on "his watch." Even though he did nothing personally that would put him to blame and in all respects performed his job competently, he held himself personally responsible because he failed to know of and therefore warn or prepare for the threat that Argentina presented. Contrast this with the attitudes of the captain of the *Exxon Valdez*, responsible for the largest oil spill in history, who professed innocence because he wasn't the one on the bridge at the time of the incident, and Darryl Gates, the Los Angeles police chief, who insisted that the problem of brutal officers was an individual problem and not one for which he should be held responsible. Of course, the explanation that one was "unaware" of wrongful behavior has been used by the highest office in the country, so it should not be surprising that it is frequently heard from administrators when faced with the wrongdoing of their subordinates.

When one makes the top leadership responsible for their subordinates' behavior, they will lead and administer with greater awareness, interaction, and responsibility. Because of this expanded responsibility, a supervisor or administrator must be concerned with anything that might affect the on-duty behavior of officers. Delattre (1989) describes a situation where an officer's wife comes to a supervisor and complains about the off-duty behavior of the officer, including alcohol use, seeing other women, and physical abuse. When this scenario was presented to an in-service class for supervisors, there were mixed feelings regarding the extent to which the supervisor should intervene in the private life of the officer. While all felt that the physical abuse was a crime and thus demanded some action, there was no agreement as to whether the supervisor should be involved absent any physical abuse. Some felt that as long as the officer performed his duties on the job without any observable effects of his off-duty behavior, then he had a right to a private life free from scrutiny. Others felt that a responsible supervisor should be concerned with such things as marital troubles and alcohol use before they led to problems on the job. The ethical justification of such a view was either utilitarian (it would prevent greater harm) or the ethics of caring (the officer may need someone to talk to and certainly the wife needs help).

An important element in determining the course of action seemed to be whether or not there was a personal relationship between the superior and the subordinate. If there was, then the supervisors seemed more willing to get involved. This seems to be a response consistent with the ethics of care in that the supervisors felt more responsible toward another individual based on the relationship between them. It also is probably indicative of a misperception of the limits of ethical leadership. A strong ethical leader should have a personal relationship with all of his or her subordinates—not just a formal, impersonal one. This personal relationship is the building block of modeling, identification, and persuasive authority.

What is strong leadership? It involves caring and commitment to the organization. A strong leader is someone who is connected with others but also has a larger vision, if you will, of goals and missions. It also implies someone with those virtues that Delattre and Delaney described. Souryal also describes ethical leaders as those with "a mental state that is characterized by vision, enlightened reasoning, and moral responsibility" (1992, 186).

CONCLUSION

In this chapter we have explored ethics and law enforcement. Many of the issues discussed in this chapter, such as discretion, authority, and power, are also relevant to the next two chapters. We looked at the influence of the police subculture on ethical behavior and its opposition to formal ethical standards. We explored reasons for the lack of consistency between the two. We then discussed various practices of police. Finally, we looked at training issues and what strong leadership and management might look like.

As we began the chapter, we will also close with the images of the use of force by the Los Angeles police. Some of us remember earlier images from the 1960s where law enforcement officers appeared on newscasts beating and using attack dogs against peaceful civil rights demonstrators. One might hope that in the same way those negative images of the 1960s led to a greater professionalization, better training, and racial and sexual integration of police departments in the 1970s, so too can the Rodney King incident lead to positive results and a new era of more ethical and thoughtful policing in the 1990s.

In the ethical dilemmas at the end of this chapter, try putting yourself in the place of police officers. As with the dilemmas in previous chapters, decide on your course of action, but then take the extra time to try and justify your action using an ethical framework. Or approach it in another way and use any ethical system and try to resolve the dilemma using the principles of the framework, whether or not you agree with them. With either procedure you will find that these dilemmas are not easy to resolve.

DISCUSSION QUESTIONS

1. What is the worst thing a police officer might do?
2. Would you rather have the police enforce every law than to practice discretion? Why?
3. Do you believe police officers are changed in any way by the job? How?
4. What methods should police use when attempting to catch drug dealers? Prostitutes? Gamblers? If you agree with the use of informants and undercover work, what ethical standards would you write for those engaged in such work?
5. What rules should guide police procedure when interrogating a suspect?

6. Should police officers receive free or half-price meals? Other gratuities? Where would you draw the line?
7. Read a book that details an ethical issue in policing (or see the movie), such as *Prince of the City* (Daley 1984), *Serpico* (Maas 1973), or *Rush* (Wozencraft 1990). Describe the ethical dilemma(s) the officer faced. How did the officer resolve them? What ethical rationale would justify the officer's decision?
8. Talk to ten police officers and ask them what their views are on police gratuities. Present two or three various hypotheticals, such as free coffee, half-price meals, or tickets to a ballgame. Then compare your findings with those of others who did the same exercise with different officers.
9. List some current innovations in crime prevention and analyze them from an ethical framework—for instance, neighborhood policing, neighborhood watch programs, groups like the Guardian Angels, private security for subdivisions and apartment buildings, use of Tazer guns, and so on.

⇥ ETHICAL DILEMMAS ⇤

Please read and respond to the following situations. Be prepared to discuss your ideas.

Situation 1

You are a rookie police officer on your first patrol. The older, experienced officer tells you that the restaurant on the corner likes to have you guys around so they always give free meals. Your partner orders steak, potatoes, and all the trimmings. What are you going to do? What if it were just coffee at a convenience store? What if the owner refused to take your money at the cash register?

Situation 2

As a patrol officer, you are only doing your job when you stop a car for running a red light. Unfortunately, the driver of the car happens to be the mayor. You give her a ticket anyway, but the next day get called into the captain's office and told in no uncertain terms that you screwed up and there is an informal policy extending "courtesy" to city politicians. Several nights later you observe the mayor's car weaving erratically across lanes and speeding. What would you do? What if the driver were a fellow police officer? What if the driver were a high school friend?

Situation 3

You are a rookie police officer who responds to a call for officer assistance. At the scene you see a ring of officers surrounding a suspect who is down on his knees. You don't know what happened before you arrived, but you see a sergeant use a Tazer on the suspect and you see two or three officers step in and take turns hitting the suspect with their nightsticks about the head and shoulders. This goes on for several minutes as you stand in the back of the circle. No one says anything that would indicate that this is not appropriate behavior. What would you do?

Situation 4

Officer A turned in an overtime slip claiming six hours of surveillance. The supervisor is suspicious of Officer A because he frequently turns in overtime slips claiming he was conducting surveillance. Surveillance is not something that always leads to a conclusion and can easily be abused. The supervisor has heard rumors that Officer A is going home and having dinner with his family during the hours he puts in for overtime. Officer A is an otherwise productive officer. You know that Officer A was at home during the time in question, and you are asked by the supervisor whether you know where Officer A really was. What would you tell him?

Situation 5

While on the witness stand you answer all the prosecutor's and defense attorney's questions. You complete your testimony and exit the courtroom knowing that you have specific knowledge that may help the defense attorney's case. You have answered all questions truthfully, but the specific question needed to help the defense was not asked. What should you do?

Situation 6

You stop someone and check his pockets and find some dope. You had no probable cause to search him but you did anyhow because you thought he might be holding. Do you find a reason to arrest him and then put in the report that you found the dope after the arrest so it won't get thrown out in court?

7

Ethics and the Courts

Many people refer to the criminal justice system as the criminal *injustice* system because of a perception that practices in this nation's courtrooms do not necessarily conform to ideals of justice. As mentioned in previous chapters, justice is a goal that may not necessarily be achieved by a legal system. Moreover, sometimes the day-to-day practices of the system may even be inconsistent with or violate the principles of law, further removing practice from the ideal. The basic elements of a justice system are an impartial fact-finding process and a fair and equitable resolution, with protection against error. Those who work in the justice system have ethical and moral duties to fulfill to protect this concept of justice.

Common perceptions of lawyers indicate that the public has little confidence in their ability to live up to the ideals of justice. In a Gallup survey reported in *U.S. News and World Report*, lawyers were rated as less ethical and less honest than police officers, doctors, television reporters, and funeral directors, among others. Only building contractors, politicians, and car salespeople had lower ratings than lawyers (Kelly 1982, 29). The public's opinion of attorneys was said to have reached a new low when it was disclosed that almost all the Watergate figures were lawyers (Davis and Elliston 1986, 43, 115). This perception of the lawyer as an amoral "hired gun" is in sharp contrast to the ideal of the lawyer as an officer of the court, sworn to uphold the ideals of justice declared sacrosanct under our system of law. Which is closer to the truth?

History indicates that the ethics of those associated with the legal process have always been suspect. Plato and Aristotle condemned the advocate because of his ability to make the truth appear false and the guilty appear innocent. This early distrust has continued throughout history; early colonial lawyers were distrusted and even punished for practicing law. For many years lawyers could not charge a fee for their services because the mercenary aspects of the profession was condemned (Papke 1986, 32). Gradually lawyers and the profession itself were accepted, but suspicion and controversy continued in the area of fees and qualifications. Partly to counteract public antipathy, lawyers formed their own organization, the American Bar Association (ABA), in 1878. Shortly afterward, this professional organization established the first ethical guidelines for lawyers.

PERCEPTIONS OF JUDICIAL PROCESSING

As mentioned before, the ideal of the justice system is that two advocates of equal ability will each engage in a pursuit of truth, guided by a neutral fact finder, with the truth emerging from the contest. Actual practices in our justice system are very different. Various descriptions profess to offer a more realistic picture of the system. One approach is to use game theory to describe judicial processing. The movement of an offender from arrest to conviction is, in some respects, played like a game. Each player has a certain role to perform, with rules and responsibilities. Also, hidden agendas (covert motivations and goals) exist. The adversarial system pits the defense attorney against the prosecutor, and the judge may be considered the umpire in this contest. The judge sets down the rules and, unless there is a jury, decides who wins the contest. The rationale for the system is that the best person wins, obviously an optimistic view. If a powerful and rich defendant is able to hire the best criminal lawyer in the country complete with several assistants and investigators, the prosecuting attorney, a public servant who may have many other cases to deal with simultaneously, is faced with stiff competition. This is the exception, of course; more commonly, a defendant must rely on an overworked public defender, a young, inexperienced attorney just starting out, or an attorney who can only make criminal law profitable through high caseloads and quick turnover. In any of these cases, the defense is matched against a public office that has greater access to evidence and some investigative assistance.

A variation on game theory is offered by Blumberg (1969), who refers to the practice of law as a confidence game because both prosecutor and defense attorney conspire to appear as something they are not—adversaries in a do-or-die situation. What is more commonly the case is that the prosecutor and the defense attorney will still be working together when the client is gone; thus their primary allegiance is not to the client, but to themselves. For defense attorneys this may involve either making the case appear more difficult than it is to justify their fee or, if the client has no resources, arbitrarily concluding a case that has merit. Attorneys may use their power for reasons other than the client's interest; in the following example cited by Blumberg (1969, 329), where all actors cooperate in the conspiracy against the client:

> [Judges] will adjourn the case of an accused in jail awaiting plea or sentence if the attorney requests such action. While explicitly this may be done for some innocuous and seemingly valid reason, the tacit purpose is that pressure is being applied by the attorney for the collection of his fee, which he knows will probably not be forthcoming if the case is concluded.

The game here is to make the client believe that the advocacy system is working for him or her while in reality it is being used against him or her. Other stories are told of attorneys asking for continuances because of a missing witness, "Mr. Green" (referring to money owed to the attorney by the client). For this charade to be successful, all players in the system must cooperate; evidently in many situations they do. Great shows of anger and emotion in the courtroom help clients believe they are getting something for their money, but such performances are belied by the jocular relationship sometimes apparent between the defense attorney and the prosecutor shortly after trial or between courtroom sessions. In fact, many defense attorneys are ex-prosecutors. This is, in some respects, helpful to their clients because they know the way the prosecutor's office works and what a reasonable plea offer would be. But one also must assume that their prosecutorial experience has shaped their perceptions of clients and what would be considered fair punishments. Moreover, their continuing relationships with prosecutors overlap into their social and personal lives and, thus, it is not surprising that allegiances are more often all lawyers against civilians, rather than defense versus prosecution.

Other authors have also used the analogy of a confidence game to describe the interaction among prosecutor, defense attorney, and client. For example, Scheingold (1984, 155) writes:

> The practice of defense law is all too often a "confidence game" in which the lawyers are "double agents" who give the appearance of assiduous defense of their clients but whose real loyalty is to the criminal courts. The defendant, from this perspective, is only an episode in the attorney's enduring relationships with the prosecutors and judges whose goodwill is essential to a successful career in the defense bar.

Another perspective describes our courts as administering *bureaucratic justice.* Each individual case is seen only as one of many for the professionals who work in the system. The goal of the system—namely, bureaucratic efficiency—becomes more important than the original goal of justice. Also, because each case is part of a workload, decision making takes on a more complicated nature. For instance, a defense lawyer may be less inclined to fight very hard for a "loser" client if he or she wants a favor for another client later in the week. The prosecutor may decide not to charge a guilty person in order to get him or her to testify against someone else. In this sense, each case is not separately tried and judged, but is linked to others and processed as part of a workload. The bureaucratic system of justice is seen as developing procedures and policies that although not intentionally discriminatory, may contribute to a perception of unfairness. For instance, a major element in bureaucratic justice is the presumption of guilt, while the ideal of our justice system is a presumption of innocence. District attorneys, judges, and even defense attorneys approach each case presuming guilt and place a priority on achieving the most expeditious resolution of the case. This is the basic rationale behind plea bargaining, whether it is recognized or not; the defendant is assumed to be guilty and the negotiation is to achieve a guilty plea while bargaining for the best possible sentence—the lowest possible is the goal of the defense while the highest possible is the goal of the prosecutor. Plea bargaining is consistent with the bureaucratic value system because it is the most efficient way of getting maximum punishment for minimum work.

Descriptions of bureaucratic justice such as the following (Scheingold 1984, 158) allow for the fact that efficiency is tempered with other values and priorities:

> The concept of bureaucratic justice . . . provides the most persuasive account of how the participants in criminal process reconcile legal and bureaucratic forces. "Bureaucratic jus-

tice unites the presumption of guilt with the operational morality of fairness." . . . All participants in the criminal process behave as if a person who is arrested is probably guilty. Nevertheless, the coercive thrust of the presumption of guilt is softened somewhat by the operational morality of fairness that leads the participants to make certain that defendants get neither more nor less than is coming to them—that defendants, in other words, get their due.

Scheingold is referring to the practice of judges, prosecutors, and defense attorneys who adapt the system to their personal standards of justice. This is exemplified by a judge who determines that an individual offender is a threat to society and so overlooks errors during trial to make sure that the individual ends up in prison. In the same way, a person who is legally guilty may get a break because it is determined that he is a decent guy who made a mistake rather than a "bad character." Moreover, in almost all cases, there may be general consensus on both sides as to what is fair punishment for any given offender. Defense attorneys who argue for unrealistically low sentences do so in a desultory and uncommitted fashion, knowing that the prosecutor would not and could not offer such a sentence. Prosecutors put up very little argument when defense attorneys ask for sentences that fit office guidelines. Instead of describing the justice system as a system that practices the presumption of innocence and takes careful steps to determine guilt, what may be more realistic is to characterize it as a system wherein all participants assume guilt, take superficial steps to arrive at the punishment phase, and operate under a value system that allocates punishment and mercy to offenders according to an informal operating standard of fairness.

One other perception of the criminal justice system is that of Samuel Walker's "wedding cake" illustration based on a model proposed by Lawrence Friedman and Robert Percival. In this scheme, the largest portion of criminal cases are presented as the bottom layers of the cake and the few serious cases as forming the top layer. The courtroom work group is believed to share definitions of seriousness and operates as a unit to keep the dynamics of the courtroom static, despite changes that are forced upon it. Changes such as the exclusionary rule, determinate sentencing, and other legislation have surprisingly little impact on court outcomes because of a shared perception of serious crime and appropriate punishment. The vast majority of crime, however, is considered trivial, and the processing of these cases involves very little energy or attention from system actors (Walker 1985).

FORMAL ETHICS FOR LAWYERS AND JUDGES

A profession, as defined earlier, involves a specialized body of knowledge, commitment to the social good, ability to regulate itself, and high social status (Davis and Elliston 1986, 13). The presence of ethical standards is essential to the definition of a profession. Formal ethical standards for lawyers and judges were originally promulgated by the ABA in the Model Code of Professional Responsibility. The original canons, adapted from the Alabama Bar Association Code of 1887, were adopted by the ABA in 1908 and have been revised frequently since then (American Bar Association, 1979). Several years ago, the ABA switched its endorsement of the Model Code as the general guide for ethical behavior to the Model Rules of Professional Responsibility, summarized in Appendix A.

Today's Model Rules cover many aspects of the lawyer's profession, including such areas as client-lawyer relationships, the lawyer as counselor, the lawyer as advocate, transactions with others, public service, and maintaining the integrity of the profession. Ethical issues in criminal law may involve courtroom behavior, suborning perjury, conflicts of interest, use of the media, investigation efforts, use of immunity, discovery and the sharing of evidence, relationships with opposing attorneys, and plea bargaining (Douglass 1981).

To enforce these ethical rules, the ABA has a standing committee on ethical responsibility to offer formal and informal opinions when charges of impropriety have been made. Also, each state bar association has the power to sanction offending attorneys by private or public censure or recommending suspension of their privilege to practice law. The bar associations also have the power to grant entry into the profession, since one must ordinarily belong to the bar association of a particular state to practice law there. Bar associations judge competence by testing the applicant's knowledge, but they also judge moral worthiness by background checks of the individual. The purpose of these restrictive admission procedures is to protect the public image of the legal profession by rejecting unscrupulous or dishonest individuals or those unfit to practice for other reasons. Many feel, however, that if bar associations were serious about protecting the profession, they would continue to monitor the behavior and moral standing of current members with the same care they seem to take in the initial decision regarding entry (Elliston 1986, 53).

Law schools have been criticized for being singularly uninterested in fostering any type of moral conscience in graduating students. Several writers have condemned the law school practice of reshaping law students so that when they emerge "thinking like a lawyer," they have mastered a type of thinking that is concerned with detail and logical analysis but gives little regard to morality and larger social issues.

Gerry Spence, for instance, a flamboyant defense attorney, brags of receiving low grades in law school—an indication, he believes, that he did not "sell out" to the mindset of bottom-line winning and profit above all else that is representative of law school indoctrination (Spence 1989). Stover (1989) writes how public interest values decline during law school. The reason for this decline seemingly has to do with the low value placed on public interest issues by the law school curriculum, which also treats ethical and normative concerns as irrelevant or trivial compared to the "bar courses" such as contract law and torts. Morality and ethics are often made light of, even in professional responsibility courses where there are more stories (humorous and otherwise) of how to get around the ethical mandates than stories of how to resolve dilemmas and maintain a sense of personal integrity.

A practicing attorney is investigated only when complaints have been lodged against him or her. The investigative bodies have been described as decentralized, informal, and secret. They do little for dissatisfied clients since typical client complaints involve competence—a vague and ill-defined term (Marks and Cathcart 1986, 72). Another study of client satisfaction found that the biggest complaint against attorneys was that too little time was given the client by the lawyer or that the lawyer was inaccessible (Arafat and McCahery 1978, 205). Neither of these complaints is likely to receive a disciplinary ruling by an ethics committee.

Many of the Model Rules involve the special relationship the attorney has with the client. The separation of professional and personal responsibility poses difficult issues. Many lawyers feel that loyalty to the client is paramount to their duties as a professional. This loyalty surpasses and eclipses individual and private decisions, and the special relationship said to exist between lawyer and client justifies decisions when the client's interests are at stake that might otherwise be deemed unacceptable. An extreme position is that the attorney is no more than the legal agent of the client. The lawyer is neither immoral nor moral, but merely a legal tool. This position is represented by the statement "I am a lawyer, first and foremost." A more moderate position is that the loyalty to the client presents a special relationship between client and lawyer, similar to that between mother and child or trusted friends. This protected relationship justifies fewer actions than the one described above. Utilitarianism supports the special relationship in that it benefits us all to have these relationships available (Fried 1986, 136). The ethics of care may also be used to support this position since the focus on the special relationship with and needs of the client is consistent with this ethical system. Many people reject this perspective and regard lawyers as individuals who must take personal responsibility for their decisions. They are perceived as the legal *and* moral agents of their clients, rather than merely the legal agent. Their personal responsibility to avoid wrongdoing precludes involving themselves in their clients' wrongdoing (Postema 1986, 168). This position is represented by the statement "I am a person first, lawyer second."

Elliott Cohen (1991), an advocate of the "moral agent" position, believes that to be purely a legal advocate is inconsistent with being a morally good person in several ways. For instance, the virtue of justice would be inconsistent with a zealous advocate who would maximize the chance of his or her client's winning, regardless of the fairness of the outcome. A pure legal agent would sacrifice values of truthfulness, moral courage, benevolence, trustworthiness, and moral autonomy. Only if the attorney is a moral agent, as well as a legal advocate, can there be any possibility of the attorney's maintaining individual morality. Cohen (1991, 135–36) suggests some principles attorneys must follow to be consistent with both goals:

1. Treat others as ends in themselves and not as mere means to winning cases.
2. Treat clients and other professional relations who are relatively similar in a similar fashion.
3. Do not deliberately engage in behavior apt to deceive the court as to the truth.
4. Be willing, if necessary, to make reasonable personal sacrifices—of time, money, popularity, and so on—for what you justifiably believe to be a morally good cause.
5. Do not give money to, or accept money from, clients for wrongful purposes or in wrongful amounts.
6. Avoid harming others in the process of representing your client.
7. Be loyal to your client and do not betray his confidences.
8. Make your own moral decisions to the best of your ability and act consistently upon them.

The rationale for these principles seems to be an amalgamation of ethical formalism, utilitarianism, and other ethical frameworks. Some may seem impossible to uphold; for instance, it may be difficult to avoid harming others when representing a client in an adversary role. There are losers and winners in civil contests, as well as in criminal law, and lawyers must accept responsibility for the fact that sometimes the loser is harmed in financial or emotional ways.

The Model Code of Professional Responsibility for attorneys dictated that they should "be temperate and dignified" and "refrain from all illegal and morally reprehensible conduct." The Model Rules expect that "a lawyer's conduct should conform to the requirements of the law, both in professional service to clients and in the lawyer's business and personal affairs." These are similar prescriptions to those found in the Law Enforcement Code of Ethics. Both groups of professionals are expected to uphold a higher standard of behavior than the general public. They provide protection and help enforce the rules of behavior for the rest of us. Since both professions have a special place in society's attempt to control individual behavior, it is not inconsistent to expect a higher standard of behavior to apply.

USE OF DISCRETION

Although the issues of force and authority do not arise with legal professionals in the same manner as they do with law enforcement and correctional professionals, the power of discretion is shared. Discretion exists at every stage of the criminal justice system; professionals at each stage have the power to use their discretion wisely and ethically, or for self-interest and other unethical purposes. In the courts, prosecutors have discretion to charge and pursue prosecution, defense attorneys have discretion to accept or refuse cases and choose trial tactics, and judges have discretion to make rulings on evidence and other trial procedures, as well as convictions and sentences.

One view of law is that it is neutral and objective. Law and the formal rules of law are the focal points of decision making (Pinkele and Louthan 1985, 9). The reality is that lawmakers, law enforcers, and lawgivers have a great deal of discretion in making and interpreting the law. Law is political in that it is responsive to power interests. Far from being absolute or objective, the law is a dynamic, ever-changing symbol of political will. Just as lawmaking and interpretation are influenced by political will and power groups, individual lawgivers and those who work in the system also have a great deal of discretion in interpreting and enforcing the law. For instance, the Supreme Court interprets constitutional or legislative intent, and these interpretations are far from being neutral or inviolate. This is not to say that discretion exists unfettered or operates in unsystematic ways. Louthan (1985, 14) offers the following observation:

> For some, discretion is "law without order," "the authority to make decisions according to one's own judgment . . . ," the "departure from legal rules"; in short, "normlessness." Others, though, would contend that while discretion may refer to a procedural context of decisions reached informally, it does not necessarily imply that decisions are made on an ad hoc

basis, without order, and without reference to some kind of directional norm. Indeed, it can be argued that discretionary behavior itself becomes routine, that the environment of decision is one in which the actor thinks as much (maybe simultaneously, maybe first) about the norms or folkways of discretion and its related currencies of informal exchange as he does about what may be required by the rule of law.

If we accept that discretion is an operating reality in the justice system, then we must ask in what ways legal professionals use this discretion. If individual value systems replace absolute rules or laws, then these individual value systems may be ethical or unethical. For instance, even if we decided that discretion is morally acceptable, there might be problems with how it is used. Judges might base their decisions on a concept of fairness, or they might instead base their decisions on a prejudiced perception that blacks are always more criminal so they deserve longer sentences or that women are not dangerous so should get probation. In these examples, the discretion is misused because prejudicial values take the place of the concept of fairness. Judges' rulings on objections are supposed to be based on rules of evidence, but sometimes there is room for interpretation and individual discretion. Some judges use this discretion appropriately and make decisions in a best effort to conform to the rules, but other judges use arbitrary or unfair criteria, such as personal dislike of an attorney, or in the case of one particular judge, awarding favorable rulings to each attorney by turns regardless of the merit of the objection.

In our legal system, discretionary decisions at the trial level can be reexamined through the process of appeal. Appeals are part of due process in that they serve as a check on the decision making of trial judges. Any gross errors will be corrected; any extremely unethical actions will result in a retrial. However, appeals are not conducted in all cases, and even in cases that are appealed, many errors go unnoticed and uncorrected. Courtroom behavior, for instance, is seldom noticed or corrected unless it extremely and blatantly violates constitutional rights.

The remainder of this chapter will explore the use of discretion in the courts by looking at the role responsibilities of the major actors in the system—namely, the defense attorney, the prosecutor, and the judge. Obviously, these actors work with a criminal code that is handed down to them by the legislature. The formation of laws, and the factors and compromises that go into a law's creation or revision, is a subject unto itself. We will address the ethical questions that arise in the implementation, rather than the creation, of law.

ETHICAL ISSUES FOR DEFENSE ATTORNEYS

The role of the defense attorney is to protect the due process rights of the defendant. Due process is supposed to minimize mistakes in judicial proceedings that might result in a deprivation of life, liberty, or property. Due process rights, including notice, neutral fact finders, cross-examination, presentation of evidence and witnesses, and so on, are supposed to minimize the risk of error. The defense attorney is present to ensure that these rights are protected—for instance, during interrogation to make sure no co-ercion is used; at lineup to make sure it is fair and unbiased; and during trial to ensure adequate defense and cross-examination. The pure role of advocate is contradictory to the reality that the defense attorney must, if he or she is to work with the other actors in the court system, accommodate their needs as well as those of clients.

Defense attorneys have a fairly negative reputation in the legal community, as well as with the general public. They are seen as incompetent and/or unable to compete on the higher rungs of the status ladder of law, those higher rungs being corporate, tax, and international law. Alternatively or additionally, they are seen as "shady" or "money grubbers" who get the guilty off by sleazy tactics. In fiction, defense attorneys are presented as either fearless crusaders who always manage to defend innocent cli-ents (usually against unethical prosecutors); or as sleazy dealmakers who are either too burned out or egoistic to care about their clients. The reality fits neither of these por-trayals. Kittel (1990) finds that the majority of defense attorneys would not change their career given an opportunity to do so and most chose their career because they were interested in the trial work it offered or for public policy reasons, as opposed to the common myth that criminal defense attorneys enter that field because they couldn't make it anywhere else.

As mentioned earlier, the system tends to operate under a presumption of guilt. Indeed, defense attorneys are often in the position of defending clients they know are guilty. The rationale for defending a guilty person is, of course, that a person deserves due process before a finding of guilt and punishment. Before punishment can be mor-ally imposed, a fair procedure must ensure the punishment is appropriate. To ensure appropriate punishment, a set of fact-finding procedures is necessary, and the defense attorney's role is to make sure the rules are followed. If defense attorneys are doing their job, then we can all be comfortable with a conviction. If they do not do their job, then we have no system of justice, and none of us is safe from wrongful prosecution. Due process protects us all by making the criminal justice system prove wrongdoing fairly; the person who makes sure no shortcuts are taken is the defense attorney.

In the early 1990s the ABA promulgated Standards for Criminal Justice. "The De-fense Function," Chapter 4, covers a multitude of issues such as the function of defense counsel, punctuality, public statements, duty to the administration of justice, access, the lawyer-client relationship, duty to investigate, control and direction of litigation, plea bargaining, trial conduct, and appeal. These standards are summarized in Appen-dix B. One sees that they are much more specific than the Law Enforcement Code of Ethics. Instead of being aspirational, these standards are guidelines for behavior. They are not, however, strict rules the violation of which would result in disciplinary action. In this section, we will explore only a few of the many different ethical issues that con-front defense attorneys in their representation of clients.

Responsibility to the Client

The basic duty defense counsel owes to the administration of justice and as an officer of the court is to serve as the accused's counselor and advocate with courage and devotion and to render effective, quality representation. (Standard 4-1.2[b])

Defense attorneys are always in the position of balancing the rights of the individual client against overall effectiveness. Extreme attempts to protect these rights will reduce the defense attorney's effectiveness for other clients. Furthermore, defense attorneys must balance the needs and problems of the client against their ethical responsibilities to the system and profession.

A lawyer is supposed to provide legal assistance to clients without regard for personal preference or interest. A lawyer is not allowed to withdraw from a case simply because he or she no longer wishes to represent the client; only if the legal action is for harassment or malicious purposes, if continued employment will result in a violation of a disciplinary rule, if discharged by a client, or if a mental or physical condition renders effective counsel impossible can a lawyer be mandatorily withdrawn. In other cases, a judge may grant permission to withdraw when the client insists upon illegal or unethical actions, is uncooperative and does not follow the attorney's advice, or otherwise makes effective counsel difficult. Legal ethics mandate that people with unpopular causes and individuals who are obviously guilty still deserve counsel, and it is the ethical duty of an attorney to provide such counsel. In fact, although many people condemn attorneys and especially the American Civil Liberties Union for defending such groups as the American Nazi Party or the Ku Klux Klan or such individuals as Charles Manson or notorious drug dealers, clearly they could not do otherwise under their own ethical principles.

Some lawyers have no problem at all with defending "unworthy" clients. Drug cases are becoming well known as lawyers' pork barrels. Many lawyers have made millions of dollars defending major drug smugglers and dealers, sometimes on a retainer. In effect, they share in the wealth generated by illegal drugs. Is it ethical to take any client able to pay large and continuing bills? It is commonly believed that anytime a criminal defendant can and will pay, a lawyer can always be found to take the case to trial and conduct innumerable appeals, no matter what the likelihood of winning.

Recently, the government has started using provisions under the Racketeer Influenced and Corrupt Organizations Statute (18 U.S.C. Sections 1961–68), usually referred to as RICO, to confiscate drug money, including fees already paid to attorneys. Defense attorneys object to this practice, protesting that it endangers fair representation for drug defendants because attorneys may be less willing to defend these clients when there is a possibility that their fees will be confiscated. Some prosecutors, it should be noted, have gone a step further and are starting to prosecute attorneys themselves if there is evidence that an attorney is engaged in a continuing conspiracy to further a criminal enterprise by his or her association with the client. This use of the RICO statute is extremely controversial, as are other uses of it that will be discussed later.

Many people are firmly convinced that the quality of legal representation is directly related to the thickness of the defendant's wallet. When people can make bail and afford private attorneys, do they receive better justice? Do defense attorneys exert more effort for clients who pay well than they do for court-appointed clients? Obviously, professional ethics would dictate equal consideration, but individual values also affect behavior. If an attorney felt confident that his or her court-appointed clients received at least adequate representation, then could one not justify a more zealous defense for a paying client? Where adequate representation is vaguely and poorly defined, this question is even more problematic.

Confidentiality

Defense counsel should not reveal information relating to representation of a client unless the client consents after consultation, except for disclosures that are impliedly authorized in order to carry out the representation and except that defense counsel may reveal such information to the extent he or she reasonably believes necessary to prevent the client from committing a criminal act that defense counsel believes is likely to result in imminent death or substantial bodily harm. (Standard 4-3.7[d])

Attorney-client privilege refers to the confidentiality that exists in the communication between the two. The confidentiality protection is said to be inherent in the fiduciary relationship between the client and the attorney, but more important is that the client must be able to expect and receive the full and complete assistance of his or her lawyer. If a client feels compelled to withhold negative and incriminatory information, he or she will not be able to receive such assistance; thus, the lawyer must be perceived as a completely confidential agent of the client. Parallels to the attorney-client relationships are relationships between spouses and the priest-penitent relationship. In these cases the relationship creates a legal entity that approximates a single interest rather than two, and a break in confidentiality would violate the Fifth Amendment protection against self-incrimination (Schoeman 1982, 260).

The only situations wherein a lawyer can ethically reveal confidences of a client are when the client consents, when disclosure is required by law or court order, when the intention of the client is to commit a crime and the information is necessary to prevent the crime, or when one needs to defend oneself or employees against an accusation of wrongful conduct. In the following situation described by Harris (1986, 116), none of these factors applied; therefore, the lawyers felt ethically bound to withhold the location of two bodies from the families of the victims.

In July 1973, Robert Garrow, a 38-year-old mechanic from Syracuse, New York, killed four persons, apparently at random. The four were camping in the Adirondack Mountains. In early August, following a vigorous manhunt, he was captured by state police and indicted for the murder of a student from Schenectady. At the time of the arrest, no evidence connected Garrow to the other deaths. . . . The court appointed two Syracuse lawyers, Francis R. Belge and Frank H. Armani, to defend Garrow.

Some weeks later, during discussions with his two lawyers, Garrow told them that he had raped and killed a woman in a mine shaft. Belge and Armani located the mine shaft and the body of the Illinois woman but did not take their discovery to the police. The body was finally discovered four months later by two children playing in the mine. In September, the lawyers found the second body by following Garrow's directions. This discovery, too, went unreported; the girl's body was uncovered by a student in December.

Belge and Armani maintained their silence until the following June. Then, to try to show that he was insane, Garrow made statements from the witness stand that implicated him in the other three murders. At a press conference the next day, Belge and Armani outlined for the first time the sequence of events.

The local community was outraged. The lawyers, however, believed they had honored the letter and spirit of their professional duty in a tough case. "We both, knowing how the parents feel, wanted to advise them where the bodies were," Belge said, "but since it was a privileged communication, we could not reveal any information that was given to us in confidence."

Their silence was based on the legal code that admonishes the lawyer to "preserve the confidence and secrets of a client." The lawyer-client "privilege" against disclosure of confidences is one of the oldest and most ironclad in the law. If the defendant has no duty to confess his guilt or complicity in a crime, it can make no sense to assert that his lawyer has such a duty. Otherwise, the argument goes, the accused will tell his lawyer at best a deficient version of the facts, and the lawyer cannot as effectively defend the client. This argument frequently seems unconvincing; it certainly did to the people of Syracuse.

The author goes on to evaluate the actions of the two lawyers under the utilitarian ethical framework and decides that they did the right thing since it would be ethically acceptable for lawyers to break client confidentiality only in cases in which a death or crime could be prevented by disclosure. This formulation is, as always, based on the greatest utility for society, and it is believed that society benefits in the long run from attorney-client confidence. Therefore, it should be sacrificed only when the confidence endangers a life.

Religious ethics might condemn the attorneys' actions since lying to the parents who sought information was a form of deception. On the other hand, in the Catholic religion, a similar ethical dilemma might arise because of the confidentiality of the priest-penitent relationship. In that example, it would be impossible for the priest to betray a confession no matter what the circumstances. Ethical formalism also is difficult to reconcile with the lawyers' actions. First of all, under the categorical imperative, the lawyers' actions must be such that we would be willing for all others to engage in similar behavior under like circumstances. Could one will that it become universal law for attorneys to keep such information secret? What if you were the parents who did not know the whereabouts of their daughter or even if she was alive or dead? It is hard to imagine that they would be willing to agree with this universal law. On the other hand, ethical formalism is also concerned with duty, and it is the duty of the attorney to protect his or her client. There may be a formulation of the confidentiality rule that could pass the universalism principle. The ethical rule that allows confidentiality to be breached to prevent future crime is consistent with both utilitarianism and ethical formalism principles.

The ethics of care would be concerned with the needs of both the client and the parents in the case described. It would perhaps resolve the issue in a less absolutist fashion than the other rationales. For instance, when discussing this case in a college classroom, many students immediately decide that they would call in the location of the bodies anonymously, thereby relieving the parents' anxiety and also protecting to some extent the confidential communication. While this compromise is unsupported by an absolute view of confidentiality since it endangers the client (he would not even be charged with the crimes if the bodies were never found), it protects the relationship of the attorney and the client and still meets the needs of the parents.

A defense attorney's ethics may also be compromised when a client insists on taking the stand to commit perjury. Disciplinary rules specifically forbid the lawyer from allowing perjury to take place; if it happens before the attorney realizes the intent of the client, the defense must not use or refer to the perjured testimony (Freedman 1986; Kleinig 1986). But if the attorney appears to disbelieve or discredit his or her client, then this behavior violates the ethical mandate of zealous defense. Pellicciotti (1990) contends that the attorney must take an active stand against perjured testimony when he or she knows that it is untruthful by trying to dissuade the client from lying if the attorney knows in advance what is contemplated, by informing the court, by withdrawing from the case, or by another means. If the attorney merely suspects the information is perjured, then Pellicciotti instructs that ethics requires the attorney to proceed and give the defendant the best defense possible, even though the attorney may himself or herself have doubts. Of course, this then raises the question as to whether it is ethical for attorneys to tell their clients, "Before you say anything, I need to tell you that I cannot participate in perjury and if I know for a fact that you plan to lie, I cannot put you on the stand." Defense attorneys often explain that they don't bother to inquire as to guilt or innocence in the first place because their clients more often than not lie to them, so they proceed with the defense wanting to know only pertinent information rather than an admission of guilt. The approach of defending someone without regard to guilt or innocence and without wanting to know may be problematic in itself.

Conflicts of Interest

Defense counsel should not permit his or her professional judgment or obligations to be affected by his or her own political, business, property, or personal interests. (Standard 4-3.5[a])

Attorneys are specifically prohibited from engaging in representations that would compromise their loyalty to their clients. Specifically, attorneys must not represent clients who may have interests that conflict with those of the attorney—for instance, a client who owns a company that is a rival to one in which the attorney has an interest. The attorney also must not represent two clients who may have opposing interests—for instance, codefendants in a criminal case, since very often one will testify against the other. The attorney would find it impossible in such a situation to represent each individual fairly. Disciplinary rules even prohibit two lawyers from a single firm from representing clients with conflicting interests. In some informal and formal decisions from ethics committees, this rule has even been used to prohibit legal aid or public defender offices from defending codefendants (American Bar Association 1986).

Although attorneys may not ethically accept clients with conflicting interests, there is no guidance on the more abstract problem that all criminal clients in a caseload have conflicting interests in that their cases are often looked upon as part of a workload rather than considered separately. Many defense attorneys make a living by taking cases from people with very modest means or taking court-appointed cases where the fee is set by the court. The defense attorney then becomes a fast food lawyer, depending on volume and speed to make a profit. What happens here, of course, is that quality may get sacrificed along the way. When lawyers pick up clients in the hallways of courtrooms and from bail bondsmen referrals, the goal is to arrange bail, get a plea bargain, and move on to the next case. Guilt or innocence has very little to do with this operation and rarely does the case come to trial.

About 90 percent of the cases in the criminal justice system are settled by a plea bargain (Senna and Siegel 1987, 310). The defense attorney's goal in plea bargaining is to get the best possible deal for the client—namely, probation or the shortest prison sentence the prosecutor is willing to give for a guilty plea. The defense attorney also has to be aware that he or she cannot push to the limit in every case, since usually the prosecutor and defense attorney have an ongoing relationship. A courtroom appearance may be an isolated event for the client, but for the defense attorney and prosecutor, it is an ongoing, weekly ritual—only the names change. Because of the nature of the continuing relationship, the defense attorney must weigh present needs against future gains. If the defense becomes known as unwilling to play ball, reduced effectiveness may hurt future clients.

Most conclude that plea bargaining, even if not exactly "right," is certainly efficient and probably inevitable. Even in those jurisdictions that have moved to determinate sentencing, what has happened is that plea bargaining has become charge bargaining instead of sentence bargaining. Should we measure the morality of an action by its efficiency? This efficiency argument is similar to that used to defend some deceptive investigative practices of police. The goals of the system—crime control or bureaucratic efficiency—may be contrary to individual rights. Obviously, plea bargaining would fail under the categorical imperative, since the individual is treated as a means in the argument that plea bargaining is good for the system. Utilitarian theory may or may not be used to justify plea bargaining, depending on how one calculates the long-term effects it has on society's views toward the justice system. It is possible that plea bargaining undermines society's sense of justice and thus cannot be justified even under utilitarianism.

Even if we do approve of plea bargaining because of its benefits to the system, what about practices that take place within plea bargaining, such as trading cases, or "train justice"? When a defense attorney has several cases to bargain, he or she may trade off on some to get better deals for others. Can any ethical system justify this practice? Clearly, conflicts of interest may exist even when clients are not related or associated in any way.

Another conflict of interest may occur if the attorney desires to represent the client's interests in selling literary or media rights. Standard 4-3.4 specifically forbids entering into such agreements before the case is complete. The temptations are obvious—if the attorney hopes to acquire financial rewards from a share of profits, his or her professional judgment on how best to defend the client may be clouded. Whether putting off signing such an agreement until the case is complete removes the possibility of unethical decisions is debatable.

Zealous Defense

Defense counsel, in common with all members of the bar, is subject to standards of conduct stated in statutes, rules, decisions of courts, and codes, canons, or other standards of professional conduct. Defense counsel has no duty to execute any directive of the accused which does not comport with law or such standards. Defense counsel is the professional representative of the accused, not the accused's alter ego. (Standard 4-1.2[e])

Few would challenge the idea that all people deserve to have their due process rights protected. What many people find unsettling, however, is the zeal with which some defense attorneys approach the courtroom contest. For instance, how diligent should the defense be in protecting the defendant's rights? An inconsistency may arise between providing an effective defense and maintaining professional ethics and individual morality. Lawyers should represent clients zealously within the bounds of the law, but the law is sometimes vague and difficult to determine. Some actions are simply forbidden. The lawyer may not engage in motions or actions to intentionally and maliciously harm others, knowingly advance unwarranted claims or defenses, conceal or fail to disclose that which he or she is required by law to reveal, knowingly use perjured testimony or false evidence, knowingly make a false statement of law or fact, participate in the creation or preservation of evidence when he or she knows or it is obvious that the evidence is false, counsel the client in conduct that is illegal, or engage in other illegal conduct. The attorney is also expected to maintain a professional and courteous relationship with the opposing attorneys, litigants, and witnesses and to refrain from disparaging statements or badgering conduct. The defense attorney must not intimidate or otherwise influence the jury or trier of fact or use the media for these purposes.

Despite these ethical rules, practices such as withholding evidence, manufacturing evidence, witness badgering, and defamation of victims' characters are commonly used tactics in the defense arsenal. For instance, the sexual history of rape victims has been brought out purely to cast doubt on the character of the rape victim and persuade the jury to believe she deserved or asked for her rape. It may be the case that the evidence against a client is so overwhelming the only thing left for the defense attorney is to try and attack the credibility of witnesses. In some cases defense attorneys go to extreme lengths to change the course of testimony, for example, by bribing witnesses or not stopping the client from intimidating the witness. These cases are rare, of course, but they are not unheard of.

Defense attorneys may sacrifice their integrity for the sake of a case. For instance, in one trial, the defense attorney and prosecutor were getting ready to try a barroom murder case. The prosecutor was able to present only one eyewitness to the shooting— the bartender. No one else in the bar was willing to testify that they saw anything. The prosecutor had other circumstantial evidence of the defendant's guilt, but the eyewitness was crucial. Unfortunately, the bartender had a ten-year-old murder conviction— a fact that would reduce his credibility in the jury's eyes. This fact could be brought out by the defense under the rules of evidence; however, the prosecutor could petition the court to have the fact suppressed and had a good chance of succeeding since it bore no relevance to the case and would be prejudicial, but she did not file the appropriate motion. Just before the trial was about to start, the prosecutor asked the defense attorney if he was going to bring out this fact on his cross-examination of the bartender. If he planned to do so, the prosecutor would have asked for a continuance and filed a motion to have it suppressed, or at least brought it out herself on direct to reduce its impact. He told her specifically and clearly that he had no intention of using that information or questioning the witness about it since it was so long ago and irrelevant to the case. When the direct examination of this witness was over and the defense attorney started his cross-examination, his first question was "Isn't it true that you were convicted of murder in 19—?" While the prosecutor may have committed an error in judgment by trusting the defense attorney, the defense attorney deliberately misled the prosecutor as to his intentions—he lied. If a defense attorney makes a practice of such tactics, he or she will quickly develop a reputation as untrustworthy and find that prosecutors will not cooperate with his requests for continuances or other favors. Zealous defense is a weak rationale for lying. When asked about his actions, the defense attorney explained that it "just slipped out" and complained that the prosecutor took these things "too seriously." This behavior is an example of an unethical decision used for short-term gain, an egoistic rationalization, and a view of due process as a game since when an opponent is offended by a lie, she is taking things "too seriously."

A recent innovation in trial tactics is the development of "scientific" jury selection. Attorneys often contend that a trial has already been won or lost once the jury has been selected. Whether or not this is true, attorneys are becoming increasingly sophisticated in their methods of choosing which members of a jury panel would make good jurors. A good juror is defined not as one who is unbiased and fair, but as someone who is predisposed to be sympathetic to that attorney's case. The ability to use these methods is limited only by a budget. Some lawyers, such as the famed "Racehorse" Haynes in Houston, have used methods such as surveying a large sample of the population in the community where the case is to be tried to discover how certain demographic groups feel about issues relevant to the case so that these findings can be used when the jury is selected. Other attorneys hire jury experts, psychologists who sit with the attorney and through a combination of nonverbal and verbal clues, identify those jury panel members who are predisposed to believe the case presented by the attorney. Another method uses a "shadow jury"—a panel of people selected by the defense attorney to represent the actual jury that sits through the trial and provides feedback to the attorney on the evidence being presented during the trial. This allows the attorney to adjust his or her trial tactics in response. Some of these methods were used in the William Kennedy Smith rape trial in Florida, which resulted in an acquittal. While attorneys have always used intuition and less sophisticated means to decide which jury members to exclude, these tactics are questioned by some as too contrary to the basic idea that a trial is supposed to start with an unbiased jury (Smith and Meyer 1987).

While bribery and suppression of evidence are not difficult to identify as unethical practices, it is more difficult to determine when a defense attorney's treatment of a witness is badgering as opposed to energetic cross-examination or when exploring a witness's background is character assassination as opposed to a careful examination of credibility. Other trial tactics include putting the opposing attorney at a disadvantage by aggressive personal attacks or allegations of incompetence. Female attorneys have reported that male opponents use paternalism in an effort to infantilize or feminize the female attorney to reduce her credibility with the jury. The line where zealous defense stops and unethical practices begin is difficult to determine.

ETHICAL ISSUES FOR PROSECUTORS

As the second line of decision makers in the system, prosecutors have extremely broad powers of discretion. The prosecutor acts like a strainer—he or she collects some cases for formal prosecution while eliminating a great many others. Because of limited resources, full enforcement of the law is impossible. Also, the severity of the criminal law may be inappropriate to some situations; thus, there is a need for discretion so that these cases may be diverted.

To guide discretion, there are ethical standards relating specifically to the role of the prosecutor. Chapter 3 of the ABA Standards for Criminal Justice covers the prosecution function; it is summarized in Appendix C. These standards cover topics similar to those for defense attorneys, but they also make special note of the unique role of the prosecutor as a representative of the court system and the state, rather than a pure advocate.

Use of Discretion

> A prosecutor should not institute, or cause to be instituted, or permit the continued pendency of criminal charges when the prosecutor knows that the charges are not supported by probable cause. A prosecutor should not institute, cause to be instituted, or permit the continued pendency of criminal charges in the absence of sufficient admissible evidence to support a conviction. (Standard 3-3.9[a])

The prosecutor must seek justice, not merely a conviction. Toward this end, prosecutors must share evidence, use restraint in the use of their power, represent the public interest, and give the accused the benefit of reasonable doubt. Disciplinary rules are more specific: they specifically forbid the prosecutor from pursuing charges when there is no probable cause and mandate timely disclosure to defense counsel of evidence, especially exculpatory evidence or evidence that might mitigate guilt or reduce the punishment.

One court has described the prosecutor's functions in the following way (*State v. Moynahan*, 164 Conn. 560, 325 A.2d 199, 206; cert. denied, 414 U.S. 976 [1973]):

> As a representative of the people of the state, [the prosecutor] is under a duty not solely to obtain convictions but, more importantly, (1) to determine that there is reasonable ground

to proceed with a criminal charge [citation omitted]; (2) to see that impartial justice is done the guilty as well as the innocent; and (3) to ensure that all evidence tending to aid in the ascertaining of the truth be laid before the court, whether it be consistent with the contention of the prosecution that the accused is guilty.

Despite these ideals of prosecutorial duty, an individual factor in prosecutorial discretion is that prosecutors want to and must win; therefore, their choice of cases is influenced by this value, whether it is ethically acceptable or not. Law enforcement considerations also influence prosecutorial action. If there is a bargain to be struck with an informant, if a lesser charge will result in testifying or uncovering information that could lead to further convictions, then this is considered in decision making. Finally, the pressure of public opinion is a factor to consider. Prosecutors may pursue cases they might otherwise have dropped if there is a great deal of public interest in the case.

Prosecutors can elect to charge or not; their decision is influenced by political pressures, the chance for conviction, the severity of the crime, prison population, a "gut feeling" of guilt or innocence, and the weight of evidence. The prosecutorial role is to seek justice, but justice doesn't mean the same thing to everyone and certainly does not entail prosecuting everyone to the fullest extent of the law. Whether to charge or not is one of the most important decisions of the criminal justice process. The decision should be fair, neutral, and guided by due process, but this is an ideal; often many other considerations enter into the decision. Prosecutors don't usually use their charging power for intimidation or harassment, but personal factors may be involved in charging, such as a particular interest in a type of crime, such as child abuse, or public pressure over a particular crime that impels the prosecutor to charge somebody quickly, as in serial rape or murder. As in charging, the decision not to charge is open to ethical questions. To give one person who participated in a brutal crime immunity to gain testimony against others is efficient, but is it consistent with justice? Should such an individual escape punishment for betraying his or her friends? To not charge business-people with blue law violations because they are good citizens is questionable if other businesses are prosecuted for other ordinances.

Various studies have attempted to describe prosecutor decision making; one cites office policy as an important influence. *Legal sufficiency* is an office policy that weeds out those cases where the evidence is not strong enough to support further action. *System efficiency* is an office policy with goals of efficiency and accountability; all decisions are made with these goals in mind, so many cases result in dismissals. Another policy is *defendant rehabilitation*, which emphasizes diversion and other rehabilitation tools rather than punitive goals. Finally, *trial sufficiency* is an office policy that encourages a permanent definition of the charge to stick with through trial (Jaccoby, Mellon, and Smith 1980).

Another study looks at the prosecutor as operating in an exchange system. The relationship between the prosecutor and the police is described as one of give-and-take. Prosecutors balance police needs or wishes against their own vulnerability. The prosecutor makes personal judgments as to which police officers can be trusted. Exchange also takes place between the prosecutor's office and the courts. When jails become overcrowded, deferred adjudication and probation may be recommended more often; when dockets become impossible, charges may be dropped. Finally, exchange takes place between defense attorneys and prosecutors, especially since many defense attorneys have previously served as prosecutors and may be personally familiar with the procedures and even the personalities in the prosecutor's office (Cole 1970).

Discretion is considered essential to the prosecutorial function of promoting individualized justice and softening the impersonal effects of the law. On the other hand, discretion is the key element in perceptions of the legal system as unfair and biased toward certain groups of people or individuals. Solutions to the problem of prosecutorial discretion may include regulation or internal guidelines. For instance, an office policy might include a procedure for providing written reasons for dropping charges; this procedure would respond to charges of unbridled discretion.

Conflicts of Interest

A prosecutor should avoid a conflict of interest with respect to his or her official duties. (Standard 3.1-3[a])

Part-time prosecutors present a host of ethical issues. A Bureau of Justice Statistics (1992) bulletin reported that 47 percent of prosecutors held their jobs as a part-time occupation. Obviously, there is the possibility of a conflict of interest. It may happen that a part-time prosecutor has a private practice, and situations may occur where the duty to a private client runs counter to the prosecutor's duty to the public. In some cases, it may be that a client becomes a defendant, necessitating the prosecutor to either hire a special prosecutor or step aside as counsel. Even when no direct conflicts of interest exist, time is always a problem for part-time prosecutors. The division of time is between the private practice, where income is correlated with hard work, and prosecutorial cases, where income is fixed no matter how many hours are spent. Obviously, this may result in a less energetic prosecutorial function than one might wish.

It is well known that the prosecutor's job is a good stepping-stone to politics, and many use it as such. In these cases, one has to wonder whether cases are taken on the basis of merit or on their ability to place the prosecutor in the public eye and help his or her career. Winning becomes more important also. The prosecutor's relationship with the press is important. The media can be enemy or friend depending on how charismatic or forthcoming the prosecutor is in interviews. Sometimes cases are said to be tried in the newspapers—the defense attorney and the prosecutor stage verbal sparring matches for public consumption. Prosecutors may react to cases and judges' decisions in the newspapers, criticizing the decision or the sentence and in the process denigrating the dignity of the system.

The RICO statute has increasingly been used as a tool to confiscate property and money associated with organized criminal activity. Once this tactic was approved by the courts, a veritable flood of prosecutions began that were designed, it seems, primarily to obtain cash, boats, houses, and other property of drug dealers. Making decisions based on the potential for what can be confiscated rather than other factors is a very real and dangerous development in this type of prosecution.

Plea Bargaining

A prosecutor should not knowingly make false statements or representations as to fact or law in the course of plea discussions with defense counsel or the accused. (Standard 3-4.1[c])

Arguments given in defense of plea bargaining include heavy caseloads, limited resources, legislative overcriminalization, individualized justice, and legal problems of cases (legal errors that would result in mistrials or dropped charges if the client did not plead) (Knudten 1978, 275). If we concede that plea bargaining is an acceptable element of judicial processing, there are ethical guidelines for its use. Prosecutors may overcharge—that is, charge at a higher degree of severity or press more charges than could possibly be sustained by the evidence—so that they can bargain down. Prosecutors may even mislead defense attorneys about the amount of evidence or the kind of evidence they have or about the sentence they can offer to obtain a guilty plea. Only 36 percent of chief prosecutors reported that explicit criteria for plea bargains were in place in 1990 (Bureau of Justice Statistics 1992). Guidelines providing a range of years for certain types of charges would help the individual prosecutors maintain some level of consistency in a particular jurisdiction.

Zealous Prosecution

The duty of the prosecutor is to seek justice, not merely to convict. (Standard 3-1.2[c])

Just as the defense attorney is at times overly zealous in defense of clients, prosecutors may be overly ambitious to attain a conviction. Often one hears of appeals based on overlooked or ignored witnesses or other evidence. When prosecutors are preparing a case, they are putting a puzzle together and any piece of evidence that doesn't fit the puzzle is sometimes conveniently ignored. Witnesses with less than credible reasons for testifying are used if they help a case. Moreover, witness preparation by both defense attorneys and prosecutors is not necessarily unethical; however, it does tend to confuse the jury by having witnesses appear with false images. Dress, behavior, and response to questions are all carefully orchestrated to present the information in the most favorable light. Witnesses are not supposed to be paid, but their expenses can be reimbursed, and this may be incentive enough to say what they think the prosecutor wants to hear.

There are very few controls on the behavior of prosecutors in the courtroom. Voters have some control over who becomes a prosecutor, but once in office most prosecutors stay in the good graces of a voting public unless there is a major scandal or an energetic competitor. In cities, most work is conducted by assistant prosecutors who are hired rather than elected. Misconduct in the courtroom is sometimes verbally sanctioned by trial judges, and perhaps an appellate decision may overturn a conviction, but these events are rare. Gershman (1991) writes that prosecutors misbehave because it works and they can get away with it. Because misconduct is only scrutinized when the defense attorney makes an objection and then files an appeal, and even then the appellate court may rule that it was a harmless error, there is a great deal of incentive to use

improper tactics in the courtroom. Although some misconduct may result in a case being overturned, very seldom does the individual prosecutor face any personal penalties.

Ordinarily, then, prosecutors' misbehavior is unchecked; it may take the form of
persistent reference to illegal evidence, leading witnesses, nondisclosure of evidence to
the defense, appeals to emotions, and so on. One prosecutor admitted that early in his
career he sometimes made faces at the defendant while his back was to the jury and the
defense attorney wasn't looking. The jury saw the defendant glowering and looking angry for no discernible reason, which led to a negative perception of his sanity, temper,
or both. Of course, the defense attorney may be engaged in other unethical actions as
well, so the contest between them becomes one of effectiveness of methods rather than
an attempt to abide by the strictures of law or ethical considerations.

Expert Witnesses

A prosecutor who engages an expert for an opinion should respect the independence of the
expert and should not seek to dictate the formation of the expert's opinion on the subject.
(Standard 3-3.3[a])

Expert witnesses, who can receive a fee, are often accused of compromising their
integrity for money or notoriety. The use of expert witnesses has risen in recent years.
Psychiatrists often testify as to the mental competency or legal insanity of an accused.
Forensic experts have for many years testified regarding factual issues of evidence. Today, criminologists and other social scientists may be asked to testify on such topics as
victimization in prison, statistical evidence of sentencing discrimination, the effectiveness of predictive instruments for riots and other disturbances, risk assessment for individual offenders, mental health services in prison, patterns of criminality, the battered
woman syndrome, and so on. When the expert is honest in his or her presentation as to
the limitations and potential bias of the material, no ethical issues arise. However, expert witnesses may testify in a realm beyond fact or make testimony appear factual
when some questions are not clearly answerable. Because of the *halo effect*—essentially,
when a person with expertise or status in one area is given deference in all areas—an
expert witness may endow a statement or conclusion with more legitimacy than it may
warrant. When expert witnesses are used, they run the risk of having their credibility
attacked by the opposing side; credibility is obviously much easier to attack when a witness has attempted to present theory or supposition as fact or conclusion, either for
ideological reasons or because of pressure from zealous attorneys. Those who always
appear on either one side or the other may also lose their credibility. For instance, a
doctor who is used often by prosecutors in one jurisdiction during capital sentencing
hearings has become known as "Dr. Death" because he always determines that the defendant poses a future risk to society, which is one of the necessary elements for the
death penalty. While he is well known to both prosecutors and defense attorneys by
reputation, juries would not be expected to know of his predilection for finding future
dangerousness and would take his testimony at face value unless the defense attorney
bring this information out on cross-examination.

Competing expert witnesses who present entirely different "facts" to the jury create an atmosphere of cynicism and distrust. Expert witnesses can and do provide valuable contributions to the trial process. Ethical dilemmas can be avoided by clearly presenting the limits and biases of the information offered.

Turning to attorneys' actions, the use of expert witnesses can present ethical problems when the witness is used in a dishonest fashion. To pay an expert for time is not unethical, but to shop for experts until one is found who benefits the case may be, since the credibility of the witness is suspect. Experts are used to prove the truth of facts in essentially the same manner as eyewitnesses are used to prove facts. When eyewitnesses differ as to what they have seen, the explanation is that someone is either wrong or lying. It is no different with expert witnesses; however, since they profess to have extensive knowledge in the area, it is more difficult to conclude they are mistaken. Another difficulty is presented when one side obtains an expert who develops a conclusion or set of findings that would help the other side. Ethics do not prohibit a civil attorney from merely disregarding the information, without notice to the opponent of information that could benefit his or her case. However, prosecutors operate under a special set of ethics since their goal is justice, not pure advocacy. Any exculpatory information is supposed to be shared with the defense; this obviously includes test results and may also include expert witness findings.

Some ethical issues prosecutors are faced with are similar to those of defense attorneys, since they are, in a way, opposite players in the same game. However, they have a qualitatively different role because of their discretionary power in the decision-making process. Their discretion to charge dramatically affects defendants' lives. Their role as an officer of the court puts them in a very powerful position and, as such, results in different ethical standards for the prosecutor.

ETHICAL ISSUES FOR JUDGES

Perhaps the most popular symbol of justice is the judge in his or her black robe. Judges are expected to be impartial, knowledgeable, and authoritative. They guide the prosecutor, defense attorney, and all the other actors in the trial process from beginning to end, helping to maintain the integrity of the proceeding. This is the ideal, but judges are human, with human failings.

Ethical Guidelines

To help guide judges in their duties, a Code of Judicial Conduct was developed by the American Bar Association. This code identifies the special ethical considerations unique to judges. The primary theme of judicial ethics is impartiality. If we trust the judge to give objective rulings, then we must be confident that his or her objectivity isn't marred by any type of bias.

Judges may let their personal prejudices influence their decisions. To head off this possibility, the ABA's ethical guidelines specify that each judge should try to avoid all appearance of bias, as well as actual bias. Judges must be careful to avoid financial involvements or personal relationships that may threaten objectivity. We expect judges, like police officers, to conform to higher standards of behavior than the rest of us. Therefore, any hint of scandal in their private lives calls into question their professional ethics also. The obvious rationale is that judges who have less than admirable personal values cannot judge others objectively, and those judges who are less than honest in their financial dealings do not have a right to sit in judgment on others.

There are a number of problematic issues in the perceived objectivity of judges. For instance, in those states where judges are elected, the judges must solicit campaign contributions. These monies are most often obtained from attorneys, and it is not at all unusual for judges to accept money from attorneys who practice before them. Does this not provide at least the appearance of impropriety? This is exacerbated in jurisdictions that use court appointments as the method for indigent representation. In these jurisdictions, judges hand out appointments to the very same attorneys who give money back in the form of campaign contributions. Obviously, the appearance, if not the actuality, of bias is present in these jurisdictions.

Use of Discretion

Judges' discretion occurs in two major areas. The first area is in the interpretation of the law in court cases. For instance, a judge may be called upon to assess the legality of evidence and make rulings on the various objections raised by both the prosecutors and the defense attorneys. A judge also writes instructions to the jury, which set up the legal questions and definitions of the case. The second area of judicial discretion is in sentencing decisions.

Judges must rule on the legality of evidence; they may make a decision to exclude a confession or a piece of evidence because of the way it was obtained and by so doing may allow the guilty to go free. The exclusionary rule has generated a storm of controversy since it may result in a guilty party avoiding punishment because of an error committed by the police. The basis for the exclusionary rule is that one cannot accept a conviction on tainted evidence. The ideals of justice reject such a conviction because accepting tainted evidence, even if obtained against a guilty party, is a short step away from accepting any type of evidence, no matter how illegal, and thus poses a threat to the whole concept of due process. The conviction is so violative of due process that it is ruled void. A more practical argument for the exclusionary rule is that if we want police officers to behave in a legal manner, we must have heavy sanctions against illegalities. If convictions are lost due to illegal evidence collection, police may reform their behavior. Actual practice provides little support for this argument, though. Police have learned how to get around the exclusionary rule, and in any event, cases on appeal are so far removed from the day-to-day decision making of the police that they have little effect on police behavior. Recent court decisions have created several exceptions to the exclusionary rule, as discussed in Chapter 4. Judges who decide to exclude evidence and set aside convictions do so by disregarding short-term effects for more abstract principles—specifically, the protection of due process.

Ethical frameworks may or may not provide a rationale for the implementation of the exclusionary rule in a particular case. Religious ethics don't give us much help unless we decide that this ethical system would support vengeance and thus would permit the judge to ignore the exclusionary rule in order to punish a criminal. On the other hand, religious ethics might also support letting the criminal go free to answer to an ultimate higher authority, since human judgment was in this case imperfect. The categorical imperative would probably support the exclusionary rule since one would not want a universal law of accepting all tainted evidence. On the other hand, one would have to agree to retrying all criminals, regardless of the severity of the crime, whenever the evidence was tainted despite the possibility of further crime or harm to individuals. Act utilitarianism would support ignoring the exclusionary rule if the crime was especially serious or if there were a good chance that the offender would not be retried successfully. The utility derived from ignoring the rule would outweigh the good. However, rule utilitarianism could be used to support the exclusionary rule, since the long-term effect of allowing illegal police behavior would be more serious than letting one criminal go free.

The judge is called upon to decide many and various questions throughout a trial. He or she, of course, has the law and legal precedent as guidance, but in most cases each decision involves a substantial element of subjectivity. Judges have the power to make it difficult for either the prosecutor or the defense attorney through their pattern of rulings on objections, evidence admitted, and even personal attitude toward the attorney, which is always noted by the jury and is influential in their decision.

The second area of judicial discretion is in sentencing. The following makes clear the small amount of training judges receive for this awesome responsibility (Johnson 1982, 20):

> Few judges have the benefit of judicial training sessions prior to embarking upon the often bewildering and frequently frustrating task of pursuing that vague, if not indefinable, entity so commonly known as justice. . . . Thus, it is not uncommon for the new judge, relying upon a philosophy often formulated hastily, to be placed in the unenviable position of pronouncing a sentence upon another human being without any special preparation.

Judges' decisions are scrutinized by public watchdog groups and appellate-level courts. One wonders, in fact, if judges aren't overly influenced by the current clamor for strict punishments. On the other hand, if judges are supposed to enact community sentiment, perhaps it is proper for them to reflect its influence. Is there one just punishment for a certain type of offender, or does the definition of what is just depend on community opinion of the crime, the criminal, and the time?

Evidence indicates that the decision making of judges actually is based on personal standards, since no consistency seems to appear between the decisions of individual judges in the same community. One study found that two judges in Louisiana had remarkably different records on numbers of convictions. The two also differed in their patterns of sentencing (Pinkele and Louthan 1985, 58). It must be noted that others have found a general consistency among sentencing practices, and the system provides a basic, if rough, fairness in sentencing.

CONCLUSION

According to the basic tenets of our law, the accused is innocent until conviction. Prosecutors, judges, and defense attorneys are all officers of the court and as such are sworn to uphold the highest principles of our law, including the basic assumption of innocence. However, in the day-to-day operations of courthouse politics and bureaucracy, the rights of individuals may compete with the goal of efficient processing.

The presence and use of discretion in the criminal justice system is pervasive; however, discretion requires decision makers to depend on individual values and ethics rather than structured laws and rules.

DISCUSSION QUESTIONS

1. If you were a prosecutor, how would you decide which cases to prosecute?
2. What are the advantages and problems with plea bargaining?
3. Should someone get a reduced sentence for testifying against a crime partner?
4. Should defense attorneys shop for lenient judges, prepare witnesses, attack the credibility of witnesses, and engage in other actions designed to get the defendant the best chance of acquittal?
5. Should prosecutors overcharge to help them in plea bargaining, make deals with informants, allow doubtful testimony from witnesses, and other actions designed to get a conviction?
6. Would you be able to defend someone you knew was guilty?
7. Using moral and ethical criteria, analyze some recent innovations designed to improve crime prevention. Such innovations as preventive detention, neighborhood justice centers that mediate rather than find guilt or innocence, the use of a waiver to adult court for violent juvenile offenders, increased sentences for gang-related or drug-related crimes, and criminalization of nonpayment of child support are possibilities to consider.
8. Using ethical and moral criteria, evaluate recent courtroom procedures. Examples include videotaped testimony, allowing television cameras in the courtroom, and victim statements during sentencing.
9. Watch a movie that presents a legal dilemma (for example, *Criminal Law, Penalty Phase, Presumption of Innocence*) and analyze the dilemma using one of the ethical frameworks discussed in this book.

⊰ ETHICAL DILEMMAS ⊱

Please read and respond to the following situations. Be prepared to discuss your ideas.

Situation 1

You are a deputy prosecutor and have to decide whether or not to charge Joe Crum with possession and sale of a controlled substance. You know you have a good case because the guy sold to the local junior high school and many of the kids are willing to testify. The police are pressuring you to make a deal because he has promised to inform on other dealers in the area if you don't prosecute. What should you do?

Situation 2

Your first big case is a multiple murder. As defense attorney for Sy Kopath you have come to the realization that he really did break into a couple's home and torture and kill them in the course of robbing them of jewelry and other valuables. He has even confessed to you that he did it. You are also aware, however, that the police did not read him his Miranda warning and he was coerced into giving a confession without your presence. What should you do? Would your answer be different if you believed he was innocent or didn't know for sure either way?

Situation 3

You are a judge who must sentence two defendants. One insisted on a jury trial and, through his defense attorney, dragged the case on for months with delays and motions. He was finally convicted by a jury. The other individual was his codefendant and pleaded guilty. They were apparently equally responsible for the burglary. How would you sentence them?

Situation 4

You are a member of a jury. The case is a child molestation case where the defendant is accused of a series of molestations in his neighborhood. You have been advised by the judge not to discuss the case with anyone outside the courtroom and especially not to talk to anyone on either side of the case. Going down in the elevator after the fourth day of the trial, you overhear the prosecutor talking to one of the police officer witnesses. They are discussing the fact that the man has a previous arrest for child molestation but it has not been allowed in by the judge as too prejudicial to the jury. You were pretty sure the guy was guilty before, but now you definitely believe he is guilty. You also know that if you tell the judge what you have heard, it will probably result in a mistrial. What would you do?

Situation 5

You are a prosecutor in a jurisdiction that does not use the grand jury system. An elderly man has administered a lethal dose of sleeping tablets to his wife, who was suffering from Alzheimer's disease. He calmly turned himself in to the police department, and the case is on the front page of the paper. It is entirely up to you whether to charge him with murder or not. What would you do?

8

The Ethics of Punishment and Correction

Throughout this text, we have followed the individual's progress through the criminal justice system. We have explored each phase of the process from the writing of laws through police enforcement to trial and conviction. We have now reached the punishment phase. After someone has been found guilty of a criminal offense, an array of possible sanctions and treatments are possible. A suspended sentence may be given, restitution or community service may be ordered, or probation with stringent or not-so-stringent conditions may be required. If the crime is serious, the offender dangerous, or both, incarceration for a period of time ranging from one day to life is a possibility. During incarceration the wrongdoer may be required to participate in treatment programs ranging from self-help groups like Alcoholics Anonymous to psychosurgery. The ultimate sanction the state can impose, of course, is death.

According to one author (Leiser 1986, 198), several elements are essential to the definition of punishment:

1. There are at least two persons—one who inflicts the punishment and one who is punished.
2. The person who inflicts the punishment causes a certain harm, or unwanted treatment, to occur to the person who is being punished.
3. The person who inflicts the punishment has been authorized, under a system of rules or laws, to harm the person who is punished in the particular way in which he/she does.
4. The person who is being punished has been judged by a representative of that authority to have done what he or she is forbidden to do or to have failed to do what he or she is required to do by some rule or law to which he or she is subject.
5. The harm that is inflicted upon the person who is being punished is for the act or omission mentioned in Condition 4.

We need also to define treatment. According to correctional terminology, treatment may be anything used to induce behavioral change. The goal is to eliminate dysfunctional or deviant behavior and to encourage productive and normal behavior patterns. In prison, treatment includes diagnosis, classification, therapy of all sorts, education, religious activity, vocational training, and self-help groups.

Punishment and even treatment are usually limited by some rationale or guideline. For instance, von Hirsch (1976, 5) presents the following restrictive guidelines:

1. The liberty of each individual is to be protected so long as it is consistent with the liberty of others.
2. The state is obligated to observe strict parsimony in intervening in criminals' lives.
3. The state must justify each intrusion.
4. The requirements of justice ought to constrain the pursuit of crime prevention (that is, deterrence and rehabilitation).

We will explore "just deserts" versus deterrence and treatment more fully in the following pages. In this chapter, we will first explore the various rationales for punishment, look at capital punishment in particular, and then examine the ethical issues related to correctional personnel, in both institutional and community corrections.

RATIONALES FOR CORRECTIONS

Does society have the right to punish or correct miscreants? If it does, where does that right come from? The rationale for corrections and treatment comes from the social contract. In the same way that the social contract forms the basis for police power, it also provides a rationale for further control in the form of corrections. To review this concept: we avoid social chaos by giving the state the power to control us. In this way we protect ourselves from being victimized by others by giving up our liberty to aggress against others. If we do step outside the bounds, the state has the right to control and punish us for our transgression.

Corrections is a schizophrenic system paying homage to several masters, including the principles of retribution, reform, incapacitation, deterrence, and rehabilitation. The long-standing argument between proponents of punishment and proponents of treatment reveals a system without a clear mandate or rationale for action. Garland (1990) writes that even the state's goal of punishment is problematic since it is marked with inconsistencies between the intent and the implementation. The "moral contradictions" are that it seeks to uphold freedom by means of its deprivation and it condemns private violence by using state violence.

Can treatment and punishment occur at the same time? Or, as many critics argue, are correctional officials paying lip service to a treatment ethic while continuing to do the same things they've always done? Public opinion toward criminals has become more punitive, resulting in the virtual abandonment of the treatment ethic and rehabilitation as a goal. Such shifts in public opinion and consequent responses raise the question whether a punishment system in which sentencing and the definition of just punishment are relative and change with time and mood can ever be an ethical or moral one. Should there be some absolute sense of what constitutes a just punishment for a particular crime? Such a principle has never been recognized.

An important question to ask is: "Who are we punishing?" Studies show that only a very small minority of individuals who commit crimes end up in prison. A larger percentage, but by no means the majority of criminal offenders, receive correctional sanctions of some other kind. Therefore, a small number of individuals receive the sanctions deserved by many; furthermore, we may assume those small numbers are not representative of the larger population. Those in our jails and prisons are there not only because they committed crimes, but also because they are poor, members of a minority group, or powerless.

Those selected for punishment tend to commit certain types of crimes, and those who commit other crimes avoid the more punitive sanctions of the corrections system. For instance, big business routinely bilks consumers out of billions of dollars annually and then chalks up the punitive fines incurred to operating expenses, yet it would not be uncommon in some jurisdictions for a shoplifter to be sent to prison. Streams and land are routinely polluted by industrial waste, but again punitive fines are the typical sanctions, and these cannot begin to restore what has been taken away in the flagrant pursuit of financial profit. Very seldom do we see executives responsible for company policy go to prison. White-collar criminals routinely receive fines, probation, or short stays in halfway houses while so-called street criminals receive prison sentences. Many people question the justification of punishment when only a very small, select group of offenders is being punished.

Our view of criminals has changed several times over the course of history. Originally, criminals were viewed as sinners with no ability to change their behavior, and therefore punishment and incapacitation were seen as the only logical ways to respond to crime. Bentham (1748–1833) and Beccaria (1738–1794) viewed the criminal as rational and as having free will, and therefore saw the threat of punishment as a deterrent. Neoclassicists such as Quetelet (1796–1874) and Guerry (1802–1866) recognized that some groups of people could not be held entirely responsible for their actions and therefore believed that they should not be punished. The insane and the young were treated differently because they were considered moral infants, not possessing the sense to refrain from wrongdoing. Then the positivist school influenced thinking to the extent that all criminal acts were believed to be merely symptoms of an underlying pathology. The following quote from the 1870 Prison Congress (cited in Mitford 1971, 104) exemplifies this view:

A criminal is a man who has suffered under a disease evinced by the perpetration of a crime, and who may reasonably be held to be under the dominion of such disease until his conduct has afforded very strong presumption not only that he is free from its immediate influence, but that the chances of its recurrence have become exceedingly remote.

The treatment programs created in the last one hundred years or so operate under the assumption that we can do something to offenders to reduce their criminal activity. That "something" may involve treating a psychological problem, such as a sociopathic or paranoid personality; addressing social problems such as alcoholism or addiction; or resolving more pragmatic problems like chronic unemployment with vocational training and job placement. Obviously, the perception of the criminal influences the rationale for correction and punishment. The two major justifications for punishment and treatment are retribution and prevention. The retributive rationale postulates that punishment is an end in itself, while the preventive approach views punishment as a means rather than an end and embraces other responses to crime. The retributive rationale is probably more consistent with a view of the criminal as rational, and the preventive rationale, with certain exceptions, is more consistent with the view of the criminal as being less responsible for his or her behavior.

Retribution

As mentioned before, the social contract provides the rationale for punishment. As long as one is a member of society, one has implicitly agreed to society's rules and also to punishment when these rules are broken.

One criticism of the social contract theory is that it is completely contingent on a consensus perspective of society. That is, the members of society are assumed to share the same goals, beliefs, and power. The ideal state is one of agreement, which is seen as entirely possible. The conflict perspective, as discussed in an earlier chapter, views society as made up of a number of conflicting groups; when one wins, the other loses, because their interests can never be the same. Obviously, the social contract theory is difficult to reconcile to a conflict perspective, since for some no advantages correspond to the sacrifice of liberties. If someone perceives himself or herself as disenfranchised from society, does the right to punish still exist? Can we still use the social contract as the rationale for punishment?

The retributive rationale for punishment is consistent with the social contract theory. Simply stated, the retributive rationale is that the individual offender must be punished because he or she deserves it. Mackie (1982, 4) describes three specific types of retribution. The first, *negative retribution*, dictates that one who is not guilty must not be punished for a crime; the second, *positive retribution*, demands that one who is guilty ought to be punished; and the third, *permissive retribution*, says that one who is guilty may be punished. This formulation states that retribution may support punishment, but also may limit punishment. There are limits to who may be punished (only those who commit crimes) and restrictions on the amount of punishment (only that sufficient to balance the wrong). Further, this formulation implies that punishment need not be administered in all cases. The exceptions, although not discussed by Mackie, may involve the concepts of diminished responsibility, mercy, or both.

Our system of justice was created to take the place of private vengeance. We do not allow victims to seek their own revenge but rather replace "hot vengeance" with "cool justice," dispassionate in its determination and distribution. The social contract supports the notion that it is intrinsically right for the state, rather than the victim's family, to execute a killer. The state has taken over the necessary task of punishment to ensure the survival of society by preventing private vengeance. Intentionally inflicting pain on another is an evil, but by explaining it as state punishment we have redefined the action as not evil and even "just."

Another retributivist justification for punishment is that it is the only way the individual can achieve salvation. In fact, we owe the offender punishment because only through suffering can atonement occur, and only through atonement or *expiatio* can the offender achieve a state of grace. Obviously, this is a religious view, but it tends to be fairly universal. One other view of retribution is that it neutralizes the advantage gained by a wrongdoer. The criminal act puts out of balance the parity of social relationships, and only a punishment or similar deprivation can restore the balance.

The question of whether to punish the crime or the criminal is long-standing and important in any discussion of retributive punishment. Bentham believed that each criminal offense deserved a measure of punishment calculated to balance the potential pleasure or profit of the criminal offense. The neoclassicists, however, allowed some characteristics of the offender to influence the punishment decision. This debate continues today with those who argue for determinate sentencing over indeterminate sentencing. Determinate sentencing punishes the offense, with the length of the sentence determined by the seriousness of the crime. Indeterminate sentencing, however, allows judges a great deal of discretion so that they can tailor the punishment to fit the individual offender. A young offender may get a second chance because he has the potential to change; a woman may receive probation instead of prison because she has an infant to take care of; a habitual criminal may be the unhappy recipient of an increased sentence because he is considered unsalvageable. This type of individualized justice is inconsistent with a retributive rationale since punishment is based on who the criminal is rather than on what the criminal did.

What is an appropriate amount of punishment? This is a difficult question, even for the retributivist. The difference between a year in prison and two years in prison is abstract. Prison may be more of a deprivation for some than for others. Should this be considered during sentencing? Punishment of any kind affects individuals differently; for instance, a whipping may be worse than death for someone with a low tolerance for pain, better than prison for someone with a great need for freedom, and perhaps even represent pleasure for someone who enjoys physical pain. Our present system of justice very seldom recognizes these individual vulnerabilities or sensitivities to various punishments.

Sentencing studies routinely show that little or no agreement exists regarding the type or amount of punishment appropriate for a wrongdoer. Disparity in sentencing is such a problem that many reforms are aimed at reducing or even eliminating judges' discretion. Yet when legislators take on the task themselves by setting determinate sentences, their decisions are arrived at by political pressure rather than from any fair and equitable standard. The basic premise of retribution is that the offender deserves punishment. However we arrive at the final decision of what punishment criminals should receive, we feel the balance is restored when they have suffered, as they have made their victims suffer.

Prevention

Three common justifications or rationales for punishment can all be subsumed under a general heading of prevention. Prevention assumes something should be done to the offender to prevent future criminal activity. The three possible goals of prevention are deterrence, incapacitation, and treatment. Each of these goals is based on certain factual assumptions, which must be considered in addition to the relevant moral questions; for instance, it is a factual question as to whether people can be deterred from crime, but it is a moral question as to what we could do to an individual to assure deterrence.

Deterrence   Specific deterrence is what is done to offenders to prevent them from deciding to commit another offense. General deterrence is what is done to an offender to prevent others from deciding to engage in wrongful behavior. The first is teaching through punishment; the second, teaching by example.

Our right to deter an individual offender is rooted in the same rationale used to support retribution. By virtue of membership in society, individuals submit themselves to society's controls. If we feel someone's actions are damaging, we will try various means to persuade him or her to cease that activity. The implicit assumption of a deterrence philosophy is that in the absence of controls, society would revert back to a jungle-like, dangerous "war of all against all"; we need the police and official punishments to keep us all in line. Under this rationale, the true nature of humankind is perceived to be predatory and only held in check by external controls. Several criminologists, such as Wilson, van den Haag, and Posner, are known as deterrence advocates who support this justification of punishment. In recent years, general deterrence has given way to specific deterrence because empirical support for the efficacy of general deterrence is lacking (von Hirsch 1985).

Von Hirsch, a punishment advocate, specifies the rationale for deterrence in the following way (1976, 54):

1. Those who violate others' rights deserve punishment.
2. There is, however, a countervailing moral obligation of not deliberately adding to the amount of human suffering. Punishment necessarily makes those punished suffer. . . .
3. The notion of deterrence, at this point, suggests that punishment may prevent more misery than it inflicts—thus disposing of the countervailing argument in Step Two.

Therefore, we see that a consequentialist uses deterrence to defend the additional misery caused by punishment.

If we were to support the rationale of specific deterrence, we would assume that punishment is effective in deterring future behavior. Unfortunately, it is very difficult to find any studies that show that anything we do to the offender, whether punishment or treatment, has any effect on subsequent behavior. Arguments are made that this ineffectiveness is due to implementation; in other words, punishment doesn't deter because it is inconsistent and slow. The amount of punishment needed for deterrence is even more problematic if we seek to deter others. First, it becomes much harder to justify. If we know that a term of imprisonment either will not deter an offender or is much more than what would be needed to deter an individual but is the amount needed to deter others, it is questionable whether this further punishment can be justified. A clear example of this situation is the so-called passion murderer; the likelihood of this person's killing again is slim, but he or she is usually given a long sentence to make it clear that killing will not be tolerated. The offender is only a tool to teach a lesson to the rest of us. Durkheim said that the value of criminals is in establishing the parameters of acceptable behavior. By their punishment, we can define ourselves as good and resolve to stay that way.

If one's goal is purely general deterrence, there does not necessarily need to be an original crime. Consider a futuristic society wherein the evening news routinely shows or describes the punishments received by a variety of criminals. The crime, or the punishments, for that matter, do not have to be real to be effective. If punishing innocent people for crimes they might do were just as effective as, or more effective than, punishing criminal offenders, this action might satisfy the ends of deterrence, but would obviously not be acceptable under any system of ethics except perhaps act utilitarianism. Actually, the reality of sentencing is not that much different from the situation just described, in that what the public hears about sentences bears little resemblance to what the offender actually serves. Although the public is becoming more sophisticated in this regard, not many know that when the judge sentences an offender to fifteen years in prison, with good time, time served, and parole, the actual prison time may be closer to three years or even less in those states that have early release policies because of severe prison overcrowding.

Incapacitation Another purpose of punishment is to prevent further crime through incapacitation. Strictly speaking, incapacitation may not be punishment at all, since the purpose is not to inflict pain but to hold an offender until there is no risk of further crime. The major issue concerning incapacitation is prediction; unfortunately, our ability to predict is not very good. Two possible mistakes may be made: releasing an offender who commits further crimes and not releasing an offender who would not. We are willing to tolerate more of the second error, but we must take some risks unless we choose to keep all offenders locked up indefinitely. However, there is no political incentive, other than the high cost of imprisonment, to take the risk. Any time an individual or agency advocates early release, they become easy targets for public censure.

Carrying the goal of incapacitation to its logical conclusion, one would not have to commit a crime at all to be declared potentially dangerous and subject to incapacitation. Our statistics can narrow some types of street crime down to a fairly identifiable subgroup in our society—unemployed, young, black males. If we wanted to reduce a large portion of crime, we could incapacitate this whole group of people. We don't because the wrong associated with punishing innocents is stronger than the right of reducing victimization. However, we now incarcerate career criminals not only for their last offense but for what they might do in the future. We justify habitual felon laws by the prediction that these criminals will continue to commit crime. Statistical studies have found that a small group of offenders commit a disproportionate share of crime, and those individuals can be identified by background characteristics such as how many crimes they have committed, how young they were when they committed their first crime, whether they are addicted to drugs, and so on (Greenwood 1982). Selective incapacitation is a policy to incarcerate these individuals for longer periods of time than other criminals since this would affect crime rates at a lower cost than longer incarceration for all. The argument is obviously utilitarian since retributive punishment would not favor disparate punishments for similar crimes. The real question is whether we ought to hold criminals for what they might do rather than what they have done.

Treatment   If we can find justification for the right to punish, can we also find justification for treatment? Treatment can be considered as one type of specific deterrence since it is an attempt to prevent future crime by changing the criminal offender. Treatment is considered to be beneficial to the individual offender as well as to society. It is a very different approach from the moral rejection implicit in retributive punishment. Treatment implies acceptance rather than rejection, support rather than hatred. On the other hand, the control over the individual is just as great as with punishment; some people, in fact, would say it is greater.

What is treatment? We sometimes consider anything experienced by a person after the point of sentencing to be treatment, including education, prison discipline, and religious services. Can treatment be experimental? Must it be effective to be considered treatment? A court was obliged to define treatment in *Knecht v. Gillman* (488 F.2d. 1136[1973]). Inmates challenged the state's right to use apomorphine, a drug that induces extreme nausea and a feeling of imminent death, as a form of aversive conditioning. In its holding, the court stated that calling something treatment did not remove it from Eighth Amendment scrutiny. In other words, one couldn't inflict pain under the label of treatment. Treatment was further defined as that which constituted accepted and standard practice and could reasonably result in cure.

What we think needs to be cured is another problem. Recall the discussion of whether our society could be characterized by consensus or conflict. Treating a deviant may be justifiable if one believes that society is basically homogeneous in its values and beliefs, but viewed from a conflict perspective, treatment may look more like brainwashing or coercive use of power. The greater intrusiveness inherent in treating the mind is sometimes considered worse than punishment.

According to some experts, treatment can only be effective if it is voluntary. It is nevertheless true that much of the treatment inmates and other correctional clients participate in is either implicitly or directly coerced. Providing treatment for those who want it is one thing; requiring participation from those who are resistant in psychotherapy, group therapy, religious activities, or chemotherapy is quite another. Is this justifiable under a retributivist ethical system? Is it consistent with a utilitarian perspective?

Just Deserts and the Justice Model

Two current rationales for punishments have been termed the *just deserts model* and the *justice model* of punishment. Early advocates of the justice model describe the perspective of the model as follows (Fogel and Hudson 1981, vii):

1. The criminal law is the "command of the sovereign."
2. The threat of punishment is necessary to implement the law.
3. The powerful manipulate the chief motivators of human behavior—fear and hope—through rewards and punishments to retain power.
4. Socialization of individuals, however imperfect, occurs in response to the commands and expectations of the ruling social-political power.
5. The criminal law protects the dominant prescribed morality (a system of rules said to be in the common and best interest of all), reflecting the enforcement aspect of the failure of socialization.

6. In an absence of any absolute system of justice or "Natural Law," no accurate etiologic theory of crime is possible, nor is the definition of crime itself historically stable.
7. Although free will may not exist perfectly, the criminal law is largely based upon its presumed vitality and forms the only foundation for penal sanctions.
8. A prison sentence represents a punishment sanctioned by a legislative body and meted out through the official legal system against a person adjudged responsible for his behavior. Although a purpose of such punishment may be deterrence or rehabilitation, more specifically, such punishment is the deprivation of liberty for a fixed period of time.
9. When corrections becomes mired in the dismal swamp of preaching, exhorting, and treating it becomes dysfunctional as an agency of justice. Correctional agencies should engage prisoners as the law otherwise dictates; as responsible, volitional, and aspiring human beings, and not conceive of them as patients.

This model may be seen as part of a backlash against the abuse of discretion that characterized the rehabilitative era; it promotes a degree of predictability and equality in sentencing by reverting back to earlier retributive goals of punishment and restricting the state's right to use treatment as a criterion for release.

The just deserts model is also retributive and bases punishment on "commensurate deserts" (von Hirsch 1976, xxvi). As the spokesman for this view, von Hirsch (1985, 138) disagrees with deterrence and punishment theorists who feel that retributive and deterrent or incapacitative goals can be combined:

> A desert rationale utilizes the criminal record in a wholly different fashion than selective incapacitation would. (1) Desert calls for primary emphasis on the seriousness of the crime, with only a secondary role (if any) given to the criminal record. Selective incapacitation, by contrast, rests almost entirely on the prior criminal history and on status factors such as employment and drug use. (2) Desert relies on convictions, whereas selective incapacitation techniques need to utilize arrests or other non-adjudicative indicia of prior offending. (3) Desert requires the sentence, to the extent that prior crimes are considered, to take into account only those features that bear on those crimes' blameworthiness, such as their number and seriousness; a selective incapacitation approach tends toward the use of other features of previous crimes that have no relevance to their reprehensibleness.

Von Hirsch does, however, approve of a system of punishment that incorporates incapacitative features in judging the weight of a crime by its recidivism potential. Offenders who commit similar crimes are punished equally, but the rank ordering of crimes is determined by recidivistic potential. This system, "categorical incapacitation," combines deserts and prevention but in a way that, according to von Hirsch, is not unjust to the individual offender (von Hirsch 1985, 150). Von Hirsch continues to disagree with the "new rehabilitationists," who he feels are trying to resurrect a rehabilitative ethic with the rationale that humane conditions during incapacitation require some treatment options. Von Hirsch believes that while treatment options may be offered within the same categories of punishments, they should never be substituted for punishment itself or be part of the equation (von Hirsch and Maher 1992).

Garland (1990) offers a different view. He believes that if social control is what is desired, then the emphasis should be placed on ways of accomplishing that purpose other than punishment after the fact. If we had a system that was better at socializing and integrating its citizens—he calls this a system of social justice and moral education—then we would not have to worry so much about punishing them. The punishment that was still necessary would be viewed as morally expressive rather than instrumental, which would be a type of retributive rather than utilitarian rationale.

ETHICAL FRAMEWORKS FOR CORRECTIONS

The various rationales for punishment just described are well established and can be found in many texts (Gerber and McAnany 1972). Ethical systems can also be discussed as rationales for the goals of punishment and correction. Ethical formalism and utilitarianism receive a disproportional amount of attention here, but the reader is urged to apply the other ethical systems as well.

Utilitarianism

Utilitarianism is often used to support the last three rationales of punishment; namely, deterrence, incapacitation, and treatment. According to utilitarianism, punishing or treating the criminal offender benefits society and this benefit outweighs the negative effect on the individual offender. This is a teleological argument because the morality of the punishment is determined by the consequences derived—namely, reduced crime. The following describes the utilitarian argument for punishment (Borchet and Stewart 1986, 316):

> Traditional utilitarian thinking has concluded that having laws forbidding certain kinds of behavior on pain of punishment, and having machinery for the fair enforcement of these laws, is justified by the fact that it maximizes expectable utility. Misconduct is not to be punished just for its own sake; malefactors must be punished for their past acts, according to law, as a way of maximizing expectable utility.
>
> The utilitarian principle, of course, has implications for decisions about the severity of punishment to be administered. Punishment is itself an evil, and hence should be avoided where this is consistent with the public good. Punishment should have precisely such a degree of severity (not more or less) that the probable disutility of greater severity just balances the probable gain in utility (less crime because of the more serious threat). The cost, in other words, should be counted along with the value of what is bought; and we should buy protection up to the point where the cost is greater than the protection is worth.

Bentham was the major proponent of the utilitarian theory of punishment and established basic guidelines for its use. Box 8-1 lists a number of his rules. Bentham believed that punishment works when it is applied rationally to rational people, but is not acceptable when the person did not make a rational decision to commit the crime, such as when the law forbidding the action was passed after the act occurred, the law was unknown, the person was acting under compulsion, or the person was an infant,

Box 8-1
BENTHAM'S RULES OF PUNISHMENT

Rule One. That the value of the punishment must not be less, in any case, than what is sufficient to outweigh that of the profit of the offense.

Rule Two. The greater the mischief of the offense, the greater is the expense it may be worthwhile to be at, in the way of punishment.

Rule Three. When two offenses come in competition, the punishment for the greater offense must be sufficient to induce a man to prefer the less.

Rule Four. The punishment should be adjusted in such manner to each particular offense, that for every part of the mischief there may be a motive to restrain the offender from giving birth to it.

Rule Five. The punishment ought in no case to be more than what is necessary to bring it into conformity with the rules here given.

Rule Six. That the quantity of punishment actually inflicted on each individual offender may correspond to the quantity intended for similar offenders in general, the several circumstances influencing sensibility ought always to be taken into the account.

Rule Seven. That the value of the punishment may outweigh the profit of the offense, it must be increased in point of magnitude, in proportion as it falls short in point of certainty.

Rule Eight. Punishment must be further increased in point of magnitude, in proportion as it falls short of proximity.

Rule Nine. When the act is conclusively indicative of a habit, such an increase must be given to the punishment as may enable it to outweigh the profit, not only of the individual offense, but of such other like offenses as are likely to have been committed with impunity by the same offender.

Rule Ten. When a punishment, which in point of quality is particularly well calculated to answer its intention, cannot exist in less than a certain quantity, it may sometimes be of issue, for the sake of employing it, to stretch a little beyond the quantity which, on other accounts, would be strictly necessary.

Rule Eleven. In particular, this may be the case where the punishment proposed is of such a nature as to be particularly well calculated to answer the purpose of a moral lesson.

Rule Twelve. In adjusting the quantum of punishment, the circumstances by which all punishment may be rendered unprofitable ought to be attended to.

Rule Thirteen. Among provisions designated to perfect the proportion between punishments and offenses, if any occur which by their own particular good effects would not make up for the harm they would do by adding to the intricacy of the code, they should be omitted.

(From Bentham 1843/1970.)

insane, or intoxicated. The utility of the punishment would be lost in these cases; therefore, punishment could not be justified (Borchert and Stewart 1986, 317).

All the rules enumerated in Box 8-1 ensure that punishments are acceptable to the utilitarian framework. The basic formula provides that the utility of punishment to society outweighs the negative of the punishment itself. Utilitarian theory also supports treatment and incapacitation if they can be shown to benefit society. If, for instance, treatment and punishment had equal amounts of utility for society, treatment would be the more ethical choice because it has a less negative effect on the individual. Likewise, if incapacitation and punishment are equally effective in protecting and providing utility to society, then the choice with the least negative utility would be the ethical one.

Ethical Formalism

Contrast the utilitarian views toward punishment discussed in the previous section with Kant's (quoted in Borchet and Stewart 1986, 322):

> Juridical punishment . . . can be inflicted on a criminal, never just as instrumental to the achievement of some other good for the criminal himself or for the civil society, but only because he has committed a crime; for a man may never be used just as a means to the end of another person. . . . Penal law is a categorical imperative, and woe to him who crawls through the serpentine maze of utilitarian theory in order to find an excuse, in some advantage to someone, for releasing the criminal from punishment or any degree of it, in line with the pharasaical proverb "it is better that one man die than that a whole people perish"; for if justice perishes, there is no more value in man living on the earth. . . . What mode and degree of punishment, then, is the principle and standard of public justice? Nothing but the principle of equality. . . . Thus, whatever undeserved evil you inflict on another person, you inflict on yourself.

Ethical formalism clearly supports a retributive view of punishment. It is deontological because it is not concerned with the consequences of the punishment but only its inherent morality. It would support the idea that a criminal is owed punishment because to do otherwise would not be according him or her equal respect as a human. The punishment, however, should not be used as a means to any other end but retribution. Treatment is not supported by ethical formalism because it uses the offender as a means to protect society.

Several arguments support this retributive rationale. First, Mackie (1982) discusses the universal aspects of punishment: the urge to react in a hostile manner to harm is an element inherent in human nature; therefore, one might say that punishment is a natural law. Another supporting argument is found in the principle of forfeiture, which postulates that when one intrudes on an innocent person's rights, one forfeits a proportional amount of one's own rights. If an aggressive move threatens a victim's liberty, by restraining or hurting a victim in some way, then the aggressor forfeits his or her own liberty; in other words, he or she forfeits the right to be free from punishment (Bedau 1982).

Ethics of Care

The ethics of care would support treatment over retributive punishment. Several authors have discussed the ethics of care in relation to the justice and corrections system. For instance, Heidensohn (1986) and Daly (1989) discuss differences in the perception of justice from a care perspective versus a retributive perspective. They discuss these as female and male perceptions, respectively. The female care perspective emphasizes needs, motives, and relationships. The corrections system, ideally, should be supported by a caring ethic since it takes into account offender needs, and community corrections especially emphasizes the relationship of the offender to the community. In this perspective, one should help the offender to become a better person, because that is what a caring and committed relationship would entail. Retributive punishment and deterrence are not consistent with the ethics of care. Some, however, say that retribution and a care ethic are not, nor should they be considered, dichotomous. Restitution, for instance, might be seen as supported by both rationales—it establishes a responsibility on the part of the offender to right his or her wrong, but the responsibility is satisfied by recompensing the victim rather than by pain or punishment. Restitution, then, can be said to meet the needs of the victim and the offender and to satisfy justice at the same time.

Rawlsian Ethics

John Rawls presents an alternative to utilitarianism and retributivism. Rawls's defense of punishment starts with Kant's proposition that no one should be treated as a means and with the idea that each should have an "equal right to the most extensive basic liberty compatible with a similar liberty to others." A loss of rights should only take place, according to Rawls, when it is consistent with the best interests of the least advantaged. Rules regarding punishment would be as follows (cited in Hickey and Scharf 1980, 169):

1. We must punish only to the extent that the loss of liberty would be agreeable were one not to know whether one were to be the criminal, the victim, or a member of the general public [the veil of ignorance]; and
2. The loss of liberty must be justified as the minimum loss consistent with the maintenance of the same liberty among others.

Furthermore, when the advantage shifts—when the offender instead of the victim or society becomes the one with the least advantage—then punishment must cease. This theory leaves a lot of unanswered questions, since it seems that if victims were chosen carefully—for instance, if only those who would not suffer financially or emotionally from victimization were selected—then the criminal, especially if he or she comes from an impoverished background, would still be at a disadvantage. On the other hand, Rawls's system does seem to be consistent with the idea that the criminal act creates an imbalance of some previous state of parity and punishment should be concerned with regaining that balance.

PUNISHMENT AND TREATMENT ALTERNATIVES

We have discarded many punishments that historically were found acceptable, such as flogging, hanging, banishment, branding, cutting off limbs, drawing and quartering, pillories and stocks, and so on. Although we still believe society has the right to punish, what we do in the name of punishment has changed substantially. We are uncomfortable with physically painful punishments and have used imprisonment to take their place.

Humane Punishment

The Supreme Court has given legal reasons for the abolition of most types of corporal punishment. The Eighth Amendment protects all citizens from "cruel and unusual" punishment. Although what is cruel and unusual is vague, several tests have been used to define the terms, such as the following, discussed in *Furman v. Georgia* (408 U.S. 238, 92 S.Ct. 2726, 33 L.Ed.2d 346 [1972]):

1. "Unusual" (by frequency): Those punishments that are rarely, if ever used thus become unusual if used against one individual or a group. They become arbitrary punishments because the decision to use them is so infrequent.
2. "Evolving standards of decency": Civilization is evolving and punishments considered acceptable in the nineteenth century are no longer acceptable in the twentieth century.
3. "Shock the conscience": A yardstick for all punishment is to test it against the public conscience. If people are naturally repelled by the punishment, then it must be cruel and unusual by definition.
4. "Excessive or disproportionate": Any punishment that is excessive to its purpose or disproportionately administered (for instance, if greater amounts of punishment are given to one group than to another or to one individual in comparison to like individuals) is considered wrong.
5. "Unnecessary": Again, we are looking at the purpose of the punishment in relation to what is done. If the purpose of punishment is to deter crime, then we should only administer an amount necessary to do so. If the purpose is to protect and the offender presents no danger, then prison should not be used.

These tests have eliminated the use of the whip and the branding iron; yet some people say that we may have done nothing to move toward humane punishment and in fact we may have moved away from it. Newman points out the possibility that corporal punishment, at least the less drastic kinds such as whipping, are actually less intrusive in a person's life than a prison sentence. In fact, physical punishment may be more of a deterrent and yet less damaging to a person's future. After all, a whipping takes perhaps days or weeks to get over but a prison sentence may last years and affect all future earnings (Newman 1978, 270). Which is the more intrusive punishment? Which is the more ethical? Which would you prefer?

A criminal offender may be sentenced to prison or probation, or assessed a fine. Under a probation sentence, an offender may be required to perform community service, pay court costs, pay restitution to the victim, find employment, attend drug treatment, or meet a number of other possible requirements. The same is true of parole. There are other innovations in corrections such as boot camps, intensive probation and parole, electronic monitoring, and so on. Some judges get creative in sentencing, such as a judge who had a probation officer nail a sign to the front door of a convicted sex offender warning children to stay away because a child molester lived there. The offender was required to leave the sign up during the term of his probation. Other punishments include license plates that notify everyone the driver has been convicted of DWI, attending church and asking forgiveness of the congregation for stealing from the church, and giving blood. One can analyze these sentences through legal rights or through ethical and moral criteria. Does natural law or some other ethical system provide a rationale to support or condemn these sentences? Should anyone—even a child molester—be subjected to such public censure? Is it fair to subject the offender's family to such a punishment?

Capital Punishment

What sets capital punishment apart from all other punishments is its quality of irrevocability. This type of punishment leaves no way to correct a mistake. For this reason, some believe that no mortal should have the power to inflict capital punishment, because there is no way to guarantee mistakes won't be made.

The major ethical positions that can support the death penalty are utilitarianism and retributivism. Because of controversy over the factual issues involved, utilitarian arguments are used both to defend and condemn capital punishment. If we believe, as do retentionists, that capital punishment is just because it deters people, then we must show proof that it does indeed deter. The abolitionists present evidence that it does not.

Arguments for the retention of the death penalty include considerations of justice and considerations of social utility. Considerations of justice involve the retributivist, deontological view that the moral order is upset by the commission of an offense, and the disorder can only be rectified by punishment equal in intensity to the seriousness of the offense. Utilitarians view the evil of capital punishment as far outweighed by the future benefits that will accrue to society. Execution, for example, might lead to such socially desirable effects as protection from the violent criminal and deterrence of other potential criminals. Walker (1985, 79) summarizes the evidence marshaled on both sides of the deterrence question and finds very little support for the proposition that executions are useful deterrents.

Abolitionists emphasize the "inherent worth and dignity of each individual." The taking of a human life is judged a morally unacceptable practice and is believed to be nothing more than vengeance (Mappes 1982, 83–87). Utilitarianism may also support the idea that executions create a net negative effect on society, because although criminals may receive what they deserve, society is negatively affected by the brutalizing image of execution. This view is consistent with the idea that violence begets violence, and far from showing societal intolerance toward murder, capital punishment is seen as actually cheapening human life and encouraging bloodlust.

Religious ethics have been used to support and condemn capital punishment. Old Testament law supporting the taking of "an eye for an eye" is used by retentionists, while the commandment "Thou shalt not kill" is used by the abolitionists. The ethical justification of capital punishment presents serious and probably unresolvable problems. It is a telling commentary that for as long as society has used capital punishment to punish wrongdoing, critics have defined it as immoral (Johnson 1991).

Questions also arise about the methods and procedures of capital punishment. Should all murderers be subject to capital punishment, or are some murderers more "justified" than others? Should we allow defenses of age, mental state, or reason? If we do apply capital punishment differentially, doesn't this open the door to bias and misuse? Unless the Supreme Court revises its current position, the legality of executions is not in question even though the procedures used to arrive at the decision to execute are still being challenged. Using moral and ethical rather than legal analysis, one might examine recent Supreme Court cases that hold that statistical differences in the use of executions do not violate the disproportionality test, that offenders who are simply crime partners rather than perpetrators of murder deserve execution, and that mental retardation can be used only as a mitigating factor in the decision to execute. The morality of capital punishment in general is still very much a topic of debate and elicits strong feelings on the part of many people.

USE OF DISCRETION AND AUTHORITY

We have previously discussed how discretion plays a part in each phase of the criminal justice system. In corrections, discretion is involved when correctional officers decide to write disciplinary tickets or deliver verbal reprimands; this is similar to police discretion in making the decision to arrest. Discretion is also involved when the disciplinary committee makes a decision to punish an inmate for an infraction: the punishment can be as serious as increasing sentence length through loss of good time, or as minor as a temporary loss of privileges. What punishment may be administered depends on state law and Supreme Court decisions related to prisoners' rights, but also largely on the discretion of disciplinary committees. A similar decision-making process would be that of a parole hearing officer in a revocation hearing. This type of discretion is similar to the discretion of the prosecutor and judge in a criminal trial.

Correctional psychiatrists, psychologists, and counselors have a responsibility to the correctional client. Like the defense attorney, they must use discretion to balance clients' needs against the larger needs of the system or institution. Their role actually may involve more ambiguity than the defense lawyer's since there is some question as to whether they owe their primary allegiance to the offender or society.

We see, then, that similarities exist between correctional personnel and the other practitioners discussed thus far. As always, when the power of discretion is present, the potential for abuse is also present. Professional ethics exist to guide individual decision makers in their use of discretion, but as with law enforcement and legal professionals, adherence to a code of ethics is influenced by the professional subculture and institutional values. Formal ethics for correctional personnel will be discussed in more detail shortly.

USE OF AUTHORITY AND POWER

Correctional officers (C.O.'s) are similar to the police in that their uniform represents the authority of the institution regardless of the person wearing it. Some C.O.'s are uncomfortable with this authority and do not know how to handle it. Some C.O.'s revel in it and misperceive the bounds of authority given to them as a representative of the state. The following statement is a perceptive observation of how some C.O.'s misuse and misperceive the authority they have (Kauffman 1988, 50):

> [Some officers] don't understand what authority is and what bounds you have within that authority. . . . I think everyone interprets it to meet their own image of themselves. "I'm a corrections officer [slams table]! You sit here! [Slam!] You sit there!" Rather than "I'm a person who has limited authority. So, you know, I'm sorry gentlemen, but you can't sit there. You are going to have to sit over there. That's just the rules," and explaining or something like that the reason why.

This officer obviously recognized that the uniform bestows the authority of rational and reasonable control, not unbridled domination. It is also true that the power of the C.O. is limited. In actuality, it is impossible to depend on the authority of the uniform to get tasks accomplished, and one must find personal resources—personal respect and authority stemming from who one is and what one stands for—in order to gain cooperation from inmates.

Some officers who perceive themselves as powerless in relation to the administration, the courts, and society in general may react to this perceived powerlessness by misusing their little bit of power over inmates. They may abuse their position by humiliating or abusing inmates.

Probation and parole officers have a different type of authority and power over offenders. They have the power to recommend release or revocation. This power is also limited since probation and parole officers' recommendations can be ignored by the judge or hearing board. Yet the implicit power an officer has over the individuals on his or her caseload must be recognized as an important element of the role, not to be taken lightly or misused.

ETHICAL ISSUES FOR CORRECTIONAL OFFICERS

Along with getting an image facelift during the rehabilitative era of the 1970s, professional security staff in corrections exchanged their old label of *guard* for the new one *correctional officer*. However, the slang terms used to describe these individuals, such as *hack, screw,* and *turnkey,* have been more resistant to change. Although increasing professionalism and greater responsibility now characterize the individuals in this occupation, correctional officers, by any name, are still perceived as operating under punitive goals and doing little to improve the negative environment of the prison.

The American Correctional Association's Code of Ethics (Box 8-2) outlines formal ethics for correctional professionals. Many similarities exist between this code and the

---

Box 8-2
AMERICAN CORRECTIONAL ASSOCIATION
CODE OF ETHICS

Preamble

The American Correctional Association expects of its members unfailing honesty, respect for the dignity and individuality of human beings, and a commitment to professional and compassionate service. To this end, we subscribe to the following principles.

Members will respect and protect the civil and legal rights of all individuals.

Members will treat every professional situation with concern for the person's welfare and with no intent of personal gain.

Relationships with colleagues will be such that they promote mutual respect within the profession and improve the quality of service.

Public criticisms of colleagues or their agencies will be made only when warranted, verifiable, and constructive in purpose.

Members will respect the importance of all disciplines within the criminal justice system and work to improve cooperation with each segment.

Subject to the individual's right to privacy, members will honor the public's right to know and will share information with the public to the extent permitted by law.

Members will respect and protect the right of the public to be safeguarded from criminal activity.

Members will not use their positions to secure personal privileges or advantages.

Law Enforcement Code of Ethics presented in Chapter 6. For instance, the importance of integrity, respect for and protection of individual rights, and service to the public are emphasized in both codes, as are the importance and sanctity of the law. Also, the prohibition against exploiting professional authority for personal gain is stressed in both codes.

Another similarity between this code and the Law Enforcement Code is the disparity that sometimes exists between the ideal behavior it describes and what actually occurs. The ACA Code of Ethics describes the ideal behavior of correctional staff; however, as was discussed in the chapter on law enforcement, subcultural values may be inconsistent with and subvert formal ethical codes. This is the case with correctional personnel also. Although the ethical code clearly calls for fair and objective treatment, integrity, and high standards of performance, the actual practices of correctional staff may be quite different.

Member will not, while acting in an official capacity, allow personal interest to impair objectivity in the performance of duty.

No member will enter into any activity or agreement, formal or informal, which presents a conflict of interest or is inconsistent with the conscientious performance of his or her duties.

No member will accept any gift, service, or favor that is or appears to be improper or implies an obligation inconsistent with the free and objective exercise of his or her professional duties.

In any public statement, members will clearly distinguish between personal views and those statements or positions made on behalf of an agency or the Association.

Each member will report to the appropriate authority any corrupt or unethical behavior where there is sufficient cause to initiate a review.

Members will not discriminate against any individual because of race, gender, creed, national origin, religious affiliation, age, or any other type of prohibited discrimination.

Members will preserve the integrity of private information; they will neither seek data on individuals beyond that needed to perform their responsibilities, nor reveal nonpublic data unless expressly authorized to do so.

Any member who is responsible for agency personnel actions will make all appointments, promotions, or dismissals in accordance with established civil service rules, applicable contract agreements, and individual merit, and not in the furtherance of partisan interests.

(Revised August 1990. Copyright American Correctional Association. Reprinted by permission from the American Correctional Association, Laurel, Maryland.)

The Correctional Subculture

The subculture of the correctional officer has never been as extensively described as the police subculture, but some elements are similar. First of all, the inmate may be considered the enemy, along with superiors and society in general. Moreover, the acceptance of the use of force, the preference toward redefining job roles to meet minimum requirements, and the willingness to use deceit to cover up wrongdoing are evident in both subcultures (Crouch 1980; Johnson 1987). Kauffman (1988, 85–112), in a perceptive study of the correctional officer's world, notes the following norms of the correctional officer subculture:

1. Always go to the aid of another officer. Similar to law enforcement, the necessity of interdependence ensures that this is a strong and pervasive norm in the correctional officer subculture. Kauffman describes a "slam" in Walpole prison as when the officer slams a heavy cell door, which reverberates throughout the prison building, bringing a dozen officers to his or her aid in minutes; an obvious parallel to the "officer down" call in law enforcement.
2. Don't lug drugs. This prohibition is to ensure the safety of other officers, as is the even stronger prohibition against bringing in weapons for inmates. The following norm against "ratting" on a fellow officer may except informing on an officer who is a known offender of this lugging norm.
3. Don't rat. In similar ways to the law enforcement subcultural code and, ironically, the inmate code, correctional officers also hate those who inform on their peers. Kauffman notes two subordinate norms: Never rat out an officer to an inmate, and never cooperate in an investigation, or worse yet, testify against a fellow officer in regard to that officer's treatment of inmates.
4. Never make a fellow officer look bad in front of inmates. This applies regardless of what the officer did, since it jeopardizes the officer's effectiveness and undercuts the appearance of officer solidarity.
5. Always support an officer in a dispute with an inmate. Similar to the previous provision, this prescribes behavior—not only should one not criticize a fellow officer, but one should support him or her against any inmate.
6. Always support officer sanctions against inmates. This is a specific version of the previous provision. This includes the use of illegal physical force as well as legal sanctions.
7. Don't be a white hat. This prohibition is directed at any behavior, attitude, or expressed opinion that could be interpreted as sympathetic toward inmates. Kauffman also notes that it is often violated and does not have the strong subcultural sanctions that accompany some of the other norms.
8. Maintain officer solidarity against all outside groups. Similar to police officers, correctional officers feel denigrated and despised by society at large. This norm reinforces officer solidarity and includes prohibitions against any other group, including the media, administration, or public.
9. Show positive concern for fellow officers. This norm promotes good will toward other officers. Two examples include: never leave another officer a problem, which means don't leave unfinished business at the end of your shift for the next officer to

handle, and help your fellow officers with problems outside the institution, meaning lending money to injured or sick officers or helping out in other ways.

Kauffman notes that this code may vary from institution to institution depending on such factors as permeability, the administration, the level of violence from inmates, architecture, and the demographic profile of officers. Distrust of outsiders, dissatisfaction, and alienation are also elements of both the police and the correctional officer subcultures. In both professions, the individuals must work with sometimes unpleasant people who make it clear that the practitioner is not liked or appreciated. Further, there is public antipathy (either real or perceived) toward the profession, which increases the social distance between criminal justice professionals and all others outside the profession. In addition, the working hours, the nature of the job, and the unwillingness to talk about the job to others outside the profession further the isolation workers feel. One additional point to be made about the occupational subculture is that both law enforcement and corrections have been changed by the entry of minorities, the college educated, and women into the ranks.

It should also be pointed out that some researchers feel this description of the correctional officer subculture is incorrect because of *pluralistic ignorance.* This refers to the idea that a few outspoken and visible members shape the perception all group members have toward the characteristics of the majority. In corrections, this may mean that a few officers endorse and publicize the subculture just described, while the majority, who are silent, privately believe in different values (Johnson 1987, 130). Kauffman found this to be true in attitudes toward the use of force and toward the value of treatment. Individually, officers expressed more positive attitudes than they held out as typical of the subculture (1988, 179). This is probably true as well in the police subculture.

Relations with Inmates

One serious threat to an officer's ethics and professionalism occurs when relationships with inmates become personal. Sykes discussed the issue of reciprocity in supervision: officers become dependent on inmates for important task completion and the smooth management of the tier; in return, C.O.'s may overlook inmate infractions and allow a certain degree of favoritism to enter their supervision style (cited in Crouch 1980, 239). When C.O.'s become personally involved with inmates, their professional judgment may be less objective. Involvement is possible because of proximity and close contact over a period of time, combined with shared feelings of victimization by the administration. Officers may start to feel they have more in common with inmates than with the administration, and that is when unethical conduct occurs, such as ignoring infractions or doing illegal favors for the inmate. McCarthy (1991) writes of this exchange system as an incentive for corruption. He also points out that lack of training, low visibility, and unfettered discretion also contribute to a variety of corrupt behaviors.

The subcultural norms against sympathizing with or becoming too friendly with inmates as described by Kauffman (1988) are indicative of the preventive steps taken to avoid this identification. An officer who identifies with inmates is not to be trusted. The subculture minimizes the possibility of cooptation by the prohibitions against friendliness and the socialization process, which results in a correctional officer's view of inmates as animalistic and not worth human sympathy. Kauffman also notes that inmates themselves make it difficult for C.O.'s to continue to hold sympathetic or friendly views. In her study, new officers were continually harassed by inmates until the neutral or positive views they held at entry were replaced with negative views. She described Walpole in the 1970s as overrun with rats and roaches, with excrement smeared on the walls and garbage ankle deep on the floors—inmates wouldn't clean up and officers could not. Extreme inmate-on-inmate violence, including mutilations and torture, was commonplace, and officers feared being thrown from the tiers, being knifed in the back, or being hit in the head by soup cans or other heavy objects thrown from the tiers above. While this description obviously is not representative of most prisons, then or now, the elements of inmate hostility, fear, and hopelessness are characteristic of all prisons.

Just as officers may act in unethical ways when they like an inmate, officers have the power to make life difficult for the inmate they do not like. These extralegal harassments and punishments may include "forgetting" to send an inmate to an appointment, making an inmate stay in keeplock longer than necessary, or pretending not to hear someone locked in a cell asking for toilet paper or other necessary items. Lombardo (1981) notes the practice of putting an inmate in keeplock on a Friday even without a supportable charge because the disciplinary committee would not meet until the following Monday to release the inmate, the use of profanity toward inmates even in front of families, not notifying an inmate of a visitor, and losing passes. Kauffman (1988) notes that during the time period she studied, officers sometimes flushed cell toilets to aggravate inmates, dumped good food into the garbage, withheld toilet paper or matches, reported "tips" of contraband in a cell that resulted in a shakedown, scratched artwork, and in other innumerable informal ways made the targeted inmate's life miserable.

Because prisoners are in a position of need, having to ask the officers for things as simple as permission to go to the bathroom, officers have the power to make inmates feel even more dependent than necessary and humiliated because of their dependency. The relative powerlessness of the officers in relation to their superiors, the administration, and society in general creates a situation where some take advantage of their only power—that over the inmate.

Even more so than police, C.O.'s work every day with large numbers of men or women who simply do not like—indeed sometimes hate—the correctional officer for no other reason than the uniform he or she is wearing. There is always the potential of injury, from an unprovoked attack, while subduing an inmate, while breaking up a fight, or from being taken hostage. Officers will say this last possibility is never far from their minds and may affect to a certain extent their supervision of inmates, since it is potentially dangerous to be personally disliked.

On the other hand, on a day-to-day basis, inmates are not that much different from anyone else; some are friendly, some are funny, some are good conversationalists. A comfortable alliance is sometimes formed between the guards and the guarded, especially in work settings, that is not unlike a foreman-employee relationship. This strange combination of familiarity and fear results in a pervasive feeling of distrust. Officers insist that "you can be friendly with inmates, but you can never trust them." Mature officers learn to live with this basic inconsistency and are able to differentiate situations where rules must be followed from those in which rules can be relaxed. Younger and less perceptive officers either take on a defensive attitude of extreme distrust or are manipulated by inmates because they are not able to tell the difference between goodwill and gaming.

Use of Force

The use of force is a legal and sometimes necessary element of correctional supervision, and most observers say that severe beatings simply do not occur in prisons today; but one still hears reports that force is used as an extralegal punishment against unruly or aggressive inmates. Part of the problem lies in the vagueness of the term *necessary force*; this may mean the resort to violence is the absolute last alternative available, or it may mean force is used when it is the most convenient way to get something accomplished (Morris and Morris in Crouch 1980, 253).

During the course of a fistfight or struggle with an inmate, officers react to violence instinctively—that is, without much rational thought as to whether a blow is necessary or gratuitous. Premeditated beatings, usually for a previous attack on a fellow officer, are harder to understand or justify. C.O.'s may view such beatings as utilitarian in that they serve as warnings to all inmates that they will receive similar treatment if they attack C.O.'s; thus, the action protects all officers to some extent from inmate aggression. Officers also might defend the action on retributive grounds, since the inmate would probably not be punished for the attack through legal channels. However, these retaliations always represent the most brutal and inhumane aspects of incarceration and damage the integrity of the correctional professional.

Kauffman (1988) notes that in prison the violence inmates perpetrate against each other desensitizes officers to violence in general, and specifically to the violence used by officers against inmates. After witnessing scores of stabbings, beatings, and mutilations, some C.O.'s begin to think of inmates as animals, undeserving of humane treatment. The nonchalant attitude toward violence adopted by both inmates and officers furthers the process whereby extreme violence is viewed as normal instead of abnormal, and concern and care for fellow human beings is viewed as deviant. The most prevalent expressed rationale for violence against inmates in Kauffman's study was protection. Officers' fears of violent, unprovoked attacks were realistic, and inmates serving life sentences had nothing to stop them from such violence except extralegal sanctions. Even those officers who did not participate in such violence had no strong desire to stop or report the violence, viewing the inmate as more often than not deserving of such punishment. While some officers actually enjoyed the violence, most conformed because of peer pressure or fear of subcultural sanctions against exposing the violence.

Loyalty and Whistle Blowing

There are many similarities between police and correctional staff in use of force abuses, the code of silence, and the feelings of isolation. There are also differences. The most striking difference between the two jobs is that C.O.'s must deal with the same people

daily in a closed, oppressive environment. While police officers have freedom of movement and can avoid peers or citizen troublemakers to a certain extent, C.O.'s have no
such luxury. If a C.O. fears an inmate, he or she must still face him or her every day. If a
C.O. violates the correctional subcultural code, the sanctions are felt more acutely because one must work closely with other C.O.'s all day long. While police officers cite the
importance of being able to trust other officers as backups in violent situations, one
could make the argument that C.O.'s need to trust each other more completely, more
implicitly, and more frequently, given the fact that violence in some institutions is pervasive and unprovoked, and the C.O. carries no weapon. An officer described to
Kauffman (1988, 207) the result of violating peer trust as follows:

> If an incident went down, there was no one to cover my back. That's a very important lesson
> to learn. You need your back covered and my back wasn't covered there at all. And at one
> point I was in fear of being set up by guards. I was put in dangerous situations purposely.
> That really happened to me.

Fear of violating the code of silence is one reason officers do not report wrongdoing. Loyalty is another. Officers feel a strong *esprit de corps* that is similar to the loyalty
previously discussed among police. This positive loyalty also results in covering for other
officers and not testifying or reporting offenses. McCarthy (1991) discusses types of corrupt behaviors in a prison including theft, trafficking in contraband, embezzlement, and
misuse of authority. These offenses largely are known and unreported by other correctional officers because of loyalty and subcultural prohibitions against "ratting."
     A pattern of complicity also prevents reporting. New officers cannot possibly fol-
low all the many rules and regulations that exist in a prison and still adequately deal
with inmates on a day-to-day basis. Therefore, before too long they find themselves involved in activity that could result in disciplinary action. Because others are usually
aware of this activity and do not inform supervisors, an implicit conspiracy of silence
develops, so that no one is turned in for anything because each of the others who might
witness this wrongdoing has engaged in behavior that could also be sanctioned
(Lombardo 1981, 79).

General Conduct and the "Good Officer"

Historically, correctional officers have been described as role models for inmates. In
reference to an early and idealistic view of who should be hired and for what reasons,
one author writes that this was a "pursuit of men with 'special gifts of personality and
character' capable of achieving the moral transformation of their fellow men merely by
the exercise of 'personal influence'" (Hawkins, cited in Crouch 1980, 55). This may be
a false hope, but it is true that no one in corrections has more day-to-day contact with
inmates than C.O.'s. For this reason, it is important to look at the types of individuals
hired to fill correctional officer positions and how they respond to the environment of
the prison.
     Officers, of course, are individuals, and the most interesting research in this area
describes the ways they respond to the demands and job pressures of corrections. Some

researchers have found that officers fall into various adaptational types: some are violence-prone, using the role of correctional officer to act out an authoritarian role; another type serves time in prison much the same way as the inmates do, avoiding trouble and hoping nothing goes wrong on their shift; other officers seek to enlarge their job description and perceive their role as including counseling and helping the inmate rather than merely locking doors and signing passes. This type of officer has been called the human service officer and incorporates the tasks of providing goods and services, acting as a referral agent or advocate, and helping with institutional adjustment problems (Johnson 1987, 142).

Not surprisingly, C.O.'s and inmates tend to agree on a description of a good officer. A good officer is described as one who treats all inmates fairly with no favoritism, but who does not always follow rules to the letter. Discretion is used judicially; when a good officer makes a decision to bypass rules, all involved tend to agree that it was the right decision. A good officer is not quick to use force, nor afraid of force if it becomes necessary. A good officer treats inmates in a professional manner and gives them the respect they deserve as human beings. In some cases such an officer will go far outside regular duties to aid an inmate who is sincerely in need; however, he or she can detect gameplaying and cannot be manipulated. These traits—consistency, fairness, and flexibility—are confirmed as valuable by research (Johnson 1987, 139). Although many officers in prisons reach this ideal, the trend today seems to be a less honorable approach to the position because of the pressures we will describe next.

Like police, correctional officers feel that court decisions and administrative goals have not supported their needs and have sacrificed their safety to meet inmates' demands. One result of the feeling that superiors and society do not protect their interests is an individualistic response to the ethical issues that may come up in the course of the job. The following presents a fairly negative view of the current officer's ethical position (Carroll, cited in Crouch 1980, 318):

> The officers are not working for the inmates, they are working for themselves. Unable to secure compliance with their directives by the enforcement of a set of impersonal rules, they seek to secure compliance by means of friendships, overlooking infractions, and providing highly desired information to inmates. Their behavior is not so much a repudiation of the goal of custodial control as it is an attempt to maintain order, and at the same time to protect themselves, in the face of institutional changes that have made order more difficult to maintain and their position more vulnerable.

Correctional officers feel criticized and even scorned by many, and it is little wonder that they adapt to their role by such means, yet it is important to understand the consequences of such a position. Kauffman (1988, 222) talked to officers who reported that they had lost their morality in the prison. These officers experienced anguish at the change that was wrought by the prison environment.

> Initially, many attempted to avoid engaging in behavior injurious to inmates by refusing (openly or surreptitiously) to carry out certain duties and by displacing their aggressions onto others outside the prison or themselves. As their involvement in the prison world grew,

and their ability to abstain from morally questionable actions within the prison declined, they attempted to neutralize their own feelings of guilt by regarding prisons as separate moral realms with their own distinct set of moral standards or by viewing inmates as individuals outside the protection of moral laws. When such efforts failed, they shut their minds to what others were doing and to what they were doing themselves.

Without a strong ethical code, correctional officers drift into relativistic egoism: what benefits the individual is considered acceptable, despite long-term effects or inconsistencies with their role and their personal value system. This results in feelings of disillusionment and anomie, and the side effects can be serious dissatisfaction and depression. To maintain a sense of morality in an inherently coercive environment is no easy task, yet a strong set of individual ethics is probably the best defense against being changed by the negative environment of the prison. To counteract these pressures, correctional managers should generate a strong anticorruption policy. This would include proactive measures such as mechanisms to investigate and detect wrongdoing, reduce opportunities for corruption, screen employees using state-of-the-art psychological tools, improve working conditions, and provide good role models in the form of supervisors and administrators (McCarthy 1991).

ETHICAL ISSUES FOR TREATMENT STAFF

Treatment specialists have their own ethical dilemmas. Although hired by the state, many feel their loyalties lie with the offender. Prison psychologists may be privy to information or confessions that they feel bound to hold in confidence even though the security of the institution may be jeopardized. The professional goal of all treatment specialists is to help the client. This may be fundamentally inconsistent with the prison environment, which emphasizes punishment.

Making the decision as to whether the individual is cured or not also involves mixed loyalties. Any treatment necessarily involves risk. How much risk one is willing to take depends on whether the public should be protected at all costs, in which case few people would be released, or whether one feels that the public must risk possible victimization in order to give offenders a chance to prove themselves.

Another dilemma is the administration of treatment programs. If a program has potential, someone must make decisions as to who gets into it. Ideally, one would want similar people in the treatment program and in a control group. However, it is sometimes hard to justify withholding the program from some people who may sincerely wish to participate. Laypersons have difficulty understanding the concepts of random selection and control groups. Pressure exists to admit anyone who sincerely wants a chance to participate despite what this might do to the experimental design.

Another more basic issue is the ethics of providing treatment to people who do not want it. Psychiatrists and psychologists especially have to reconcile their professional ethics in two fields, corrections and psychiatry, and at times this is hard. Psychiatrists in corrections, for instance, often feel that they are being used for social control rather than treatment. Disruptive inmates, although needing treatment, pose security risks to prison officials, and thus intervention, especially chemotherapy, often takes the form of control rather than treatment.

Psychologists have their own ethical code, and some principles seem especially relevant to corrections. For instance, under the principle of responsibility, psychologists are instructed to prevent the distortion, misuse, or suppression of their psychological findings by the institution or agency by which they are employed. This obviously affects institutional psychologists, who may feel that their findings are compromised by custody concerns. For instance, something confessed to in a counseling session may be used in parole reports to prevent release, findings may be used to block transfer, behavior brought out in psychological testing may be punished, and so on ("Ethical Principles" 1981, 633).

Other principles involve the treatment of clients: "In their professional roles, psychologists avoid any action that will violate or diminish the legal and civil rights of clients or of others who may be affected by their actions" ("Ethical Principles" 1981, 634). This principle may be applicable to certain treatment programs in prison that restrict inmates' liberty or choice; for instance, some of the behavior modification programs have been questioned legally and ethically. Many treatment professionals feel behavior modification has been subverted by the prison environment. Although it is extremely effective in inducing behavioral change, some professionals feel uneasy participating in a program oriented to punishment in an environment that is already one of deprivation. The coercive power inherent in the prison setting creates the potential for unethical practices by treatment personnel. The fact that prisoners are captive audiences makes them attractive subjects for experimentation of all kinds. Most programs ask for volunteers rather than force participation, but in a prison environment the assumption is always implicit that release is tied to compliance, and therefore what may appear as voluntary action may be the result of no choice at all.

The psychologist's or psychiatrist's responsibility to innocent victims is being scrutinized more closely today. That is, what is the ethical responsibility of a counselor when an offender threatens future violence toward a particular victim? As in the legal profession, confidentiality is an issue for psychologists. Their ethical principles state:

> Psychologists have a primary obligation to respect the confidentiality of information obtained from persons in the course of their work as psychologists. They reveal such information to others only with the consent of the person or the person's legal representative, except in those unusual circumstances in which not to do so would result in clear danger to the person or to others. Where appropriate, psychologists inform their clients of the legal limits of confidentiality. ("Ethical Principles" 1981, 636)

Some psychiatrists find it hard to be associated with something as damaging as prison and feel a moral resistance to involvement with prison treatment efforts, given the negative effects that are inevitable. Thomas (cited in Tanay 1982, 386) writes:

> The length of sentences and the nature of maximum security prisons combine to damage the personalities of the prisoners to such a degree as to make it especially difficult for them to function as autonomous and independent individuals in a free society following their

release. I believe that whenever a man serves three or more years in a maximum security prison, the experience will usually have a lasting deleterious effect on his personality.

Even for those who feel comfortable working in prison, in many instances treatment and security concerns clash. The treatment professional must choose between two value systems. To emphasize security concerns puts the psychiatrist or counselor in the role of a custodian with professional training used only to better control inmate behavior. To emphasize treatment concerns puts professionals in an antagonistic role vis-à-vis the security staff, and they may find themselves in situations where these concerns directly conflict. For instance, if the superintendent demands to see a client's file to support a disciplinary committee's decision, should the psychiatrist surrender the information that was given in confidence? In answer to this dilemma, the psychiatrist or psychologist should probably never allow the inmate to assume that information regarding rule infractions or potential wrongdoing can ever be confidential. On the other hand, if inmates are aware that counselors and psychologists can offer no confidentiality protections, then the treatment process may be affected. The issues that confront treatment personnel in prison seem to always involve the conflicting goals of punishment and treatment.

MANAGEMENT ISSUES

Administrators are removed from day-to-day contact with inmates, but their power over decision making may actually be greater than that of line staff. Administrators make decisions regarding budget allocations, programs, and rules and procedures. Administrators in correctional facilities emphasize the goal of control—that is, keeping the facility out of the newspapers and minimizing negative publicity. Because of this emphasis, administrators may be faced with difficult choices. For instance, all treatment programs using outside people are potential security risks. An easy solution would be to prohibit all outsiders from entering the prison. Obviously, few prison administrators are this stringent in their control, but the choice may be made in specific instances to limit entry based on convenience and security. The decision to limit entry could probably be justified under a utilitarian framework, but other ethical systems may not support it.

Another dilemma decision makers face is the balance between cost and inmate or officer need. If inmates' programming is weak, clothing is minimal, or medical care is inadequate, or if officers' safety is compromised because too few are employed or too much overtime is mandated, a decision maker must at some point decide priorities. Obviously, administrators often have no choice since they can only work within the budget given. However, situations do arise in governmental agencies where workers are told there is no money in the budget for needed items like office supplies and equipment or overtime pay, yet at the same time administrators do have the budget to order expensive new office furniture for themselves or go on expensive training weekends.

This discrepancy between what administrators say and what workers see is demoralizing to those in the helping professions who try to make do with increasingly smaller budgets. Moral leadership is exhibited by those administrators who share the sacrifices.

Administrators have found themselves forced to change after prisoners' rights lawsuits have resulted in court mandates to change. The implementation of court-ordered changes has often been halting and superficial, showing that compliance to the letter may be different from compliance to the spirit. Is this response to court-ordered change an ethical one? Administrators also have found themselves in the position of testifying in court about conditions or the actions of their employees. They may change their testimony to protect themselves or others; in this situation their ethical dilemma is similar to that of police officers testifying about undercover activities.

The fate of a rabble-rouser is well illustrated by Tom Murton (1982), who found his career sidetracked when he was hired by the Arkansas Department of Corrections and proceeded to expose much of the corruption and brutality present on the Cummins and Tucker prison farms. Individuals are often forced to make a choice between their career and challenging unethical or illegal practices. For administrators, this dilemma may appear more often since the scope of their knowledge is broader than that of line staff. Often the career path of an administrator, with its investment of time and energy and the mandate to be a "company man," creates an immersion in bureaucratic thinking to the point that an individual loses sight of ethical issues. How he or she decides on a course of action may be influenced by the definitions placed on the situation—that is, whether or not the decision is perceived to be ethical in nature.

Another issue for correctional managers is what to do when faced with a worker alleging sexual harassment. The type of behavior defined as constituting a "hostile work environment" was common when women first entered as officers in prisons for males. Women officers reported behavior such as C.O.'s making sexual references and disparaging comments to them in front of inmates, "setting them up" by having inmates masturbate when they were sent down the tier, putting up posters with naked women and sexual messages, and even more serious behaviors such as assaults and attempted rapes. Today, the behavior women experience is not so blatant, but some still do experience problems. When a correctional manager is approached by a female subordinate who is in a work environment where other officers or workers conduct themselves in a manner that makes her uncomfortable, there is a tendency to encourage her to handle it herself and not rock the boat. All administrators fear negative publicity and lawsuits, and if a problem such as sexual harassment can be swept under the rug, there is a great temptation to do so. Even ethical administrators face conflicting duties. They have a duty to the organization—to keep it from having to defend itself against a lawsuit—but also to the employee—to help the employee undertake the best course of action, and that might be to pursue charges. An ethical resolution to the problem may be to talk to the individuals involved, punish them, or encourage the complainant to pursue internal or external sanctions.

Administrators may be responsible for officers who are accused of committing wrongs against inmates, such as brutality or harassment. In this situation, there are difficulties in making a stand. If the administrator supports the officer (publicly or privately) he or she is in effect condoning that behavior and allowing it to continue. If the administrator exposes the officer and subjects him or her to punishment, then there is a possibility that the administrator will lose the trust and allegiance of other officers who feel betrayed. The ideal situation, of course, would be one where everyone involved would not condone such behavior and would resolve it satisfactorily. Realistically, this is usually not the case. The best an administrator can probably do is to make it clear to all what will not be tolerated and serve as a role model; when wrongdoing is exposed, to treat the individuals involved fairly with due process and an opportunity to change; and if sanctions are deemed necessary, to administer them fairly and without favoritism.

It is often reported that officers feel that moving up in correctional ranks is determined more by who you know than by your qualifications. While this may be true to a certain degree in any bureaucracy, if it is prevalent it can serve to demoralize workers and contribute to an environment where people rationalize their own behavior by saying, "It doesn't matter, I can't get ahead here anyway." Administrators should obviously promote on the basis of qualifications rather than favoritism. Assignments should not be determined by friendships or other unfair criteria. Any power or discretion that administrators and managers wield by virtue of their position should not be viewed as personal power to be used for personal reasons. The rationale for every decision should be what is best for the organization, meaning what would best meet the organization's goals, not simply ensure the organization's survival.

A controversy currently exists over the issue of private corrections. While punishment is a state function, some states are now entering into contracts with private companies. Private prisons are either built and then leased to the state, or in some cases, actually run by the private corporation, who bills the state for the service. Many have objected to the profit motive entering into corrections and point to a number of ethical issues raised by private "profiteers." First, there are potential abuses of the bidding process, as in any situation where the government contracts with a company for services or products. Money may change hands to ensure that one organization receives the contract, companies may make informal agreements to "rig" the bids, and other potential corrupt practices may go on. In Texas, officials in a private corrections company were indicted for violating competitive bidding procedures (*Houston Post*, October 31, 1991, 26A). The laws at issue were murky; however, in essence the issue was whether by creating a nonprofit organization that contracted with the counties to build several prisons, the companies created a monopoly and eliminated the counties' ability to receive competitive bids for materials or services. Legal as well as ethical issues abound when private and public motives are mixed.

In the building phase, private corporations may cut corners and construct buildings without meeting proper standards for safety. Many examples exist in the private sector where inspectors have been bribed to ignore defects in materials or building. Managing the institution also raises the possibility that a private contractor will attempt to maximize profits by ignoring minimum standards of health and safety and will, if necessary, bribe inspectors or monitors to overlook the deficiencies. It has certainly happened in other areas, such as nursing homes, that those who contract with the state government and receive state monies, reap large profits by subjecting clients to inhumane conditions (Merlo 1992).

In a more general sense, some feel that punishment and profit are not compatible with one another, and linking the two historically has led to a variety of abuses (such as the contract labor system in the South). Although the decision to use private corporations is made by legislators, correctional administrators are faced with a variety of ethical dilemmas because of it, such as whether to support the idea, whether to accept a part-time position as a consultant to a private corporation when one has decision-making authority over issues that concern the corporation, and so on.

ETHICAL ISSUES IN PROBATION AND PAROLE

Probation and parole present different ethical issues from those discussed thus far. The rationale of community corrections is supported by the ethics of care. Community corrections promotes the needs of the offender and his or her relationship to the community. It is not banishment, as in a prison sentence, but rather control and care in the community or a reintegration back into the community. Of course, other ethical frameworks may also be used to support the concept of community corrections. Because this correctional alternative costs much less than institutional corrections, a utilitarian rationale can be used. It is better for both society and the offender if the cheapest method of controlling and correcting behavior can be found. Even ethical formalism can be used to provide a rationale for community corrections if the offender's crime can be viewed as only deserving a sentence to community corrections as opposed to prison. Souryal writes that community corrections "signifies a moral concern for the individual, one that is consistent with the natural law ethics of 'dignity of man,' the constitutional ethics of individualized treatment and *perhaps* [italics in original] the religious ethics of redemption" (1992, 356).

Community corrections has a more positive and helpful image than institutional corrections. Yet, even in this subsystem of the criminal justice system, the ideals of justice and care become diluted by bureaucratic mismanagement and personal agendas. Professionals in community corrections do not have the same power to use physical force as police and correctional officers do, but they do have a great deal of nonphysical power over the clients they control. Their authority and power can be used wisely and ethically or become subverted to personal ends.

Formal ethical guidelines for probation and parole officers are provided by the ACA code previously presented. Probation and parole officers are considered more professional than correctional officers: they typically have at least a bachelor's degree if not a graduate degree, they are subject to fewer organizational controls in the form of rule books and policies, and they have a great deal of discretion in the completion of their duties. The formal ethics of the profession is summarized by the ideal of service—to the community and to the offender—and herein lies the crux of most of the ethical issues that present themselves. Whether to favor meeting offenders' needs over community needs or vice versa is at the heart of a number of different ethical dilemmas for the probation and parole officer. Other ethical issues are more similar to those encountered in the other subsystems discussed; they primarily revolve around decisions to substitute personal values and goals for organizational ideals.

In this section we will briefly discuss some of the themes that have been touched on before—discretion, occupational subculture, and treatment of clients. While our treatment of these subjects may be more cursory than what has been accorded to other criminal justice professionals in this text, this by no means implies that these are less important.

Use of Discretion

Discretion in probation is used at the point of sentencing: probation officers make recommendations to judges concerning sentencing. Discretion is also used during supervision, probation officers decide when to file violation reports, decide what recommendation to make to the judge during revocation hearings, and make numerous decisions along the way regarding the people on their caseload. Parole boards also make decisions regarding release, and parole officers have the same discretion in managing their caseload that probation officers do. What are the criteria used for these decisions? Usually, the risk to the public is the primary factor, but other considerations also intrude. Some of these other considerations may be ethical; some may not. How would one evaluate the criteria of race, crime, family ties, the crowding in institutions, the status of the victim, or the publicity of the crime?

While probation officers write presentence reports to help judges sentence, research has found that there may be errors in the information presented and some officers are not as thorough as others in gathering information. This may not make much difference if it is true, as some have found, that probation officers' recommendations and judges' decisions are almost completely determined by the present offense and prior record anyway (Whitehead 1991).

Some practices that have been uncovered in both probation and parole are clearly unethical and even illegal. Peter Maas (1983) describes high-level corruption in Tennessee, where parole releases were being sold and traded for political favors. Obviously, this behavior is unethical and illegal, but other ethical questions are more subtle. In a recent controversy in Texas, ex-parole board members were found to have sold their services as parole consultants to inmates and inmates' families in order to help them obtain a favorable release decision. While the practice evidently was not against any state law, and those who participated described their help as simply explaining the process and helping the inmate prepare a presentation to the board, many viewed it as unethical. There is at least the possibility that what the inmate was buying was the ex-parole board member's influence, which derived from friendship, collegiality, or something else. Anytime government officials go into the private sector and trade on their status as ex-officials, we feel uncomfortable. There are specific laws against influence peddling at some levels of government reflecting this discomfort. In some situations, the possibility of private gain may influence how the official performs his or her job while in office, as in the case of military leaders who make decisions on buying from contractors and have plans to become vice-presidents for these companies when they retire. In other instances, the ability to provide an open door or inside information is considered unfair when used only for those who are willing to pay, as in the case of ex-White House staff who sell their services as consultants to foreign countries or corporations. The situation with ex-parole officials in Texas was brought to light when a serial killer was arrested for yet another murder while out on parole; when how he obtained parole was investigated, it was discovered that one of these parole consultants had been hired by the inmate. Was the consultant using his contacts in an ethical manner?

Office Subculture

The subculture of probation and parole officers has never been as extensively documented as that of police and correctional officers. Due to differences between these professions, the subculture of the former is not as pervasive or strong as that of the latter. First, probation and parole officers do not feel as isolated as police or correctional officers do. They experience no stigmatization, they have normal working hours, they do not wear a depersonalizing uniform, and they have a less obviously coercive relationship with their clients. These factors reduce the need for a subculture. On the other hand, one can probably identify some norms that might be found in any probation or parole office. First, there is a norm of cynicism toward clients. The subculture promotes the idea that clients are inept, deviant, and irredeemable. Probation and parole professionals who express positive attitudes toward client capacity for change are kidded as naive and guileless. Second, there is a pervasive subcultural norm of lethargy or minimal work output. This norm is supported by the view that officers are underpaid and overworked. Third, a norm of individualism can be identified. This relates to the idea that while parole and probation officers may seek opinions from other professionals in the office, there is an unspoken rule that each runs his or her own caseload; to offer unsolicited opinions about decisions another person makes toward his or her client violates this norm of autonomy.

Probation and parole officers have been described as adapting different roles on the job. In the same way that police have been described by the watchman, caretaker, and law enforcer typology, probation and parole officers have been described by their orientation to the job and individual adaptation to organizational goals. For instance, Souryal (1992) summarizes other literature in his description of the following types: the punitive law enforcer, the welfare/therapeutic practitioner, the passive time server, and the combined model. Different ethical issues can be discussed in relation to each of these types. For instance, the punitive law enforcer may need to examine the ethical use of authority. The welfare/therapeutic worker may need to think about natural law rights of privacy and autonomy. The passive time server needs to be aware of ethical formalism and concerns of duty. Some of these issues will be discussed more fully in a moment.

As is the case for many of the other criminal justice professionals we have discussed in the book, parole and probation officers often have a great deal of flexibility in their day. They leave the office to make field contacts; they often don't work on weekdays since weekends are more conducive to home visits. While this flexibility is necessary if they are to do the job, some abuse it and use the freedom to accomplish personal tasks or spend time at home. Some offices have attempted to prevent this behavior by instituting measures such as time clocks and strict controls on movements, but these controls are inconsistent with professionalism and not conducive to the nature of the task. Other offices develop norms that accept unethical practices and lethargy. Once this occurs it becomes a difficult pattern to change. If it is already present, a single officer will have a hard time not falling into the pattern. If all officers feel overwhelmed by their caseloads and the relative lack of power they have to do anything about failure, then the result may be that they throw up their hands and adapt a "Who cares?" attitude. If the supervisor does not exhibit a commitment to the goal of the organization and instead is a petty bureaucrat or does not encourage workers, then there is an inevitable deterioration of morale.

Whitehead (1991) discusses workers' frustration over incompetents being promoted, low wages, and high caseloads that leads to burnout. Souryal (1992) notes that low pay, a public view that probation and parole are ineffective, and the politicization of parole and probation are factors in professionals' feeling that their role is ambiguous, contradictory, and politically vulnerable. Disillusionment becomes almost inevitable. While these things exist in many organizations, they are especially problematic in a profession that requires a great deal of emotional investment on the part of the practitioner. If the organization does not encourage and support good workers, then it is no wonder that what develops is an informal subculture that encourages minimum effort and treats organizational goals with sarcasm and cynicism.

Caseload Supervision

Discretion is as important during supervision as it is in the recommendation to release or sentence to prison. Many probation and parole officers do not submit violation reports automatically upon discovery of offender infractions. Some, in fact, may give the offender second or even third chances before initiating the revocation process. The discretion to decide when to write a violation report is a powerful element in the control the officer has over the offender, but it obviously can be misused. If the officer excuses serious violations, such as possessing a firearm or continuing drug use, and the decision to do so is based on personal favoritism, fear, or bribery, then that officer is putting the community at risk. If the officer sincerely believes the offender made a mistake and is a good risk, there is still a danger to the community. Is the decision any more ethical because of the officer's belief in the offender? Would it be more ethical to go by the book and always submit violation reports when the offender commits any violation, including a technical condition?

Probation and parole officers are presented with other dilemmas in their supervision of offenders. For instance, often the offender acquires a job without the employer's knowledge of his or her previous criminality. Is it the duty of the officer to inform the employer and thereby risk the continued employment of the offender? What about when offenders become personally involved with others and refuse to tell them about their past history? Does the probation or parole officer have a duty to the unwary party? What is the probation and parole officer's responsibility to the offender's family? If they are unwilling to help the offender and perhaps fear his or her presence, should the parole officer find a reason for revocation? Again, these questions revolve around competing loyalties to public and client. The correctional professional must balance these interests in every decision; often, these decisions are not easy to make.

There have been isolated instances of parole or probation officers encouraging those on their caseload to commit crimes to share in the profits, in effect running a burglary ring, but these events are extremely rare. What is more common is the officer who is burned out and not doing much at all.

CONCLUSION

In this chapter we have touched on some rationales for punishment and treatment and some of the ethical issues correctional personnel face. These individuals have much in common with other criminal justice practitioners, especially in the area of discretion, but they also are in a unique position in that they hold power over the most basic aspects of life for confined inmates or over the freedom of those in community corrections. This position allows correctional officers either to intensify the humiliation incarcerated adults feel or to make the prison experience more tolerable for those who serve time. The difficult decisions for correctional officers arise from the personal relationships that develop with inmates, the trust that is sometimes betrayed, the favors that seem harmless, and the coercive environment that makes violence normal and humanity abnormal. Correctional treatment personnel have their own problems in resolving conflicts between loyalty toward clients and toward the system. To be in a helping profession in a system geared for punishment is a difficult challenge for anyone, and the temptation to retreat into bureaucratic compliance is ever present. Probation and parole personnel face some ethical issues similar to those faced by other criminal justice professionals, as well as unique issues not found in institutional corrections, related to their power over offenders' freedom.

One final note: although this chapter has discussed officers mistreating inmates and correctional professionals engaging in other unethical conduct, this should not be taken to imply that correctional professionals are generally or pervasively unethical. The corrections system only operates as well as it does because of the caring, committed, honest people who choose it as a career.

DISCUSSION QUESTIONS

1. What do you feel is the primary goal of our corrections system?
2. If you knew for certain that prison did not deter, would you still be in favor of its use? Why? What about capital punishment?
3. If we could predict future criminals, would you be willing to incapacitate them for society's protection?

4. Should we have guidelines for what we do in the name of treatment? What should they be?
5. State your opinion about the use of capital punishment and the reasons why you believe the way you do. Now take the opposite side and give the reasons for the opposing view.
6. Watch a movie or read a book that deals with correctional issues (*Brubaker, Marie*). What are the ethical issues presented? How would you resolve them using one of the ethical frameworks discussed in this book?
7. Analyze some of the correctional practices in existence today (or that could potentially be considered) under the ethical frameworks. Look at such things as electronic monitoring, castration for sex offenders, behavior modification, chemotherapy for violent offenders, boot camps for youthful offenders, and private corrections.

⊣ ETHICAL DILEMMAS ⊢

Please read and respond to the following situations. Be prepared to discuss your ideas.

Situation 1

You are a prison guard supervising a tier. One of the inmates comes to you and asks a favor. Because he is a troublemaker, his mail privileges have been taken away. He wants you to mail a letter for him. You figure it's not such a big deal and besides, you know he could make your job easier by keeping the other inmates on the tier in line. What would you tell him?

Situation 2

As a new C.O. you soon realize that there is a great deal of corruption and graft taking place in the prison. Guards routinely bring in contraband for inmates in return for money, food bought for the inmates' mess hall finds its way into the trunks of staff cars, and money is being siphoned from inmate accounts. You are not sure how far up the corruption goes. Would you keep your mouth shut because they're just inmates anyway? Would you go to your supervisors? What if, in exposing the corruption, you implicated yourself? What if you implicated a friend?

Situation 3

You are a prison psychologist and during the course of your counseling session with one drug offender, he confesses he has been using drugs. Obviously, this is a serious violation of prison rules. Should you report him? What if he told you of an impending escape plan?

Situation 4

You are a probation officer and have a caseload that presents a variety of different types of people. One of the offenders is a young woman who was involved in drugs through her boyfriend. You have managed to get her through a drug treatment program and believe she is straight. As it happens, she lives in your neighborhood and you have developed a kind of social friendship with her—she babysits for you sometimes and often eats dinner with you and your family. While you would ordinarily never think of mixing your social life with your job, this relationship has developed because she seems like someone that you otherwise might have been friendly with—in fact, she is about your age and even went to a rival high school. One day you are making a home visit to one of the other probationers in your caseload and he tells you that he has seen this young woman at a crack house. What would you do? What would you do if she came to you and confessed that she had started using drugs again? Would you do anything differently if it were another client?

⊰ 9 ⊱

Professionalism,
Pride, and Ethics
for Real People

In the course of this book we have explored ethical issues in each of the subsystems of the criminal justice system. We have discovered that some themes run through all of these subsystems—the ethical use of authority, power, force, and discretion; subcultural barriers to ethical decision making; and the importance of ethical leadership. In this final chapter we will reiterate these themes in a discussion of why ethics is so extremely important in criminal justice. Also, we will offer some final thoughts on how to decide what is ethical, given an ethical dilemma. Finally, we will address the more basic question, "Why be ethical?"

ETHICS AND CRIMINAL JUSTICE

As stated before, professionals in all areas of criminal justice have awesome power over people's lives. Criminal law and the system to implement it deal with all the fundamental questions that have concerned philosophers down through the ages. In criminal justice we must wrestle with questions of responsibility and excuse, the limits of the state's right to control the individual, the ethical use of force, and the appropriate use of discretion. Box 9-1 summarizes a description of the connections between philosophy and criminal justice presented by Murphy (1985, 4).

While professionals and practitioners may get bogged down with day-to-day problems and bureaucratic agendas may cause them to lose sight of larger goals, foremost in their minds should be the true scope and meaning of the power inherent in the criminal justice system. That power demands and depends on each person's maintaining high standards of ethical behavior. It is the people within a justice system who make it just or corrupt.

To protect citizenry from misuse and abuse of the power inherent in a justice system, personnel in the system must have a strong professional identity. There is a continuing debate over whether police officers can be described as professionals; there is even more debate over whether correctional officers can be described as such. These arguments miss a central point. Whether one calls the men and women who wear these uniforms professionals, practitioners, or some other term, the fact is they have immense power over other people's lives. This power must be recognized for what it is and held as a sacred trust. A professional is one whose job involves more than earning a paycheck and who has an interest in the public good. While this may not be true of all those who seek careers in the criminal justice system, it is certainly true for most. Consistently, research has shown that people who are interested in careers in criminal justice are attracted to the interaction with others and the helping aspects of the career. So whether we call them professionals or something else, this ideal of a career in criminal

---

Box 9-1
PHILOSOPHY AND CRIMINAL JUSTICE

1. *The intersection of law and morals:* Criminal law deals with issues that are at the heart of morality: excuse and justification, responsibility, duty and obligation, good and evil, right and wrong. A study of the legal use of a certain concept will also illuminate the moral use of that concept.
2. *The moral centrality of the topic of punishment:* The concept of punishment affects and is affected by a number of other moral concepts: blame, praise, reward, responsibility, mercy, forgiveness, justice, charity, obligation, and rights.
3. *Metaphysical involvement:* It is impossible to discuss the nature of a just system of responsibility and excuse without also discussing the mind-body problem, the problem of free will and determinism, and other metaphysical issues.
4. *Political philosophy:* If the central problem of political philosophy is coming to terms with the nature and justification of coercion, then punishment is state coercion in its most obvious form. Thus, political philosophy must come to terms with punishment.
5. *Philosophy and empirical science:* While philosophical theories are not themselves empirical, and philosophers are not usually engaged in assessing the confirmation of empirical claims, falsity may undercut their own theories. Therefore, they have an obligation to keep informed of relevant work in the scientific community.
6. *Practical urgency:* If philosophy is to be socially useful, then the issues of punishment and responsibility seem to provide an area in which philosophical work can have practical social utility.

(*Source:* Murphy 1985, 4)

justice as a vocation rather than simply a way to earn a paycheck should be nourished and developed. Instead, what often happens is that the bureaucracy and leadership stifle and destroy the ideals of those who enter as criminal justice practitioners.

HOW TO MAKE AN ETHICAL DECISION

John Rawls presents a somewhat abstract procedure for deciding moral issues. He explains that moral principles can be developed through inductive logic. The method to discover these moral principles is through the considered moral judgments over a number of cases by a number of moral judges. These individuals would have the following characteristics: they would possess common sense (that is, they would not intellectualize the problem at hand, but would be reasonable), they would have open minds, they would know their own emotions, and they would have sympathetic knowledge of humans. The cases given them to decide would be such that the judges would not be harmed or benefited in any way by their decision, to ensure neutrality. The cases would present real conflicts of interest, but conflicts that were not too difficult and that were likely to present themselves in ordinary life. The judges would be presented with all relevant facts in the matter so that they could make a reasoned judgment. The judgments should be certain and they should be stable; that is, other judges at other times should be able to arrive at the same judgments. Finally, the judgments should be intuitive. The reason for this is that ethical principles are to be derived from a series of judgments, and if judges were already using predetermined rules, there would be no way to derive general rules from the judgments. Rawls (1957, 180) describes the procedure so far:

> Up to this point I have defined, first a class of competent judges, and, second, a class of considered judgments. If competent judges are those persons most likely to make correct decisions, then we should take care to abstract those judgments of theirs which, from the conditions and circumstances under which they are made, are most likely to be correct.

The next step is to formulate an explication of the total range of judgments. An *explication* is a set of principles described as follows (Rawls 1957, 182):

> If any competent man were to apply them intelligently and consistently to the same cases under review, his judgments, made systematically nonintuitive by the explicit and conscious use of the principles, would be, nevertheless, identical, case by case, with the considered judgments of the group of competent judges.

These explications must be written in ordinary language in the form of principles, and they must be comprehensive in solving the range of moral judgments. In other words, the decisions of the moral judges are as important as any common principles that were used in their decision making. In this way, we can identify the principles of these moral judges and apply them to other moral questions (Rawls 1957).

Obviously, Rawls's proposal is more rhetorical device than usefι ethical issues. The basic premise of this exercise, however, is to disco ciples used to decide moral questions. This is fundamental to any moral dilemmas. The ethical systems we have discussed throughout principles similar to the explications Rawls seeks through moral juuges. ror instance, ethical formalism presents basic principles for moral decision making in the form of the categorical imperative. The rules of the categorical imperative match some of the definitional components of Rawls's explications, since they are in the form of principles and are comprehensive.

In a mathematical analogy, sampling distributions are used in statistical analyses to represent probabalistically the pattern of variation that might be expected from the total population of interest. Similarly in Rawls's proposal, the particular explications of these moral judges' responses to the different moral dilemmas are important primarily in how the responses contribute to and predict the pattern of the whole.

While Rawls's effort to delineate the steps needed to arrive at moral principles is logically appealing, it does not help an individual make personal decisions when confronted with ethical dilemmas. Other writers have attempted to provide more pragmatic guidelines for use in decision making. A method proposed by Nash (1981, 81) helps individuals make business decisions. She suggests asking the following questions before making a difficult decision:

1. Have you defined the problem accurately?
2. How would you define the problem if you stood on the other side of the fence?
3. How did the situation occur in the first place?
4. To whom and to what do you give your loyalty as a person and as a member of the corporation?
5. What is your intention in making this decision?
6. How does this intention compare with the probable result?
7. Whom could your decision or action injure?
8. Can you discuss the problem with the affected parties before you make your decision?
9. Are you confident that your position will be as valid over a long period of time as it seems now?
10. Could you disclose without qualm your decision or action to your boss, your CEO, the board of directors, your family, your society as a whole?
11. What is the symbolic potential of your action if understood? If misunderstood?
12. Under what conditions would you allow exceptions to your stand?

Although these guidelines are for business decisions, they also apply to other fields. Basically, the questions are designed to lead individuals to analyze their behavior and its implications. They rely on a realization of unethical conduct and the fact that if made public, unethical conduct would make the individual feel uneasy. Of course, it is assumed that there is a commonly agreed-upon definition of right and wrong. The general principles that can be drawn from these questions are obvious. First, we are interested in attaining all the facts of the situation; this includes the effects of the decision on oneself and others. It is important to understand hidden motivations and indirect effects. Second, the concept of scrutiny works well to evaluate the decision taken; one must be comfortable with public disclosure, or else there may be some ethical problems with the decision. Along with this concept goes the notion that others should be able to make the same decision and have it judged acceptable. Finally, the concept of rationale or reason implies that the individual decision is based on a larger set of moral or ethical principles.

Let us apply these guidelines to a criminal justice example. If a police officer were confronted with an opportunity to accept some type of gratuity, either a dinner or a more expensive present, the officer should first evaluate all the facts. Is anything expected in return? Is the gift really a gift, or a payment for some service? Would the officer be comfortable if others knew of the gift or gratuity? Finally, could the officer reconcile the decision to take the gratuity with a larger set of moral principles?

Krogstand and Robertson (1979) describe three principles of ethical decision making. The first is the *imperative principle*, which directs a decision maker to act according to a specific, unbending rule. The second is the *utilitarian principle*, which determines the ethics of conduct by the good or bad consequences of the action. The third is the *generalization principle*, which is based on the question: "What would happen if all similar persons acted this way under similar circumstances?" These should sound familiar because they are, respectively, religious or absolutist ethics, utilitarianism, and ethical formalism. Ethical frameworks, if recognized, can be a great aid in individual decision making. If one is familiar with these ethical principles, then any specific dilemma can be analyzed using the ethical framework as a guideline.

To question one's general ethical behavior is a challenging self-survey. The following set of questions takes a general approach to evaluating one's ethics. It is from the American Society for Public Administration (1979, 22–23) but has been adapted where necessary to apply to those who work in the criminal justice field.

1. Do I confront difficult ethical decisions directly and attempt to think through the alternatives and the principles involved? Am I inclined to make decisions on grounds of convenience, expediency, pressure, impulse, or inertia?
2. Do I systematically review my behavior and question whether what I do is consistent with my professional values?
3. If someone asked me to explain my professional ethics, what would I say?
4. Have my values and ethics changed since I began working in the field? If so, why and how have they changed? What are the primary influences that have changed my thinking?
5. Looking ahead to the remainder of my career, are there particular areas of my ethical conduct to which I would like to pay closer attention?
6. Do I ever find myself in situations in which providing equitable treatment of clients, members of my organization, or members of other organizations creates ethical conflicts? How do I handle such dilemmas? Can I perceive any consistent pattern in my behavior?
7. Where do my professional loyalties ultimately lie? With the Constitution? The law? My organization? My superiors? My clients? The general public? Do I feel torn by these loyalties? How do I deal with the conflicts?

8. Do I ever confront situations in which I feel that it is unfair to treat everyone in the same way? How do I determine what to do in those cases? How do I decide what is fair?
9. When I am responsible for some activity that turns out inappropriately or not as I desired, do I accept full responsibility for it? Why? How?
10. Do I ever dismiss criticism of my actions with the explanation that I am only "following orders"? Do I accept any responsibility for what happens in these circumstances?

The simplest formulation of questions on which to base an ethical decision is: Does it affect others? Does it hurt others? Would I want it done if I were on the other side? Would I be proud of the decision? These four simple questions may be sufficient to address most ethical issues.

In the second chapter of this book the ethics of virtue was discussed. Part of this ethical framework is the idea that one's character is most relevant to ethical decision making. That is, good character is comprised of virtues such as honesty, trustworthiness, generosity, and so on. Bad character, obviously, would be the absence or opposite of these traits. If one has a bad character, then one is unlikely to perceive ethical dilemmas, since one will go through life in essence an egoist, making choices influenced by one's negative character traits. If one has a good character, then one does not perceive ethical dilemmas in some situations either, since it is second nature for one to do the honorable thing, whether it be not steal or tell the truth or whatever. Most people in the criminal justice field (or indeed any profession) have basically good characters; some do not. In some situations, even those who have formed habits of honesty, truthfulness, and integrity are sincerely perplexed as to the correct course of behavior. These situations occur because the behavior choice seems so innocuous or trivial (for example, whether to accept free coffee) or seems so difficult (for example, how to reconcile demands of loyalty to friends versus loyalty to the organization or society). In these instances where basically good people have trouble deciding what to do, the ethical frameworks provided in this volume might help them analyze their choices. It must also be accepted that in some dilemmas, there are no good choices.

In any organization, there are those who will almost always make ethical choices, those who will usually make unethical ones, and those who can be influenced one way or the other. The best course of action is to identify those in the second group and encourage them to find other employment or at least remove them from temptation. Then, organizational leaders must create an atmosphere for the third group that encourages ethical decision making. This can be done by promoting ethical administrators, rewarding morally courageous behavior, and providing clear and powerful organizational policies that emphasize worthwhile goals and honest means.

For criminal justice practitioners, ethical decisions arise from the exercise of discretion and the use of power. Criminal justice practitioners find themselves faced with ethical choices when balancing friendship against institutional integrity—that is, when friends and colleagues engage in inappropriate or illegal behavior or rulebreaking. There are also ethical choices to be made when balancing client (offender) needs against bureaucratic efficiency and institutional goals. In each of these areas, the individual professional must make a choice. How that choice is made depends on recognizing the situation as one involving ethics, and recognizing one's values and one's ethical system.

In conclusion, the individual should become aware of the implications of day-to-day choices—sharpen his or her ethical antennae, so to speak. Small decisions become larger life positions in a slow, cumulative way. When faced with a choice of behavior, one should first examine all possible solutions to the problem and be aware of direct and indirect effects of each response. Often, ethical issues that arise from the nature of the criminal justice professional's role are not recognized for what they are. The individual may limit analysis of a problem to finding a short-term solution or making a quick decision, in which case the larger issues or the situation's ethical implications are never addressed. It becomes easy to rationalize unethical behavior in this way by the explanation that it only happened once or that the action taken was the easiest.

Then, one should determine whether any solutions would be viewed as unacceptable if made public and for what reason. If an individual would be uncomfortable talking about an action, then chances are it is questionable. Too often, unethical decisions are protected by a shroud of secrecy, and then the secrecy is defended by pleading institutional or agency confidentiality. On an individual level, unethical behavior is almost always hidden, and further unethical behavior may follow to cover up what has already been done. Probably the best signal that something is wrong is when a person hesitates to make it public knowledge.

Finally, the individual must be able to reconcile the decision with her or his personal set of values or ethical system. Hopefully, the ethical concepts, discussions, and issues we have presented in this volume have helped clarify these decision processes. When one has to make a difficult decision about a moral issue, although one has recourse to value systems passed on by family and advice and counsel from friends and colleagues, ultimately the decision made should be one the individual is willing to take responsibility for and be proud of.

———•◆•———

WHY BE ETHICAL?

After completing a class on ethics, which involved detailed explanations and applications of the ethical systems discussed in this book, an individual responded with the question, "Why should we?" Meaning, why should anyone be ethical or moral? There is a long version and a short version of the answer to this question. The long version is that philosophers down through the ages have examined, debated, and analyzed this same question. The ethical systems can be seen as not only answering the question "What is good?" but also the question "Why be good?" Under ethical formalism the answer is that the world works better, and it is rational to do one's duty and live up to the categorical imperative. Under utilitarianism, the answer is that it is better for everyone, including the individual, to do what benefits the majority. Under the ethics of care, the answer is that we naturally and instinctively have the capacity to care and be concerned with others. Each of the other frameworks also provides answers. One dominant theme emerges from all the ethical systems—that we are connected to each other in fundamental and emotional ways. The golden rule, the universalism principle under the categorical imperative, rule utilitarianism, even enlightened egoism recognize this connection. The theme running through all these ethical systems is empathy and caring for each other. One senses this interconnectedness intuitively or can explain it rationally. The reason we should act ethically can be explained rationally (ethical formalism and utilitarianism) or intuitively (ethics of care, religion).

Professional ethics is merely an application of moral systems to a particular set of questions or a specific environment. The basis of all professional ethical codes is the same: to be a good professional, one must be a good person. This chapter may be criticized as too short, too superficial, too uninformative. My response is that for everyone other than philosophers most of these issues are simple. How does one act ethically? Make ethical choices. How does one know what they are? Most of the time the answer is easy—no one needs to tell a police officer that stealing or taking a bribe is wrong, and no one needs to tell a correctional officer that beating up a helpless inmate is wrong. Rationalizations are developed because we know these actions are wrong. For those choices that are truly difficult, people of goodwill, using rationality and sensitivity, can apply any ethical system and come up with an ethical solution. It may not be the best, not everyone may agree, but it will allow the individual to be satisfied that he or she made a choice based on ethics rather than egoism. Finally, why be ethical? The short answer was given by someone in a class who said "So you can sleep at night." Simplistic, perhaps, but no less accurate.

To become cynical and pessimistic in the field of criminal justice is all too easy. Organizational, peer, and societal pressures seem to conspire against ethical decision making. It takes each individual person to say, "I am responsible for my actions and I will try to make the right choice." If there are enough of these people, then law enforcement, the courts, and corrections can represent the best of democratic ideals and we can be proud to be associated with a system that has the goal as well as the reality of justice.

DISCUSSION QUESTIONS

1. Select the most difficult ethical dilemma in the previous chapters and try to answer it again using the questions given by Laura Nash.
2. Now select an ethical or moral dilemma from your own life and try to resolve it using any guidelines derived from this volume. Be explicit about the procedure you used to arrive at a decision and the decision itself.

❧ A ❧

Summary of and Selections from the ABA Model Rules of Professional Responsibility

Preamble, Scope, and Terminology

This section states that a lawyer is a representative of clients, an officer of the legal system, and a public citizen having special responsibility for the quality of justice. A lawyer has a duty to zealously assert his or her client's position, consistent with requirements of honest dealing with others. The lawyer should act as a mediator when appropriate. The lawyer should always be competent, prompt, and diligent. He or she should maintain confidentiality. It is the lawyer's duty to uphold the law and the legal process. A lawyer should improve the administration of law; this includes providing aid to those who cannot afford legal assistance. Because lawyers are largely self-governing, each has a responsibility to observe the rules of professional conduct and aid in securing their observance by other lawyers.

The rules of professional conduct are partly obligatory and partly permissive. If a rule is phrased as "shall" or "shall not," it is an imperative and may be the subject of a disciplinary action. Other rules using "may" provide guidance, but the individual may use his or her own discretion. The rest of this section explains the relationship between the rules and other laws and governing documents.

Client-Lawyer Relationship

1.1 Competence Lawyers shall provide competent representation—up-to-date legal knowledge, skill, preparation, and diligence. A lawyer can take a case that presents new legal issues, if willing to do reasonable preparation and study.

1.2 Scope of Representation A lawyer must accept the client's direction in certain decisions regarding the case. For criminal cases, it is the client's decision whether to submit a plea, whether to waive jury trial, and whether to testify. A lawyer shall not help a client or advise him or her in any way to commit a criminal act.

1.3 Diligence Demands due diligence and promptness in serving the client.

(Adapted and summarized from the *ABA Model Rules of Professional Responsibility*, copyright 1991 by the American Bar Association. All rights reserved. Reprinted with permission.)

1.4 Communication   Adequate communication with the client regarding the case is required.

1.5 Fees   Lawyers' fees must be reasonable, taking into consideration the time and skill required, as well as the difficulty.

1.6 Confidentiality   Lawyers must never reveal information relating to representation of a client unless the client consents after consultation; unless it is to stop the client from committing a criminal act that the lawyer believes is likely to result in imminent death or substantial bodily harm; or to establish a claim or defense on behalf of the lawyer in a controversy between the two of them.

1.7 Conflict of Interest   A lawyer shall not represent two clients who may have competing interests, or if the client's interest may conflict with his or her own interests, unless the client consents after consultation.

1.16 Declining or Terminating Representation   A lawyer must withdraw from representation if to continue would involve violation of the rules of professional conduct or if the lawyer's physical or mental condition materially impairs the lawyer's ability or if the lawyer is discharged. Other than the above conditions, a lawyer may only withdraw if the withdrawal does not result in adverse effects for the client or if the client persists in criminal or fraudulent plans, the client has used the lawyer to commit a crime or fraud, the client insists on objects that are repugnant or imprudent to the lawyer, the client hasn't lived up to obligations and the lawyer has warned of the consequences of such an action, the representation will result in an unreasonable financial burden on the lawyer, or for other good cause. If ordered to do so by a tribunal, the lawyer must continue representing the client even if good cause for withdrawal exists.

Counselor

2.1 Advisor   A lawyer shall exercise independent judgment and give candid advice, giving consideration to moral, economic, social, political, and legal factors.

2.2 Intermediary   A lawyer may act as intermediary between clients if they both know of the risks of such representation and still give their consent, and the lawyer believes such representation can be impartial and fulfill responsibilities to each party.

Advocate

3.1 Meritorious Claims and Contentions   A lawyer shall not bring or defend a proceeding or legal issue that is frivolous or without merit. There must be at least a good faith argument for an extension, modification, or reversal of existing law. A lawyer for the defendant in a criminal proceeding, or the respondent in a proceeding that could result in incarceration, may nevertheless so defend the proceeding as to require that every element of the case be established.

3.2 Expediting Litigation   Make reasonable efforts to expedite litigation.

3.3 Candor toward the Tribunal   A lawyer shall not knowingly make a false statement of material fact or law or fail to disclose a material fact when disclosure is necessary to avoid assisting a criminal or fraudulent act by the client, or fail to disclose legal authority in the controlling jurisdiction that is directly adverse to the position of the client, or offer evidence that the lawyer knows to be false. If such material evidence becomes known to the lawyer as false after it has been entered, reasonable remedial measures must be taken.

3.4 Fairness to Opposing Party and Counsel   A lawyer shall not unlawfully obstruct opponents' access to evidence or alter, destroy, or conceal potential evidence, nor ask someone else to do so. Further, a lawyer cannot falsify evidence, allow anyone to testify falsely, disobey an obligation under the rules of a tribunal, make frivolous discovery requests, allude to anything in trial that will not be supported by admissible evidence, assert personal knowledge of facts in issue, state personal opinions as to the justness of a cause, the credibility of a witness, the culpability of a civil litigant, or the guilt or innocence of the accused, or request another person other than the client's relative not to give information to another party.

3.5 Impartiality and Decorum of the Tribunal   A lawyer shall not attempt to influence a judge, juror, prospective juror, or other official, or communicate ex parte with any person, or engage in disruptive conduct.

3.6 Trial Publicity   A lawyer shall not make public statements that may materially prejudice an adjudicative proceeding.

3.7 Lawyer as Witness   A lawyer can't be an advocate in a trial in which he or she will also be a witness.

3.8 Special Responsibilities of a Prosecutor   Duties include pursuing charges only supported by probable cause, making reasonable efforts to assure that the accused understands his or her rights, make timely disclosures to the defense of all evidence that tends to negate the guilt of the accused or mitigates the offense. A lawyer should not force a lawyer to give information about a client unless the prosecutor believes it isn't privileged information, it is related to an ongoing investigation, and there is no other way to get the information.

Transactions with Persons Other than Clients

4.1 Truthfulness in Statements to Others   A lawyer may not make a false statement of material fact or law to third persons or fail to disclose information to third parties necessary to prevent a crime or fraud committed by the client.

4.2 Communication with Person Represented by Counsel   A lawyer shall not communicate with a party who is represented by counsel without that counsel's presence, unless consent is given.

Public Service

6.1 Pro Bono Publico Service   A lawyer should provide public service in the form of no fee or reduced fee to poor clients.

6.2 Accepting Appointments   A lawyer should not refuse appointments by a tribunal unless such representation is likely to cause the lawyer to violate professional rules of conduct, create an unreasonable financial burden on the lawyer, or is a case or client that is so repugnant to the lawyer as to endanger the client-lawyer relationship.

Maintaining the Integrity of the Profession

8.1 Bar Admission and Disciplinary Matters   An applicant to the bar or lawyers who communicate in support of a bar application must not knowingly make a false statement of fact or fail to disclose any necessary fact to correct a misapprehension.

8.2 Judicial and Legal Officials   A lawyer shall not make any statements about judicial officers known to be false or with reckless disregard for the truth.

8.3 Reporting Professional Misconduct   A lawyer having knowledge that another lawyer or a judge has violated any of the rules of professional conduct that raises a substantial question as to that lawyer's honesty, trustworthiness, or fitness as a lawyer in other respects, shall inform the appropriate authority.

8.4 Misconduct   It is professional misconduct for a lawyer to violate any of the rules, assist others to do so, commit a criminal act that reflects adversely on the lawyer's honesty, trustworthiness, or fitness as a lawyer, engage in conduct that is dishonest or prejudicial to the administration of justice, state or imply an ability to influence improperly a government agency or official, or knowingly assist a judge or judicial officer in conduct that is a violation of applicable rules or law.

8.5 Jurisdiction   A lawyer admitted to practice in this jurisdiction is subject to the disciplinary authority of this jurisdiction although engaged in practice elsewhere.

⚜ B ⚜

Summary of the ABA Standards for the Defense Function

PART 1. General Standards

1.1 The Function of the Standards   These standards are intended to be used as a guide, not as criteria for the judicial evaluation of alleged misconduct.

1.2 The Function of Defense Counsel   Counsel for the accused is an essential component of the administration of criminal justice. Basic duty is to serve as the accused's counselor and advocate. Defense counsel in a capital case should respond by making extraordinary efforts on behalf of the accused. Defense counsel should seek to reform and improve the administration of criminal justice. Defense counsel should not intentionally misrepresent matters of fact or law to the court. Defense counsel should disclose to the tribunal legal authority in the controlling jurisdiction known to defense counsel to be directly adverse to the position of the accused and not disclosed by the prosecutor. It is the duty of defense counsel to know and be guided by the standards of professional conduct.

1.3 Delays; Punctuality; Workload   Defense counsel should act with reasonable diligence and promptness in representing a client, should avoid unnecessary delay, should be punctual, should not intentionally misrepresent facts or otherwise mislead the court in order to obtain a continuance, should not intentionally use procedural devices for delay for which there is no legitimate basis, and should not carry a workload that interferes with the rendering of quality representation.

1.4 Public Statements   Defense counsel should not make or authorize an extrajudicial statement that will have a substantial likelihood of prejudicing a criminal proceeding.

1.5 Advisory Councils on Professional Conduct   An advisory body should be established.

1.6 Trial Lawyer's Duty to Administration of Justice   The bar should encourage the widest possible participation in the defense of criminal cases by lawyers. All qualified lawyers should stand ready to undertake the defense of an accused regardless of public hostility toward the accused or personal distaste for the offense charged or the person of the defendant. Qualified law-

---

yers should not seek to avoid appointment by a tribunal to represent an accused except for good cause, such as: representing the accused is likely to result in violation of applicable ethical codes or other law, representing the accused is likely to result in an unreasonable financial burden on the lawyer, or the client or crime is so repugnant to the lawyer as to be likely to impair the client-lawyer relationship or the lawyer's ability to represent the client.

PART 2. Access to Counsel

2.1 Communication   Every jurisdiction should guarantee by statue or rule of court the right of an accused person to prompt and effective communication with a lawyer.

2.2 Referral Service for Criminal Cases   Every jurisdiction should have a referral service for criminal cases, which should be publicized.

2.3 Prohibited Referrals   Defense counsel should not give anything of value to a person for recommending the lawyer's services, and should not accept a referral from any source, including prosecutors, law enforcement personnel, victims, bondsmen, or court personnel, where the acceptance of such a referral is likely to create a conflict of interest.

PART 3. Lawyer-Client Relationship

3.1 Establishment of Relationship   Defense counsel should seek to establish a relationship of trust and confidence with the accused and should discuss the objectives of the representation and whether defense counsel will continue to represent the accused if there is an appeal. Defense counsel should explain the necessity of full disclosure of all facts known to the client for an effective defense, and explain the extent to which counsel's obligation of confidentiality makes privileged the accused's disclosures.

3.2 Interviewing the Client   Defense counsel should seek to determine all relevant facts known to the accused without seeking to influence the direction of the client's responses. Defense counsel should not instruct the client or intimate to the client in any way that the client should not be candid in revealing facts so as to afford defense counsel free rein to take action that would be precluded by counsel's knowing of such facts.

3.3 Fees   Defense counsel should not charge an illegal or unreasonable fee; should not imply that his or her compensation is for anything other than professional services rendered; should not divide a fee with a nonlawyer; and should not charge a contingent fee.

3.4 Obtaining Literary or Media Rights from the Accused   Prior to the conclusion of all aspects of the matter giving rise to his or her employment, defense counsel should not enter into any agreement or understanding with a client by which defense counsel acquires an interest in literary or media rights to a portrayal or account based in substantial part on information relating to the employment or proposed employment.

3.5 Conflicts of Interest   Defense counsel should not permit his or her professional judgment or obligations to be affected by his or her own political, financial, business, property, or personal interests. Ordinarily defense counsel should decline to act for more than one of several codefendants except in unusual situations.

3.6 Prompt Action to Protect the Accused   Defense counsel should inform the accused of his or her rights at the earliest opportunity and take all necessary action to vindicate such rights.

3.7 Advice and Service on Anticipated Unlawful Conduct   It is defense counsel's duty to advise a client to comply with the law. Defense counsel should not counsel a client in or knowingly assist a client to engage in conduct that defense counsel knows to be illegal or fraudulent; and should not agree in advance of the commission of a crime that he or she will serve as counsel for the defendant.

3.8 Duty to Keep Client Informed   Defense counsel should keep the client informed and should explain developments in the case to the extent reasonably necessary to permit the client to make informed decisions regarding representation.

3.9 Obligations of Hybrid and Standby Counsel   Defense counsel whose duty is to actively assist a pro se accused should permit the accused to make the final decisions on all matters.

PART 4. Investigation and Preparation

4.1 Duty to Investigate   Defense counsel should conduct a prompt investigation and should not seek to acquire possession of physical evidence where the sole purpose is to obstruct access to such evidence.

4.2 Illegal Investigation   Defense counsel should not knowingly use illegal means to obtain evidence or information.

4.3 Relations with Prospective Witnesses   Defense counsel should not use means to embarrass, delay, or burden a third person; should not compensate a witness, other than an expert; and should not discourage or obstruct communication between prospective witnesses and the prosecutor.

4.4 Relations with Expert Witnesses   Defense counsel should respect the independence of the expert and should not pay an excessive fee for the purpose of influencing an expert's testimony.

4.5 Compliance with Discovery Procedure   Defense counsel should make a reasonably diligent effort to comply with a legally proper discovery request.

4.6 Physical Evidence   Defense counsel who receives a physical item under circumstances implicating a client should disclose the location of or should deliver that item to law enforcement authorities only if required by law or court order, or if the item is contraband, possession of which is itself a crime. Defense counsel should return the item to the source and should also prepare a written record of these events.

PART 5. Control and Direction of Litigation

5.1 Advising the Accused   Defense counsel should advise the accused with complete candor, including a candid estimate of the possible outcome.

5.2 Control and Direction of the Case   Decisions to be made by the accused include what pleas to enter, whether to accept a plea agreement, whether to waive jury trial, whether to testify in his or her own behalf, and whether to appeal. Strategic and tactical decisions should be made by defense counsel.

PART 6. Disposition without Trial

6.1 Duty to Explore Disposition without Trial   Defense counsel should explore the possibility of early diversion, may engage in plea discussions, should not recommend to a defendant acceptance of a plea unless appropriate investigation and study of the case has been completed.

6.2 Plea Discussions   Defense counsel should keep the accused advised, should not knowingly make false statements, and should not seek concessions favorable to one client by any agreement that is detrimental to the legitimate interests of a client in another case.

PART 7. Trial

7.1 Courtroom Professionalism   Defense counsel should support the authority of the court and the dignity of the trial and should not engage in unauthorized ex parte discussions with or submission of material to a judge.

7.2 Selection of Jurors   Defense counsel should prepare himself or herself prior to trial, should neither harass nor unduly embarrass potential jurors or invade their privacy, and should not intentionally use the voir dire to present factual matter that defense counsel knows will not be admissible at trial.

7.3 Relations with Jury   Defense counsel should not intentionally communicate privately with persons summoned for jury duty or impaneled and should not intentionally make comments to or ask questions of a juror after the trial for the purpose of harassing or embarrassing the juror.

7.4 Opening Statement   Defense counsel's opening statement should be confined to a statement of the issues.

7.5 Presentation of Evidence   Defense counsel should not knowingly offer false evidence and should not ask legally objectionable questions.

7.6 Examination of Witnesses   The interrogation of all witnesses should be conducted fairly, objectively, and with due regard for the dignity and legitimate privacy of the witness, and without seeking to intimidate or humiliate the witness unnecessarily. Defense counsel's belief or knowledge that the witness is telling the truth does not preclude cross-examination.

7.7 Argument to the Jury   Defense counsel may argue all reasonable inferences from the evidence in the record but should not express a personal belief or opinion.

7.8 Facts Outside the Record   Defense counsel should not intentionally refer to or argue on the basis of facts outside the record.

7.9 Posttrial Motions   Defense counsel's responsibility includes presenting appropriate posttrial motions to protect the defendant's rights.

PART 8. After Conviction

8.1 Sentencing   Defense counsel should become familiar with all of the sentencing alternatives available to the court and should present to the court any ground that will assist in reaching a proper disposition favorable to the accused.

8.2 Appeal   Defense counsel should explain the meaning and consequences of the court's judgment and defendant's right of appeal and should give the defendant his or her professional judgment as to whether there are meritorious grounds for appeal. Defense counsel should take whatever steps are necessary to protect the defendant's rights of appeal.

8.3 Counsel on Appeal   Appellate counsel should not seek to withdraw from a case solely on the basis of his or her own determination that the appeal lacks merit but should endeavor to persuade the client to abandon a wholly frivolous appeal or to eliminate contentions lacking in substance. Appellate counsel has the ultimate authority to decide which arguments to make on appeal and should inform the client of his or her pro se briefing rights.

8.4 Conduct of Appeal   Appellate counsel should be diligent in perfecting appeals and should be accurate.

8.5 Postconviction Remedies   After a conviction is affirmed on appeal, appellate counsel should determine whether there is any ground for relief under other postconviction remedies.

8.6 Challenges to the Effectiveness of Counsel   If defense counsel is satisfied that another defense counsel who served in an earlier phase of the case did not provide effective assistance, he or she should not hesitate to seek relief for the defendant on that ground.

⇥ C ⇤

Summary of the ABA Standards for the Prosecution Function

PART 1. General Standards

1.1 The Function of the Standards   These standards are intended to be used as a guide, not as criteria for the judicial evaluation of alleged misconduct.

1.2 The Function of the Prosecutor   The prosecutor is an administrator of justice, an advocate, and an officer of the court; the prosecutor must exercise sound discretion in the performance of his or her functions.

1.3 Conflicts of Interest   A prosecutor should avoid a conflict of interest with respect to his or her official duties. He or she should not represent a defendant in criminal proceedings in a jurisdiction where he or she is also employed as a prosecutor, cannot participate in a matter in which he or she participated personally and substantially while in private practice, and should not recommend the services of a particular defense counsel to accused.

1.4 Public Statements   A prosecutor should not make or authorize an extrajudicial statement that will have a substantial likelihood of prejudicing a criminal proceeding.

1.5 Duty to Respond to Misconduct   Where a prosecutor knows that another person associated with the prosecutor's office is engaged in action, intends to act, or refuses to act in a manner that is a violation of a legal obligation to the prosecutor's office or a violation of law, the prosecutor should follow the policies of his or her office. He or she should ask the person to reconsider the action or inaction or should refer the matter to higher authority.

PART 2. Organization of the Prosecution Function

2.1 Prosecution Authority to Be Vested in a Public Official
2.2 Interrelationship of Prosecution Offices within a State
2.3 Assuring High Standards of Professional Skill
2.4 Special Assistants, Investigative Resources, Experts

2.5 Prosecutor's Handbook; Policy Guidelines and Procedures
2.6 Training Programs
2.7 Relations with Police
2.8 Relations with the Courts and Bar   A prosecutor should not intentionally misrepresent matters of fact or law to the court, should carefully strive to preserve the appearance as well as the reality of the correct relationship, and should not engage in unauthorized ex parte discussions with or submission of material to a judge. A prosecutor should strive to develop good working relationships with defense counsel in order to facilitate the resolution of ethical problems.
2.9 Prompt Disposition of Criminal Charges   A prosecutor should avoid unnecessary delay in the disposition of cases and should not intentionally use procedural devices for delay.
2.10 Supercession and Substitution of Prosecutor
2.11 Literary or Media Agreements   A prosecutor, prior to conclusion of all aspects of a matter, should not enter into any agreement or understanding by which the prosecutor acquires an interest in literary or media rights.

PART 3. Investigation for Prosecution Decision

3.1 Investigative Function of Prosecutor   The prosecutor has an affirmative responsibility to investigate suspected illegal activity when it is not adequately dealt with by other agencies. A prosecutor should not invidiously discriminate against or in favor of any person on the basis of race, religion, sex, sexual preference, or ethnicity in exercising discretion to investigate or prosecute. He or she should not knowingly use illegal means to obtain evidence and should not discourage or obstruct communication between prospective witnesses and defense counsel.
3.2 Relations with Victims and Prospective Witnesses   A prosecutor should not compensate a witness, other than an expert. He or she should advise a witness who is to be interviewed of his or her rights against self-incrimination and the right to counsel whenever the law so requires, should seek to insure that victims and witnesses who may need protections against intimidation are advised of and afforded such protections where feasible, and should seek to insure that victims of serious crimes or their representatives are given timely notice of judicial proceedings relating to the victims' case. Where practical, the prosecutor should seek to insure that victims of serious crimes or their representatives are given an opportunity to consult with and to provide information to the prosecutor prior to the decision whether or not to prosecute, to pursue a disposition by plea, or to dismiss the charges.
3.3 Relations with Expert Witnesses   A prosecutor should respect the independence of the expert and should not pay an excessive fee for the purpose of influencing the expert's testimony.
3.4 Decision to Charge   Prosecutors should establish standards and procedures for evaluating complaints to determine whether criminal proceedings should be instituted.
3.5 Relations with Grand Jury   A prosecutor may appropriately explain the law and express an opinion on the legal significance of the evidence but should give due deference to its status as an independent legal body.
3.6 Quality and Scope of Evidence Before Grand Jury   A prosecutor should only present evidence that is appropriate and authorized under law. He or she should not knowingly fail to disclose evidence that tends to negate guilt or mitigate the offense.
3.7 Quality and Scope of Evidence for Information
3.8 Discretion as to Noncriminal Disposition   The prosecutor should consider in appropriate cases the availability of noncriminal disposition.

3.9 Discretion in the Charging Decision   A prosecutor should not institute criminal charges when the prosecutor knows that the charges are not supported by probable cause. He or she is not obliged to present all charges that the evidence might support.

3.10 Role in First Appearance and Preliminary Hearing

3.11 Disclosure of Evidence by the Prosecutor   A prosecutor should not intentionally fail to make timely disclosure to the defense of the existence of all evidence or information that tends to negate the guilt of the accused or mitigate the offense charged or that would tend to reduce the punishment of the accused. He or she should not fail to make a reasonably diligent effort to comply with a legally proper discovery request.

PART 4. Plea Discussions

4.1 Availability for Plea Discussions   The prosecutor should have and make known a general policy or willingness to consult with defense counsel concerning disposition of charges by plea, should not engage in plea discussions directly with an accused who is represented by defense counsel, and should not knowingly make false statements or representations as to fact or law in the course of plea discussions.

4.2 Fulfillment of Plea Discussions   A prosecutor should not make any promise or commitment of a specific sentence or a suspension of sentence and should not imply a greater power to influence the disposition of a case than is actually possessed.

4.3 Record of Reasons for Nolle Prosequi Disposition

PART 5. The Trial

5.1 Calendar Control   Control over the trial calendar should be vested in the court.

5.2 Courtroom Professionalism   The prosecutor should support the authority of the court and the dignity of the trial courtroom by strict adherence to codes of professionalism and by manifesting a professional attitude toward the judge, opposing counsel, witnesses, defendants, jurors, and others in the courtroom.

5.3 Selection of Jurors   The prosecutor should prepare himself or herself prior to trial, should neither harass nor unduly embarrass potential jurors or invade their privacy, and should not intentionally use the voir dire to present factual matter that the prosecutor knows will not be admissible at trial.

5.4 Relations with Jury   A prosecutor should not intentionally communicate privately with persons summoned for jury duty or impaneled and should not intentionally make comments to or ask questions of a juror after the trial for the purpose of harassing or embarrassing the juror.

5.5 Opening Statement   The prosecutor's opening statement should be confined to a statement of the issues.

5.6 Presentation of Evidence   A prosecutor should not knowingly offer false evidence and should not ask legally objectionable questions.

5.7 Examination of Witnesses   The interrogation of all witnesses should be conducted fairly, objectively, and with due regard for the dignity and legitimate privacy of the witness, and without seeking to intimidate or humiliate the witness unnecessarily. A prosecutor should not use the power of cross-examination to discredit or undermine a witness if the prosecutor knows the witness is testifying truthfully.

5.8 Argument to the Jury   The prosecutor may argue all reasonable inferences from the evidence in the record but should not express a personal belief or opinion.

5.9 Facts Outside the Record   The prosecutor should not intentionally refer to or argue on the basis of facts outside the record.

5.10 Comments by Prosecutor After Verdict   The prosecutor should not make public comments critical of a verdict, whether rendered by judge or jury.

PART 6. Sentencing

6.1 Role in Sentencing   The prosecutor should seek to assure that a fair and informed judgment is made on the sentence and to avoid unfair sentence disparities.

6.2 Information Relevant to Sentencing   The prosecutor should assist the court in basing its sentence on complete and accurate information for use in the presentence report.

Glossary

act utilitarianism   type of utilitarianism that determines goodness of a particular act by measuring the utility for all, but only on that act and without regard for future actions

age of reason   legal age at which a person is said to have the capacity to reason and thus to understand the consequences of her or his action

bureaucratic justice   concept referring to the goal of efficiency over justice; policy of assuming guilt and moving cases through the system quickly with the least amount of work

categorical imperative   part of ethical formalism as formulated by Kant; states that one should act in such a way that one wills it to be a universal law and should treat each person as an ends and not as a means

civil disobedience   voluntary, nonviolent disobedience of established laws based on moral beliefs

cognitive dissonance   psychological term referring to the discomfort that is created when behavior and attitude or belief are inconsistent; the inclination is to change one or the other to achieve congruence

concept   idea or notion that cannot be proven

crime control model   Packer's concept of a criminal justice system that maximizes crime control at the expense of personal liberties or due process

cultural relativism   ideas that many values and behaviors differ from culture to culture, but are functional to the culture that holds them

deontological   study of duty or moral obligation emphasizing the intent of the actor or goodwill as the element of morality; character of the person (as in virtue-based ethics) or consequences of the action (as in utilitarianism) are not seen as important

deterrence (general)   an attempt to discourage or prevent some group or nonspecific individual from committing an act; for instance, to do something to one offender that should discourage the rest of society from committing any crime

deterrence (specific)   an attempt to discourage or prevent a particular individual from committing an act; for instance, to deter a criminal offender from committing any more crime

discretion   the power to make a decision or a choice

distributive justice   component of justice concerned with the allocation of the goods and burdens of society to its respective members

due process   constitutionally mandated (Sixth and Fourteenth Amendments) procedural steps designed to eliminate error in governmental deprivation of protected liberty, life, or property; that is, right to a neutral hearing body, presentation of evidence, cross-examination and confrontation of accusers, appeal, and so on

due process model   Packer's concept of a criminal justice system that emphasizes procedural protections (see *due process*) over crime control

egoism   ethical system that claims that good results from pursuing self-interest (see also *psychological egoism*)

enlightened egoism   concept that egoism may look altruistic since it is in one's long-term best interest to help others (since then they will help one)

entrapment   legal term referring to police misconduct that results in a crime being committed that would not otherwise have occurred but for the police conduct

ethical formalism   ethical system espoused by Kant that depends on duty; holds that the only thing truly good is a good will, and that what is good is that which conforms to the categorical imperative

ethical system   systematic ordering of moral principles, also called moral theory or moral philosophy

ethics   study of what constitutes good or bad conduct

ethics of care   ethical system that defines good as meeting needs and preserving and enriching relationships

ethics of virtue   ethical system that bases ethics largely on character and possession of virtues

exclusionary rule   court-created rule of evidence that excludes evidence obtained through illegal means

expiation   atonement

free will   freedom of choice or freedom to make individual decisions without external forces influencing decisions

gratuities   gifts given because of occupation or role of the recipient

group think   psychological term referring to the tendency of a group that works together and develops a common mind-set to agree on ideas that are problematic or even irrational using objective evaluation

halo effect   psychological term referring to the tendency to believe a person who is an expert in one area is knowledgeable about other areas as well; giving greater weight to opinion because of irrelevant expertise

hedonistic calculus   Bentham's formulation of the amount of punishment (pain) necessary to outweigh the anticipated profit (pleasure) of a criminal act; using this calculus, the state should be able to deter crime

hypothetical imperative   a statement of contingent demand: *if* I want something, *then* I must work for it; contrasted with the categorical imperative, which states that one must conform to the imperative with no "ifs"

imperfect duties   general moral values that do not specify acts; for instance, to be charitable

incapacitate   to make incapable; in corrections, to hold someone for any length of time in order to prevent him or her from committing crime

just deserts model   model of punishment advocated by von Hirsh that states that the only appropriate punishment is proportional to the seriousness of the crime and rejects treatment as a correctional policy related to sentencing

justice   the quality of being just, impartial, or fair; the principle or ideal of just dealing or right action

justice model   model of punishment advocated by Fogel that is similar to the just deserts model and states that treatment can be made available but should not influence sentence

lex salica   compensation-based justice; payment or atonement

lex talionis   vengeance-oriented justice concerned with equal retaliation (an eye for an eye . . .)

mala in se   wrong in itself; refers to natural crimes or acts that are condemned by all cultures throughout all time

mechanical solidarity   Durkheim's concept of societal solidarity as arising from similarities among its members

mens rea   legal concept meaning guilty mind, the mental state necessary for culpability

meta-ethics   discipline investigating the meaning of ethical terms

modeling   learning theory concept that people learn behaviors, values, and attitudes through relationships; they identify with another person and want to be like that other person and so pattern their behavior, expressions, beliefs after that person; transitory to the extent that the relationship is transitory

morals   judgment of good and bad conduct

natural law   concept of the laws of nature such as gravity; such laws are discovered by reason but exist apart from humankind; natural laws also govern morality and human nature

normative ethics   study of what is right and wrong in particular situations

order maintenance   type of police work not related to crime control; such as responding to family disturbance, neighbor dispute, lost child, health problem, traffic, and such

organic solidarity   Durkheim's concept of societal solidarity as arising from differences among people, as exemplified by the division of labor

pantheism   view that all existence is made up of attributes of God; God is everything

paternalistic laws   those laws that protect the individual against the dangers of his or her own actions; seat belt laws, helmet laws, and such

plea bargaining   practice of exchanging promises to recommend reduced sentence, reduced charge, or dropping some charges in return for a guilty plea

pluralism   idea that power groups form and reform coalitions, which in turn affect the social and political structure of society

pluralistic ignorance   idea that in any occupational subculture or group of people, the vocal minority appear to represent the beliefs of the majority and the majority believe that they do, but when polled, private beliefs are different and opposite from what the majority believe everyone believes; for instance, prison correctional officers privately believe in more treatment principles than what they express or what they believe others agree with

positive law   laws written and enforced by society (contrasted to *natural law*)

principle of forfeiture   states that one gives up one's right to be treated under the principles of respect for persons to the extent that one has abrogated someone else's rights; for instance, self-defense is acceptable according to the principle of forfeiture

principle of the golden mean   Aristotle's concept of moderation, that one should not err toward excess or deficiency; associated with the ethics of virtue

procedural justice   component of justice that concerns the steps taken (due process) to reach a determination of guilt and punishment

psychological egoism   concept that humans naturally and inherently seek self-interest, and that they can do nothing else because it is their nature

quid pro quo   something for something

rationality   the quality or state of being rational (having reason or understanding); ability to judge the consequences of one's actions

rectificatory (or commutative) justice component of justice concerning business dealings where unfair advantage or undeserved harm has occurred and justice is the recompense or righting of such a wrong

reinforcement reward

religious ethics ethical system that is based on religious concepts of good and evil; what is good is that which is God's will

retributive justice concerns the determination and methods of punishments

rule utilitarianism type of utilitarianism that determines the goodness of an action by measuring the utility of that action made into a rule for behavior

selective incapacitation policy of identifying high-risk offenders and incarcerating them for longer periods of time based on perceived risk

social contract theory concept developed by Hobbes, Rousseau, and Locke, stating that the state of nature is a "war of all against all" in which life is nasty, brutish, and short; to protect being victimized by those who are stronger, each member gives up some liberties in return for protection; the contract is between society, which promises protection, and the individual, who promises to abide by laws and punishments if laws are broken

substantive justice concept of just deserts; appropriate amount of punishment for the crime

supererogatories actions that are commendable but not considered moral duties required to be a moral person

teleological study of ends; teleological system is one concerned with consequences or ends of an action to determine goodness

treatment (correctional) that which constitutes accepted and standard practice and could reasonably result in cure

treatment ethic the idea that crime is a symptom of an underlying pathology that can be treated (also *rehabilitative ethic*)

universalism concept of absolute truths or truths that hold for all people over all time

utilitarianism ethical system which claims that the greatest good is that which results in the greatest happiness for the greatest number; major proponents are Bentham and Mill (see also *act utilitarianism* and *rule utilitarianism*)

utility good or benefit

values measure of worth or priority

veil of ignorance John Rawls's heuristic device used to determine justice: if one were ignorant of one's position in society—i.e., whether one was born to a wealthy or poor family—then one's ideas of just distribution of resources would be more objective and truthful

victim precipitation concept related to victim's participation in the criminal act; victim plays a role and is not a passive object to the criminal's action; precipitation can range from instigating the victimization to merely making it possible—i.e., being an attractive target

Annotated Bibliography

The following books have been selected for special notation because their content relates directly to criminal justice ethics. The interested reader is encouraged to pursue further reading in this subject matter through these books and others.

Braswell, Michael, Belinda McCarthy, and Bernard McCarthy, eds. *Justice, Crime and Ethics.* Cincinnati, OH: Anderson, 1991.

This book of readings covers the three subsystems of the criminal justice system as well as offering an introductory section with articles describing ethical systems, and sections on criminal justice research and crime control policy. There are eighteen articles in all by such authors as John Whitehead, Robert Johnson, Ernest van den Haag, Lawrence Sherman, Howard Cohen, and Jerome Skolnick.

Cohen, Howard, and Michael Feldberg. *Power and Restraint: The Moral Dimension of Police Work.* New York: Praeger, 1991.

This book deals only with law enforcement ethics. The authors use the social contract as the basic perspective for the justification of law enforcement and as the grounding for law enforcement ethics. They discuss the moral dimensions of the police role in society and develop moral standards for policing. The second half of the book presents four dilemmas; the authors analyze a number of possible alternatives to resolve the dilemmas.

Delattre, Edwin. *Character and Cops: Ethics in Policing.* Washington, DC: American Enterprise Institute for Public Policy Research, 1989.

This is a single-authored book on law enforcement ethics. Delattre uses a virtue-based ethical system to examine major issues of law enforcement ethics. He discusses different types of police corruption, leadership issues, training, and the Dirty Harry problem, among other issues. His basic premise is that the character of police officers is formed by habits of honesty or dishonesty, industriousness or sloth.

Heffernan, William, and Timothy Stroup, eds. *Police Ethics: Hard Choices in Law Enforcement.* New York: John Jay Press, 1985.

This book of readings presents a number of excellent articles on law enforcement ethics, many of which have been used in the writing of this book. For example, articles by Ferdinand Schoeman and Gary Marx are among others in a section on undercover operations, and Wren's article on whistle blowing and loyalty is here with others in a section on fidelity to law. Other sections focus on discretion, deadly force, and the future of policing. This book provides articles on affirmative action and sexual integration—two topics not addressed in other ethics presentations.

Schmalleger, Frank, ed. *Ethics in Criminal Justice: A Justice Professional Reader*. Bristol, IN: Wyndham Hall Press, 1990.
This book of readings is slightly different from the others in that it has more articles (four) on teaching ethics. There are also articles on public defenders, defense attorneys, police, and private security.

Schmalleger, Frank, and Robert Gustafson, eds. *The Social Basis of Criminal Justice: Ethical Issues for the 80's*. Washington, DC: University Press of America, 1981.
This was one of the first books published in the area of criminal justice ethics. The articles cover the subsystems of the criminal justice system, including prosecutorial ethics, prison system, law enforcement, and the parole board. The authors also provide an analysis of the articles as a close to the book.

Souryal, Sam. *Ethics in Criminal Justice: In Search of the Truth*. Cincinnati, OH: Anderson, 1992.
This is the latest book published in the area of criminal justice ethics. The author spends about half the book dealing with classical philosophical issues—knowledge and reasoning, the nature of reality, the nature of morality, ethical systems—and then discusses issues in law enforcement and corrections with reference to principles he presented in the first half of the book.

Bibliography

Adams, Virginia. 1981. How to keep 'em honest. *Psychology Today,* Nov., 52–53.

Albert, Ethel, Theodore Denise, and Sheldon Peterfreund. 1984. *Great traditions in ethics.* Belmont, CA: Wadsworth.

Allen, H., and C. Simonsen. 1986. *Corrections in America: An introduction.* New York: Macmillan.

American Bar Association. 1979. *Annotated code of professional responsibility.* Chicago: American Bar Association.

American Bar Association. 1986. *Informal opinions, committee on ethics and professional responsibility.* Chicago: American Bar Association.

American Society for Public Administration. 1979. *Professional standards and ethics: A workbook for public administrators.* Washington, DC: American Society for Public Administration.

Arafat, Ibtihaj, and Kathleen McCahery. 1978. The relationship between lawyers and their clients. In *Essays on the theory and practice of criminal justice,* ed. R. Rich, 193–219. Washington, DC: University Press.

Attorney General's Commission on Pornography. 1986. *Final report.* Washington, DC: Government Printing Office.

Aubert, Vilhelm. 1969. *Sociology of law.* London: Penguin.

Baelz, Peter. 1977. *Ethics and beliefs.* New York: Seabury Press.

Baier, Annette. 1987. Hume, the women's moral theorist. In *Women and moral theory,* ed. E. F. Kittay and D. Meyers, 37–51. Totawa, NJ: Rowman, Littlefield.

Barker, Thomas, and David Carter. 1991. *Police deviance.* Cincinnati, OH: Anderson.

Barry, Vincent. 1985. *Applying ethics: A text with readings.* Belmont, CA: Wadsworth.

Beauchamp, Tom. 1982. *Philosophical ethics.* New York: McGraw-Hill.

Beccaria, Cesare. 1977. *On crimes and punishments,* 6th ed., trans. Henry Paolucci. Indianapolis: Bobbs-Merrill.

Bedau, Hugo. 1982. Prisoners' rights. *Criminal Justice Ethics* 1(1): 26–41.

Bentham, Jeremy. 1970. The rationale of punishment. In *Ethical choice: A case study approach,* ed. R. Beck and J. Orr. New York: Free Press. (Original work published 1843)

Blumberg, Abraham. 1969. The practice of law as a confidence game. In *Sociology of law,* ed. V. Aubert, 321–31. London: Penguin.

Borchert, Donald, and David Stewart. 1986. *Exploring ethics.* New York: Macmillan.

Bossard, Andre. 1981. Police ethics and international police cooperation. In *The social basis of criminal justice: Ethical issues for the 80's,* ed. F. Schmalleger and R. Gustafson, 23–38. Washington, DC: University Press.

Bowie, Norman. 1985. *Making ethical decisions.* New York: McGraw-Hill.

Boyce, William, and Larry Jensen. 1978. *Moral reasoning: A psychological-philosophical integration.* Lincoln: University of Nebraska Press.

Brehm, J. W., and A. R. Cohen. 1982. *Explorations in cognitive dissonance.* New York: Wiley.

Brown, Michael. 1981. *Working the street.* New York: Russell Sage Foundation.

Bureau of Justice Statistics. 1992. *Prosecuters in state courts, 1990.* Washington, DC: U. S. Department of Justice.

Callahan, Daniel. 1982. Applied ethics in criminal justice. *Criminal Justice Ethics* 1(1): 1, 64.

Clinard, Marshall, et al. 1985. Illegal corporate behavior. In *Exploring crime,* ed. J. Sheley, 205–18. Belmont, CA: Wadsworth.

Cohen, Elliott. 1991. Pure legal advocates and moral agents: Two concepts of a lawyer in an adversary system. In *Justice, crime and ethics,* ed. M. Braswell, B. McCarthy, and B. McCarthy, 123–63. Cincinnati, OH: Anderson.

Cohen, Howard. 1985. A dilemma for discretion. In *Police ethics: Hard choices in law enforcement,* ed. W. Heffernan and T. Stroup, 69–83. New York: John Jay Press.

Cohen, Howard. 1986. Exploiting police authority. *Criminal Justice Ethics* 5(2): 23–31.

Cohen, Howard, and Michael Feldberg. 1991. *Power and restraint: The moral dimension of police work.* New York: Praeger.

Cole, George. 1970. The decision to prosecute. *Law and Society Review* 4 (Feb.): 313–43.

Commission on Obscenity and Pornography. 1970. *Report of the Commission on Obscenity and Pornography.* New York: Random House.

Crouch, Ben, ed. 1980. *Keepers: Prison guards and contemporary corrections.* Springfield, IL: Charles C Thomas.

Daley, Robert. 1984. *Prince of the city.* New York: Berkley.

Daly, Kathleen. 1989. Criminal justice ideologies and practices in different voices: Some feminist questions about justice. *International Journal of the Sociology of Law* 17: 1–18.

Davis, Michael. 1991. Do cops really need a code of ethics? *Criminal Justice Ethics* 10(2): 14–28.

Davis, Michael, and Frederick Elliston. 1986. *Ethics and the legal profession.* Buffalo: Prometheus Books.

Delaney, H. R. 1990. Toward a police professional ethic. In *Ethics in criminal justice,* ed. F. Schmalleger, 78–95. Bristol, IN: Wyndham Hall Press.

Delattre, Edwin. 1989. *Character and cops: Ethics in policing.* Washington, DC: American Enterprise Institute for Public Policy Research.

Douglass, John Jay. 1981. Prosecutorial ethics. In *The social basis of criminal justice: Ethical issues for the 80's,* ed. F. Schmalleger and R. Gustafson, 109–71. Washington, DC: University Press.

Dror, Yehezkel. 1969. Law and social change. In *Sociology of law,* ed. V. Aubert, 90–100. London: Penguin.

Durkheim, Emile. 1969. Types of law in relation to types of social solidarity. In *Sociology of law,* ed. V. Aubert, 17–29. London: Penguin.

Elias, Robert. 1986. *The politics of victimization.* New York: Oxford University Press.

Elliston, Frederick. 1986. The ethics of ethics tests for lawyers. In *Ethics and the legal profession,* ed. M. Davis and F. Elliston, 50–61. Buffalo: Prometheus Books.

Elliston, F., and M. Feldberg. 1985. *Moral issues in police work.* Totawa, NJ: Rowman & Allanheld.

Ethical principles for psychologists. 1981. *American Psychologist* 36 (June): 633–38.

Ewin, R. E. 1990. Loyalty and the police. *Criminal Justice Ethics* 9(2): 3–15.

Feibleman, James. 1985. *Justice, law, and culture.* Boston: Martinus Nijhoff.

Feinberg, Joel, and Hyman Gross. 1977. *Justice: Selected readings.* Princeton: Princeton University Press.

Fink, Paul. 1977. *Moral philosophy.* Encino, CA: Dickinson.

Fogel, David, and Joe Hudson. 1981. *Justice as fairness.* Cincinnati, OH: Anderson.

Freedman, Monroe. 1986. Professional responsibility of the criminal defense lawyer: The three hardest questions. In *Ethics and the legal profession,* ed. M. Davis and F. Elliston, 328–39. Buffalo: Prometheus Books.

Fried, Charles. 1986. The lawyer as friend. In *Ethics and the legal profession,* ed. M. Davis and F. Elliston, 132–57. Buffalo: Prometheus Books.

Fuller, Lon. 1969. *The morality of law.* New Haven: Yale University Press.

Galston, William. 1980. *Justice and the human good.* Chicago: University of Chicago Press.

Garland, David. 1990. *Punishment and modern society.* Chicago: University of Chicago Press.

Gerber, R., and P. McAnany. 1972. *Contemporary punishment: Views, explanations and justifications.* Notre Dame, IN: Notre Dame Press.

Gershman, Bennet. 1991. Why prosecutors misbehave. In *Justice, crime and ethics,* ed. M. Braswell, B. McCarthy, and B. McCarthy, 163–77. Cincinnati, OH: Anderson.

Gilligan, Carol. 1982. *In a different voice: Psychological theory and women's development.* Cambridge, MA: Harvard University Press.

Gilligan, Carol. 1987. Moral orientation and moral development. In *Women and moral theory,* ed. E. F. Kittay and D. Meyers, 19–37. Totawa, NJ: Rowman, Littlefield.

Gold, Jeffrey, Michael Braswell, and Belinda McCarthy. 1991. Criminal justice ethics: A survey of philosophical theories. In *Justice, crime and ethics,* ed. M. Braswell, B. McCarthy, and B. McCarthy, 3–25. Cincinnati, OH: Anderson.

Gottfredson, Michael, and Travis Hirschi. 1990. *A general theory of crime.* Stanford, CA: Stanford University Press.

Greenwood, Peter. 1982. *Selective incapacitation.* Santa Monica, CA: Rand Institute.

Harris, C. E. 1986. *Applying moral theories.* Belmont, CA: Wadsworth.

Heidensohn, Frances. 1986. Models of justice: Portia or Persephone? Some thoughts on equality, fairness and gender in the field of criminal justice. *International Journal of the Sociology of Law* 14: 287–98.

Hersh, F., et al. 1979. *Developing moral growth: From Piaget to Kohlberg.* New York: Longman.

Hickey, Joseph, and Peter Scharf. 1980. *Toward a just correctional system.* San Francisco: Jossey-Bass.

Hopfe, Lewis. 1983. *Religions of the world.* New York: Macmillan.

Hornum, Finn, and Frank Stavish. 1978. Criminology theory and ideology: Four analytical perspectives in the study of crime and the criminal justice system. In *Essays on the theory and practice of criminal justice,* ed. R. Rich, 143–61. Washington, DC: University Press.

Jaccoby, Joan, Leonard Mellon, and Walter Smith. 1980. *Policy and prosecution.* Washington, DC: Bureau of Social Science Research.

Johnson, Charles, and Gary Copus. 1981. Law enforcement ethics: A theoretical analysis. In *The social basis of criminal justice: Ethical issues for the 80's,* ed. F. Schmalleger and R. Gustafson, 39–83. Washington, DC: University Press.

Johnson, Leslie. 1982. Frustration: The mold of judicial philosophy. *Criminal Justice Ethics* 1(1): 20–26.

Johnson, Robert. 1987. *Hard time: Understanding and reforming the prison.* Pacific Grove, CA: Brooks/Cole.

Johnson, Robert. 1991. A life for a life? Opinion and debate. In *Justice, crime and ethics,* ed. M. Braswell, B. McCarthy, and B. McCarthy, 199–210. Cincinnati, OH: Anderson.

Kamisar, Yale, Wayne LeFave, and Jerold Israel. 1980. *Modern criminal procedure: Cases, comments and questions.* St. Paul, MN: West.

Kania, Richard. 1988. Police acceptance of gratuities. *Criminal Justice Ethics* 7(2): 37–49.

Kant, Immanuel. 1949. *Critique of practical reason,* trans. Lewis White Beck. Chicago: University of Chicago Press.

Kant, Immanuel. 1981. Ethical duties to others: Truthfulness. In *Lectures on ethics,* ed. L. Infield, 224–32. Indianapolis, IN: Hackett.

Kaplan, Morton. 1976. *Justice, human nature and political obligation.* New York: Free Press.

Karmen, Andrew. 1984. *Crime victims: An introduction to victimology.* Pacific Grove, CA: Brooks/Cole.

Kauffman, Kelsey. 1988. *Prison officers and their world.* Cambridge, MA: Harvard University Press.

Kelly, Orr. 1982. Corporate crime: The untold story. *U.S. News and World Report,* Sept. 6, 25–30.

Kessler, Gary. 1992. *Voices of wisdom: A multicultural philosophy reader.* Belmont, CA: Wadsworth.

Kittel, Norman. 1990. Criminal defense attorneys: Bottom of the legal profession's class. In *Ethics in criminal justice,* ed. F. Schmalleger, 42–62. Bristol, IN: Wyndham Hall Press.

Kleinig, John. 1986. The conscientious advocate and client perjury. *Criminal Justice Ethics* 5(2): 3–15.

Klockars, Carl. 1983. The Dirty Harry problem. In *Thinking about police: Contemporary readings,* ed. C. Klockars, 428-38. New York: McGraw-Hill.

Klockars, Carl. 1984. Blue lies and police placebos. *American Behavioral Scientist* 27(4): 529–44.

Knudten, Mary. 1978. The prosecutor's role in plea bargaining: Reasons related to actions. In *Essays on the theory and practice of criminal justice,* ed. R. Rich, 275–95. Washington, DC: University Press.

Kohlberg, Lawrence. 1976. Moral stages and moralization. In *Moral development and behavior: Theory, research and social issues,* ed. T. Lickona, 31–53. New York: Holt, Rinehart & Winston.

Kohlberg, Lawrence. 1983. *Essays in moral development, Vol. 2. The psychology of moral development.* New York: Harper & Row.

Kohlberg, L., and D. Candel. 1984. The relationship of moral judgment to moral action. In *The psychology of moral development,* ed. L. Kohlberg, 498–582. San Francisco: Harper & Row.

Kottak, Conrad Philip. 1974. *Anthropology: The exploration of human diversity.* New York: Random House.

Kramer, Ronald. 1982. The debate over the definition of crime: Paradigms, value judgments, and criminological work. In *Ethics, public policy and criminal justice,* ed. F. Elliston and N. Bowie, 33–59. Cambridge, MA: Oelgeschlager, Gunn & Hain.

Krisberg, Barry. 1975. *Crime and privilege: Toward a new criminology.* Englewood Cliffs, NJ: Prentice-Hall.

Krogstand, Jack, and Jack Robertson. 1979. Moral principles for ethical conduct. *Management Horizons* 10(1): 13–24.

Leiser, Burton. 1986. *Liberty, justice and morals.* New York: Macmillan.

Lickona, T., ed. 1976. *Moral development and behavior: Theory, research and social issues.* New York: Holt, Rinehart & Winston.

Lombardo, Lucien. 1981. *Guards imprisoned: Correctional officers at work.* New York: Elsevier.

Louthan, William. 1985. The politics of discretionary justice among criminal justice agencies. In *Discretion, justice and democracy: A public policy perspective,* ed. C. Pinkele and W. Louthan, 13–19. Ames: Iowa State University Press.

Lucas, J. R. 1980. *On justice.* Oxford, England: Oxford University Press.

Maas, Peter. 1973. *Serpico.* New York: Viking Press.

MacIntyre, Alasdair. 1991. *After virtue.* South Bend, IN: University of Notre Dame Press.

Mackie, J. L. 1977. *Ethics: Inventing right and wrong.* New York: Penguin.

Mackie, J. L. 1982. Morality and the retributive emotions. *Criminal Justice Ethics* 1(1): 3–10.

Maestri, William. 1982. *Basic ethics for the health care professional.* Washington, DC: University Press.

Malloy, Edward. 1982. *The ethics of law enforcement and criminal punishment.* Lanham, NY: University Press.

Mappes, Thomas. 1982. *Social ethics.* New York: McGraw-Hill.

Margolis, Joseph. 1971. *Values and conduct.* New York: Oxford University Press.

Marks, F. Raymond, and Darlene Cathcart. 1986. Discipline within the legal profession. In *Ethics and the legal profession,* ed. M. Davis and F. Elliston, 62–105. Buffalo: Prometheus Books.

Marx, Gary. 1985a. Police undercover work: Ethical deception or deceptive ethics? In *Police ethics: Hard choices in law enforcement,* ed. W. Heffernan and T. Stroup, 83–117. New York: John Jay Press.

Marx, Gary. 1985b. Who really gets stung? Some issues raised by the new police undercover work. In *Moral issues in police work,* ed. F. Elliston and M. Feldberg, 99–129. Totawa, NJ: Rowman & Allanheld.

Marx, Gary. 1992. Under-the-covers undercover investigations: Some reflections on the state's use of deception. *Criminal Justice Ethics* 11(1): 13–25.

Matthews, John, and Ralph Marshall. 1981. Some constraints on ethical behavior in criminal justice organizations. In *The social basis of criminal justice: Ethical issues for the 80's,* ed. F. Schmalleger and R. Gustafson, 9–22. Washington, DC: University Press.

McAnany, Patrick. 1981. Justice in search of fairness. In *Justice as fairness,* ed. D. Fogel and J. Hudson, 22–51. Cincinnati, OH: Anderson.

McCarthy, Bernard. 1991. Keeping an eye on the keeper: Prison corruption and its control. In *Justice, crime and ethics,* ed. M. Braswell, B. McCarthy, and B. McCarthy, 239–53. Cincinnati, OH: Anderson.

Merlo, Alida. 1992. Ethical issues and the private sector. In *Corrections: Dilemmas and directions,* ed. P. Benekos and A. Merlo, 23–27. Cincinnati, OH: Anderson.

Metz, Harol. 1990. An ethical model for law enforcement administrators. In *Ethics in criminal justice,* ed. F. Schmalleger, 95–103. Bristol, IN: Wyndham Hall Press.

Milgram, Stanley. 1963. Behavioral study of obedience. *Journal of Abnormal and Social Psychology* 67: 371–78.

Mitford, Jessica. 1971. *Kind and usual punishment.* New York: Vintage.

Muir, William. 1977. *Police: Street corner politicians.* Chicago: University of Chicago Press.

Murphy, Jeffrie. 1985. *Punishment and rehabilitation.* Belmont, CA: Wadsworth.

Murphy, Paul, and Kenneth T. Moran. 1981. The continuing cycle of systemic police corruption. In *The social basis of criminal justice: Ethical issues for the 80's,* ed. F. Schmalleger and R. Gustafson, 87–101. Washington, DC: University Press.

Murton, Thomas. 1982. *The dilemma of prison reform.* New York: Irvington Publications.

Nash, Laura. 1981. Ethics without the sermon. *Harvard Business Review*, Nov.–Dec., 81.

Nettler, Gwen. 1978. *Explaining crime.* New York: McGraw-Hill.

Newman, Graeme. 1978. *The punishment response.* New York: Lippincott.

Noddings, Nel. 1986. *Caring: A feminine approach to ethics and moral education.* Berkeley: University of California Press.

Papke, David. 1986. The legal profession and its ethical responsibilities: A history. In *Ethics and the legal profession,* ed. M. Davis and F. Elliston, 29–49. Buffalo: Prometheus Books.

Pellicciotti, Joseph. 1990. Ethics and criminal defense: A client's desire to testify untruthfully. In *Ethics in criminal justice,* ed. F. Schmalleger, 67–78. Bristol, IN: Wyndham Hall Press.

Pinkele, Carl, and William Louthan. 1985. *Discretion, justice and democracy: A public policy perspective.* Ames: Iowa State University Press.

Platt, Anthony. 1977. *The child savers.* Chicago: University of Chicago Press.

Postema, Gerald. 1986. Moral responsibility in professional ethics. In *Ethics and the legal profession,* ed. M. Davis and F. Elliston, 158–79. Buffalo: Prometheus Books.

Power, C., and L. Kohlberg. 1980. Faith, morality and ego development. In *Toward moral and religious maturity,* ed. J. Fowler and C. Bursselmans, 311–72. Morristown, NJ: Silver Burdett.

Quetelet, L. A. J. 1969. *A treatise on man and the development of his faculties.* Gainesville, FL: Scholars, Facsimiles and Reprints.

Quinney, Richard. 1969. *Crime and justice in America.* New York: Little, Brown.

Quinney, Richard. 1974. *Critique of the legal order.* New York: Little, Brown.

Raphael, D. D. 1980. *Justice and liberty.* London: Athlone Press.

Rawls, John. 1957. Outline of a decision procedure for ethics. *Philosophical Review* 66: 177–97.

Rawls, John. 1971. *A theory of justice.* Cambridge, MA: Belknap Press.

Reasons, Charles. 1973. The politicalization of crime, the criminal and the criminologist. *Journal of Criminal Law, Criminology and Police Science* 64 (March): 471–77.

Reiman, Jeffrey. 1990. *Justice and modern moral philosophy.* New Haven, CT: Yale University Press.

Rich, Robert. 1978. *Essays on the theory and practice of criminal justice.* Washington, DC: University Press.

Scheingold, Stuart. 1984. *The politics of law and order.* New York: Longman.

Schoeman, Ferdinand. 1982. Friendship and testimonial privileges. In *Ethics, public policy and criminal justice,* ed. F. Elliston and N. Bowie, 257–72. Cambridge, MA: Oelgeschlager, Gunn & Hain.

Schoeman, Ferdinand. 1985. Privacy and police undercover work. In *Police ethics: Hard choices in law enforcement,* ed. W. Heffernan and T. Stroup, 133–53. New York: John Jay Press.

Schoeman, Ferdinand. 1986. Undercover operations: Some moral questions about S.804. *Criminal Justice Ethics* 5(2): 16–22.

Sellin, Thorsten. 1970. The conflict of conduct norms. In *The sociology of crime and delinquency,* ed. M. Wolfgang, L. Savitz, and N. Johnston, 186–89. New York: Wiley.

Senna, Joseph, and Larry Siegel. 1987. *Introduction to criminal justice.* St. Paul, MN: West.

Sheley, Joseph, ed. 1985. *Exploring crime.* Belmont, CA: Wadsworth.

Sherman, Lawrence. 1981. *The teaching of ethics in criminology and criminal justice.* Washington, DC: Joint Commission on Criminology and Criminal Justice Education and Standards, LEAA.

Sherman, Lawrence. 1982. Learning police ethics. *Criminal Justice Ethics* 1(1): 10–19.

Sherman, Lawrence. 1985a. Becoming bent: Moral careers of corrupt policemen. In *Moral issues in police work,* ed. F. Elliston and M. Feldberg, 253–73. Totawa, NJ: Rowman & Allanheld.

Sherman, Lawrence. 1985b. Equity against truth: Value choices in deceptive investigations. In *Police ethics: Hard choices in law enforcement,* ed. W. Heffernan and T. Stroup, 117–33. New York: John Jay Press.

Skolnick, Jerome. 1982. Deception by police. *Criminal Justice Ethics* 1(2): 40–54.

Skolnick, Jerome, and Richard Leo. 1992. The ethics of deceptive interrogating. *Criminal Justice Ethics* 11(1): 3–13.

Smith, Dwight. 1982. Ideology and the ethics of economic crime control. In *Ethics, public policy and criminal justice,* ed. F. Elliston and N. Bowie, 133–56. Cambridge, MA: Oelgeschlager, Gunn & Hain.

Smith, Steven, and Robert Meyer. 1987. *Law, behavior and mental health.* New York: New York University Press.

Souryal, Sam. 1992. *Ethics in criminal justice: In search of the truth.* Cincinnati, OH: Anderson.

Spence, Gerry. 1989. *With justice for none.* New York: Penguin.

Stefanic, Martin. 1981. Police ethics in a changing society. *The Police Chief,* May, 62–64.

Sterba, James. 1980. *The demands of justice.* Notre Dame, IN: University of Notre Dame Press.

Stitt, B. Grant, and Gene James. 1985. Entrapment: An ethical analysis. In *Moral issues in police work,* ed. F. Elliston and M. Feldberg,129–47. Totawa, NJ: Rowman & Allanheld.

Stover, Robert. 1989. *Making it and breaking it: The fate of public interest commitment during law school,* ed. H. Erlanger. Urbana: University of Illinois Press.

Swift, Andrew, James Houston, and Robin Anderson. 1993. *Cops, hacks, and the greater good.* Academy of Criminal Justice Science Conference. Kansas City, Missouri.

Tanay, E. 1982. Psychiatry and the prison system. *Journal of Forensic Sciences* 27(2): 385–92.

Thompson, Dennis. 1980. Paternalism in medicine, law and public policy. In *Ethics teaching in higher education,* ed. D. Callahan and S. Bok, 3–20. Hastings, NY: Hastings Center.

Toch, Hans. 1977. *Living in prison.* New York: Free Press.

Toch, Hans, and J. Douglas Grant. 1991. *Police as problem solvers.* New York: Plenum Press.

Toch, Hans, J. Douglas Grant, and Raymond Galvin. 1975. *Agents of change: A study in police reform.* New York: Wiley.

Tonry, Michael, Lloyd Ohlin, and David Farrington. 1991. *Human development and criminal behavior.* New York. Springer Verlag.

von Hirsch, Andrew. 1976. *Doing justice.* New York: Hill & Wang.

von Hirsch, Andrew. 1985. *Past or future crimes.* New Brunswick, NJ: Rutgers University Press.

von Hirsch, Andrew, and Lisa Maher. 1992. Can penal rehabilitation be revived? *Criminal Justice Ethics* 11(1): 25–31.

Walker, Samuel. 1985. *Sense and nonsense about crime.* Pacific Grove, CA: Brooks/Cole.

Webster's Ninth New Collegiate Dictionary. 1991. Springfield, MO: Merriam.

Whitehead, John. 1991. Ethical issues in probation and parole. In *Justice, crime and ethics,* ed. M. Braswell, B. McCarthy, and B. McCarthy, 253–73. Cincinnati, OH: Anderson.

Williams, Gregory. 1984. *The law and politics of police discretion.* Westport, CT: Greenwood Press.

Wilson, James Q. 1976. *Varieties of police behavior.* New York: Atheneum.

Wozencraft, Kim. 1990. *Rush.* New York: Random House.

Wren, Thomas. 1985. Whistle-blowing and loyalty to one's friends. In *Police ethics: Hard choices in law enforcement,* ed. W. Heffernan and T. Stroup, 25–47. New York: John Jay Press.

Index